SEXUALITY AND RELATIONSHIPS IN THE LIVES OF PEOPLE WITH INTELLECTUAL DISABILITIES

by the same author

**Exploring Experiences of Advocacy by
People with Learning Disabilities**
Testimonies of Resistance
*Edited by Duncan Mitchell, Rannveig Traustadottir, Rohhss
Chapman, Louise Townson, Nigel Ingham and Sue Ledger*
ISBN 978 1 84310 359 2
eISBN 978 1 84642 511 0

of related interest

Active Support
**Enabling and Empowering People
with Intellectual Disabilities**
Jim Mansell and Julie Beadle-Brown
ISBN 978 1 84905 111 8
eISBN 978 0 85700 300 3

Learning Difficulties and Sexual Vulnerability
A Social Approach
Andrea Hollomotz
ISBN 978 1 84905 167 5
eISBN 978 0 85700 381 2

**Preventing the Emotional Abuse and Neglect
of People with Intellectual Disability**
Stopping Insult and Injury
Sally Robinson
ISBN 978 1 84905 230 6
eISBN 978 0 85700 472 7

Person-Centred Teams
**A Practical Guide to Delivering Personalisation
Through Effective Team-work**
Helen Sanderson and Mary Beth Lepkowsky
ISBN 978 1 84905 455 3
eISBN 978 0 85700 830 5

SEXUALITY AND RELATIONSHIPS IN THE LIVES OF PEOPLE WITH INTELLECTUAL DISABILITIES

STANDING IN MY SHOES

EDITED BY ROHHSS CHAPMAN, SUE LEDGER
AND LOUISE TOWNSON WITH DANIEL DOCHERTY

Jessica Kingsley *Publishers*
London and Philadelphia

Appendix 2 adapted with kind permission from the Family Planning Association.
Appendix 3 adapted with kind permission from Fanstore and Andrews, *Leaning Disabilities, Sex and the Law* 2009, pp.3–5.
Appendix 4 reproduced with kind permission from Dr Tuppy Owens.

First published in 2015
by Jessica Kingsley Publishers
73 Collier Street
London N1 9BE, UK
and
400 Market Street, Suite 400
Philadelphia, PA 19106, USA

www.jkp.com

Library of Congress Cataloging in Publication Data
Sexuality and relationships in the lives of people with intellectual disabilities: standing in my shoes / edited by Rohhss Chapman, Sue Ledger and Louise Townson, with Daniel Docherty.
    pages cm
 Includes bibliographical references and index.
 ISBN 978-1-84905-250-4 (alk. paper)
 1. People with mental disabilities--Sexual behavior. 2. Sex instruction for people with mental disabilities. I. Chapman, Rohhss.
 HQ30.5.S4835 2015
 306.7087--dc23

                              2014015114

British Library Cataloguing in Publication Data
A CIP catalogue record for this book is available from the British Library

ISBN 978 1 84905 250 4
eISBN 978 0 85700 530 4

Printed and bound in Great Britain by Bell & Bain Ltd, Glasgow

CONTENTS

PART 2 A UK EXPERIENCE

APPENDICES

ACKNOWLEDGEMENTS

We would like to acknowledge all the people who have helped and encouraged us during our work on this book. They are in no way responsible for any errors or misrepresentations, which are entirely our responsibility.

Special thanks and appreciation go to all the people who so generously shared their stories. Without their involvement the book would not have been possible. We are deeply indebted to them for their enthusiastic participation and the insights and knowledge gained through their contribution.

The preparation of this book has taken place over several stages; we wish to thank the many organisations, groups and individuals who have contributed in various ways from the initial planning and proposal stages through to the final edits and critical reading.

The book would never have happened without the unstinting support, encouragement and enthusiasm of colleagues from the Open University Social History of Learning Disability Research group and associated research networks, especially the Carlisle People First Research Team. In particular thanks are due to Dorothy Atkinson, Liz Tilley and Jan Walmsley, Caroline Gilchrist, Derek Statton, Carson Stewart and Chloe Brownlee Chapman for their specific roles in discussing and reviewing the final manuscript. Thanks also to Casey Chapman for his illuminating conversations.

Andrew Holman of Inspired Services kindly allowed us to use his picture bank, we are very grateful.

We are also grateful to Stephen Jones for his patience and advice and to others from Jessica Kingsley Publishers, particularly Emma Holak.

Finally, we want to thank our family and friends for their unfailing support and practical help, especially Louise's Mam and Dad. Without all their help and support this book would never have been written.

The book is dedicated to the memory of Rohhss's sister Anna Margeurite Fields and all the other people labelled with intellectual disabilities and their allies whose stories are at its core. We very much hope that it will help in bringing about positive changes in people's lives.

A NOTE ON TERMINOLOGY IN THIS BOOK

Overview

- This section explains labels and terms used in this book.

- We are using the general term 'people with intellectual disabilities'.

- It is hard to find a term everyone will agree with.

- In the past, people used terms that other people can find very upsetting.

- We decided to keep these in the book as they play an important part in understanding history.

The publishers

This publication uses the term 'intellectual disabilities'. This term was recommended by our publishers, Jessica Kingsley, as being the one which would be most easily understood by an international audience. In accordance with this guidance, we have used the term 'intellectual disabilities' in our editorial chapters and footnotes.

People First terminology

However, living in the UK, we are more familiar with using the term 'people with learning difficulties'. This is terminology adopted by self-advocacy and People First groups.[1] This terminology acknowledges that everyone has things that they find hard to learn or understand, and that the person should be seen before the label: 'The term "learning difficulties" implies that people want to learn and recognises that all people have some learning difficulty one way or another' (Goodley 2000, p.123).

---

1   See, for example, www.peoplefirstltd.com/why-learning-difficulty.php.

In the 1980s, the early days of self-advocacy in the UK, People First printed a T-shirt that proclaimed 'Label Jars Not People'. In addressing terminology, we recognise that even when chosen collaboratively and carefully, labels remain problematic for the people who are subject to them. This is perhaps particularly true in respect of the label of 'intellectual disabilities', which encompasses a very diverse group of people, living in different circumstances with very varied aspirations.

Differences within countries

Even within one country there are many differences of language depending on where a person or an organisation's values lie. The term 'learning disabilities' is the term preferred by the UK Government and as such is widely used within policy guidance and services. Accordingly, it is used in this book when referring to specific policy documents or services. Likewise although 'People First language' is preferred by self-advocates in Australia, the Government refers to 'intellectual disabilities'.

Historical terminology and different minority groups

Some chapters involve documentation of history and encounter labels previously used to describe people. Consultation with self-advocates with intellectual disabilities (Atkinson *et al.* 2010), in common with views expressed by other minorities with a history of oppression, for example Jewish people (Feldman 2010), Black people (Martin 2010), and gay men (Houlbrook 2010), emphasises the importance of preserving derogatory and abusive terminology as a significant part of preserving and understanding their history. Whilst respecting this position, we realise that such terms remain offensive to many people and have therefore used them only when necessary for historical accuracy or for citing the names of earlier publications. However, the purpose of this book is to better understand people's experiences of sexuality and relationships. Labels of various kinds often play a key part in shaping experience and opportunity within services and wider society. In this respect, the labels that people lived with required acknowledgement and attention within the book.

Labels preferred by chapter authors

We recognise that the use and choice of labels remains a very emotive subject and an area where language and its usage are constantly changing and evolving. To maintain authenticity of voice and respect the wishes of contributors, individual chapters employ the terms preferred by their authors. Due to this variety in language, each chapter will include a note on terminology to explain the usage in that particular chapter.

References

Atkinson, D., Holland, C., Humber, L., Ingham, N., Ledger, S. and Tilley, E. (2010) *Developing a 'Living Archive' of Learning Disability Life Stories: Project Report.* Milton Keynes: Open University.

Feldman, D. (2010) 'The importance of language.' Paper given at 'Diverse Histories – One Archive, The National Archives and The Royal Historical Society Gerald Aylmer Seminar', London, 21 April.

Goodley, D. (2000) *Self-advocacy in the Lives of People with Learning Difficulties.* Buckingham and Philadelphia: Open University Press.

Houlbrook, M. (2010) 'How to find sources for diverse histories?' Paper given at 'Diverse Histories – One Archive, The National Archives and The Royal Historical Society Gerald Aylmer Seminar', London, 21 April.

Martin, S.I. (2010) 'The importance of language.' Paper given at 'Diverse Histories – One Archive, The National Archives and The Royal Historical Society Gerald Aylmer Seminar', London, 21 April.

PART I

THE INTERNATIONAL PERSPECTIVE

CHAPTER 1

INTRODUCTION TO THE BOOK
Standing in My Shoes

Rohhss Chapman, Louise Townson and Sue Ledger with Daniel Docherty

Overview

- The purpose of the book is to understand people with intellectual disabilities' experiences of sexuality and relationships.

- Life story research with people with intellectual disabilities has become more common but has not been widely used in the area of sexuality and relationships.

- This book aims to fill this gap by drawing upon life stories to promote understanding and inform development of future support.

- The book asks if history can help us to understand how sexuality and relationship issues are addressed today.

- We set out five research questions to frame our exploration of intellectual disability, sexuality and relationships.

- We explain how the book is divided into two parts and introduce each chapter of Part 1.

The writing process

This chapter was written by Rohhss, Louise and Sue with ideas also contributed by Daniel Docherty, which were recorded and later transcribed by Louise. We have written the chapter in sections as a conversation between us, to reflect the process of co-writing. We use the words 'intellectual disabilities' in our discussion as editors.

Introduction

LOUISE

When we talk or think about relationships, there can be many different kinds, such as family, friends, work colleagues and acquaintances, boyfriends or girlfriends, or same-sex relationships. These are the types of relationships people have and that may be taken for granted in their lives.

For people with intellectual disabilities, their experience of relationships can be very different. By this I mean a number of people in their lives may be people who are paid to be there: support staff and professionals. Many people, for various reasons, don't have family contact. Even long-lasting friendships can be difficult to sustain because whatever setting the person is in, friendships and relationships can be seen as a bad thing or something too difficult to support.

There are also boundaries set up between staff and people they support which can get in the way and prevent them from being friends. I think this is wrong because people, regardless of whether they have a label or not, have the same rights to any kinds of relationship as anyone else.

Even today research is being done by academics and by students on their degree courses which find that attitudes from staff towards the sexuality of intellectually disabled people are very negative. I think a lot of this is because people such as support workers and teachers are worried about what can go wrong in relation to risk, and whether they will be held responsible. To my mind, they 'overthink' a lot of the issues.

DANIEL

I got involved to show it's a slow process and to try to change people's minds. It's about people [with intellectual disabilities] taking control. Who has the right to abort a baby or decide for someone to be sterilised just because they have a learning difficulty?

ROHHSS

Sexuality and relationships are a vital part of human existence regardless of whether you are labelled as having intellectual disabilities or not. For all of us, being loved, loving a partner, valuing and being valued by others, and not being lonely, are of key importance to our development as individuals and how we manage our lives. These elements affect our ability to feel connected and belong in the communities and families in which we live.

The right to build relationships and to have a family life is enshrined in the Human Rights Act (1998) which has been in force in the UK since 2000. The United

Nations Convention on the Rights of Persons with Disabilities (2006), ratified by the UK Government in 2009, also clearly endorses the right to relationships, marriage and a family life. Across the globe there are many laws and policies advocating the rights intellectually disabled people are entitled to, which are outlined in Chapter 2. However, in reality, we know that intellectually disabled people and their allies still have to challenge the status quo in their countries in order to achieve what is rightfully theirs at a local level.

Last Christmas I visited an old friend and was talking about this book as we discussed our respective plans for the coming year. To my surprise she was rather taken aback that I was involved in such a project. Hesitantly she said, 'Yes but, surely if you have learning difficulties then you are not really able to have…sexual relationships?' This is a commonly held view, however liberal thinking we assume people to be. It was clearly something she had never questioned.

SUE

Last year I had a similar experience. I was out with a group of parents from my daughter's playgroup whom I hadn't seen for some time. We were catching up on what we had all been doing. I said that I'd been working on a project that looked at how people with intellectual disabilities were supported to make decisions about contraception and parenting. One of the group seemed genuinely astonished. She asked, 'Can they have relationships and become parents? I'm sorry; it's never occurred to me, I've never seen any people with their own children.'

This friend had strongly supported the inclusion of a child with Down's syndrome at the local nursery and had gone out of her way to ensure her own children included the little boy in playground games and play dates. Yet for her the issue of adult relationships, including sexual relationships and the choice to parent, was obviously a completely different thing. It simply hadn't occurred to her and she really struggled with her own feelings about it.

From another viewpoint, in the 1990s I supported a group for women with intellectual disabilities. I remember one of the women saying, 'A lot of us would like a boyfriend but it isn't always allowed.' Another woman replied, 'A lot of us would really like a baby but it isn't allowed.' Some of those discussions were written up for a book, *Know Me as I Am* (Atkinson and Williams 1990). My friend's reaction brought back these words and the struggle they defined. It also made me question how much has really changed in terms of attitudes towards the sexuality of people with intellectual disabilities more than 20 years down the line.

In England, *Valuing People* policy (Department of Health 2001, 2009) highlights that people with intellectual disabilities have the right to information and accessible resources on sexuality, sexual health and safer sex. This applies whether or not they are having a sexual relationship and it clearly states the need for services to provide support with relationships, including sexual relationships. Now that policy rhetoric has moved on, it is easy to assume that within services people are being sensitively and ably supported. *But are they?*

Why are we focusing on life story accounts?

LOUISE

It is important for people with intellectual disabilities to be able to tell their story in whatever way suits that individual. Sadly for many people this isn't always possible. For instance, if a person has lived for many years in an institution then they don't always know their own history or why they were sent there. There can be very heavy reliance on family members, advocates, staff or documentation to fill in the gaps. But staff are busy and many don't think about the importance of personal history to the people they work with. They assume that people don't need to know their history or that they aren't interested. Everyone has a past and has the right to be informed of that past, whether it was good or bad.

Basically we want to get people's stories 'out there' because we are tired of negative attitudes towards intellectually disabled people. It's really important to do this because if we don't act now then things will never change.

SUE

The idea for this book came from discussions at the 2007 Social History of Learning Disability conference at the Open University, UK, titled 'Learning Disability, Relationships and Sexuality: Past and Present'. The following quote is from a paper presented by co-editor Daniel Docherty at this conference: 'We have finished now but I still see him sometimes. Looking to the future I'd like to be with somebody; to be in a relationship. But I think it's going to be quite hard' (Docherty 2007).

In his presentation and the discussion that followed Daniel described the barriers he had encountered as he tried to develop intimate relationships whilst living in a long-stay hospital, a group home and supported living. Courageously he shared how people's reactions had made him feel 'different', isolated and very lonely. His moving life story account made a deep impression on an international audience that included people with intellectual disabilities, families, advocates, paid supporters, managers and academics.

At the conference there was a strong sense that listening to these, often absent, accounts of sexuality and relationships from people with intellectual disabilities and their allies was fundamental to understanding the issues and bringing about genuine change. Although life story methods have become more common in intellectual disability research over the past two decades, until recently, few reflections about relationships, sex and sexuality have emerged from these accounts (Ledger and Tilley 2010). In writing this book we address this gap by specifically seeking out 'insider accounts' from people with intellectual disabilities and their allies. In doing so, we aim to share stories of success and promote positive change.

Sex, relationships and absent voices

SUE

As an editorial team we are all members of the Social History of Learning Disabilities (SHLD) Research Group at the Open University. This is an inclusive research group that brings together people with intellectual disabilities, families, practitioners and academics to explore the recent history of intellectual disability. The group does this through drawing on life stories and expert witness accounts from people with intellectual disabilities. We work together, collaboratively.

A central aim of the SHLD group has been to document the past with a strong focus on influencing future policy. Since it was established in 1994, the group has published extensively in the field of intellectual disability history, inclusive research, policy and practice.[1] A strong focus of the research has been the telling of a more inclusive account, using 'insider' stories to counterbalance over-reliance on 'official' versions of history as represented through policy, service documents and government reports (Appendix 1 provides examples of publications from the SHLD group).

On partnership and confidentiality

ROHHSS

Working together has been a strong feature of SHLD work. Our partnership as authors and editors – that is, two researchers labelled as having intellectual disabilities and two academics – is based on a commitment to *working together*. It is largely embedded from our experiences of working within the self-advocacy movement, a range of SHLD projects, and, for three of us, the women's movement. This is combined with the inclusive research approach that Sue and I (with Louise) took up for our PhDs in 2000 at the Open University. Therefore the book follows two strands of inquiry; the process is considered as significant as the subject matter.

---

1   In 2012 two SHLD partnership projects were chosen by a Department of Health panel (with strong representation from people with intellectual disabilities and their families) as an example of excellence in co-production to improve the lives of people with learning disabilities and their families (www.gov.uk/government/publications/learning-disabilities-good-practice-project-report).

This book is co-edited by people with intellectual disabilities. In addition, most of the chapters are co-authored by people with intellectual disabilities, or solely authored. In so doing, the design of the book introduces multiple layers of co-writing and co-editing, each raising their own issues of partnership working, ethics and ownership. This has resulted in a multiplicity of voices and accounts and, accordingly, no two chapters have taken exactly the same path in their construction. The book contributes to the literature on partnership working and we discuss the process of co-editing in more detail in Chapter 21.[2]

Working together on life history accounts also raises issues around confidentiality. Although we discuss this in more detail in Chapter 21, we need to affirm at the start that these issues have been considered in depth. Some people have kept their real names, some have given pseudonyms and some have not used surnames or have changed locations. All of these decisions have been taken within the groups alongside the authors. Some changed their minds during the process. Because of the critical nature of ethics and confidentiality in this work, we have informed the reader of the context at the start of each chapter.

What should we keep in mind while reading the book?

SUE

During the 1990s a number of abuse investigations (see for example Buckinghamshire County Council 1998) and mounting research evidence drew attention to people with intellectual disabilities as a group particularly vulnerable to sexual abuse. In the light of this, McCarthy and Thompson (2010, p.21) highlight that: 'it is not possible to address sexual issues with people with intellectual disabilities without considering the risk of sexual abuse'. In the UK responses to sexual abuse are generally led by adult protection policies and procedures (see Chapter 11). By drawing upon lived experiences, the book provides insight into how safeguarding practices, designed to protect people from harm, are impacting on people's lives. We fully acknowledge that people need protection from harm and to feel safe; but the question is, *how*? In this book people with intellectual disabilities repeatedly emphasise a need to sensitively balance protection against the value of developing relationships. We anticipate that this discussion will be of interest to families, front line staff and practitioners.

---

2   Chapter 21 can be read prior to Chapter 3 if readers wish to understand how decisions regarding partnership and anonymity are approached.

LOUISE

Some people may not agree with some of the issues they read about in this book but will need to remember that each author comes from their own culture or religion which might set out how things are in that particular country. An example of this would be in discussing arranged marriages. That is something I personally cannot really understand – marrying someone you don't even know. However, that has been the practice in certain cultures for centuries and it is not up to me to determine it wrong, even though I may question it.

Often there have been negative attitudes, particularly from staff in long-stay institutions, that seem to be ingrained, suggesting to people that sexuality and relationships are 'dirty' and 'not nice'. A lot of this experience comes out in the stories we hear from our authors.

DANIEL

We also need to remember a lot of information is hidden. When I was living in the hospital (an institution in Northwest England) they didn't call it sex; they called it 'Percy Filth'. Staff don't encourage anyone to have a relationship, because it's open to abuse. Staff don't even know what the rules are; they have to cover their backs because there could be all sorts of allegations made.

When I was institutionalised (in the 1960s) there were male staff bathing females. There is a lot more choice now. Before, you were given a male member of staff whether you were female or not and you had to put up with it. I can remember a story of when a group of men were being taught how to shave; it wasn't a man that taught you, it was a woman!

There seem to be a lot of excuses for people not talking about sex, but not talking about it can make people more distressed.

Who are the allies in this work?

SUE

Many of the authors in this book are *allies*: people who are fully committed to supporting change for equality, who have networked and researched together over the years. Importantly, parents and family carers and advocates can be great allies for sexuality work. Although many staff assume that parents will be opposed to sex and relationships education, research evidence suggests that the majority of parents welcome this (McCarthy and Thompson 2010). In the UK there are many examples of parents leading planning and support groups concerning sexual issues (Kerr-Edwards and Scott 2003, 2007). In other cultures (see Chapter 7 from Japan) we learn how it is parents who have got together to set up advocacy groups and campaign for change. Our use of the term *allies* embraces the many families who have supported people with intellectual disabilities with a range of sexuality and relationships issues. The enormous impact of their support – both emotional and practical – and its key role in enabling people to develop their sexuality are recurrent themes across many of the stories.

The stories in the book also reveal how for many families the initial involvement of a family member with intellectual disabilities in a relationship can lead to a lot of concern. Some family carers may be opposed to sex education and others may feel worried that their son or daughter is developing a strong tie with someone outside the family – a transfer of affection to a place where they perhaps have less influence and where there are often concerns about exploitation and the person's ability to cope (see Chapter 4, Ebba and Jonni's story, and Rie's story from Japan in Chapter 7). The coming together of family carers can help people struggling with issues of sexuality to feel supported (Family Planning Association 2013).

We hope that the stories shared in the book will be of interest to family carers, enabling people to hear about ways in which families have approached sexuality and relationships and how families have worked together to achieve the best way forward for their relative.

LOUISE

However, families are not the only allies. We also hear from advocacy supporters, practitioners, managers and academics. All of these people have supported people with intellectual disabilities to share their experiences and often bring about change too.

ROHHSS

Inspired by Daniel's story, the main purpose of this book is to challenge everyday notions that sex and relationships, which should be open to all of us, are highly problematic for people with intellectual disabilities to achieve.

Unlike my old school friend and the mother Sue described, most of the people choosing to read this book will have probably thought about some of these issues before. They may be involved in a course that addresses relationships and sexuality or be supporting intellectually disabled people where practical work is needed. In this respect, hearing personal stories of achievement and challenge articulated by both intellectually disabled people themselves and their allies is crucial.

Several factors have combined to enable us to bring together this edited collection and we gratefully acknowledge the work of all the chapter authors as well as the many people variously involved in projects or research that the authors have referenced throughout the book. The collection combines personal accounts from a range of cultures with reflection from people with intellectual disabilities, academics and practitioners on sexuality and relationships, inclusive research, co-writing and life history approaches. In doing so it contributes to the literature on sexuality, policy and practice. It should be of interest to academics, practitioners and students from a wide range of disciplines, in addition to people with intellectual disabilities and their families, advocacy groups, front line staff, managers, commissioners and policy makers.

Our research questions

ROHHSS

In compiling the book we reflected back on our original aims, our commitment to an inclusive approach to this subject, our interest in life stories and an historical approach. We formulated five research questions to guide the framework, analysis and discussion.

1. Does history help us to understand people with intellectual disabilities' experiences of sexuality and relationships today?

2. What have people's own experiences been?

3. How do allies effectively support people in their aspirations around sexuality and relationships?

4. What can partnership working and life story methodology contribute to this field?

5. What are the implications for policy and practice?

We hold onto these questions throughout the book, making reference to them in the editorial chapters. In Chapter 23, we summarise our findings in relation to each of the research questions. A key purpose is to gain a clearer understanding of people's experiences in order to shed light on areas that inform delivery of improved future support. This will include consideration of our findings in relation to increasingly personalised/individualised support for adults with intellectual disabilities.

Design of the book

ROHHSS, LOUISE AND SUE

The book is divided into two parts. Part 1 presents an international perspective through a range of stories from authors 'around the globe'. In Part 2 the focus shifts to explore diversity within relationships through the experiences of people living in the UK, primarily in England, in greater detail. Presenting the text in this way allows the UK experience to be set in an international context through the links to our historical overview.

Our focus on lived history accounts means that the experiences of sex and relationships discussed are either current or from a fairly recent historical period. Walmsley and Rolph (2001) state the importance of examining how previous generations approached people requiring long-term support in order to understand the present. Social meanings are recursive; the past continues to speak to the present (Giddens 1984).

Building on this approach we have chosen to ground these accounts of sex and relationships through reference to the treatment of people with intellectual disabilities during the twentieth and early twenty-first centuries. To facilitate comparison across cultures authors in Part 1 are drawn from a range of countries.

Chapter 2 introduces the global aspect of the book and explains how the stories came from people within our research networks.

Chapter 3, by historian Lee-Ann Monk, provides an overview of the treatment of people with intellectual disabilities across the twentieth and early twenty-first centuries. This is in keeping with our commitment to making links between history and current practice. Her documentation of the historical practice of mass sterilisation, including the practice of sterilisation as a condition of institutional release, serves as a very sobering reminder of the extent of oppression endured by people with intellectual disabilities during the very recent past.

Chapter 4 explores the impact of sterilisation on the life of one couple. Sigurjøn Grétarsson (Jonni) and Eyglø Ebba Hreinsdøttir, husband and wife, tell the stories of their respective upbringings, how they met and what their relationship has meant to them.

Chapter 5 hears from the Clare Inclusive Research Group who discuss Irish law about sex between people with intellectual disabilities, its impact on their lives and the steps they have taken to campaign for change.

Chapter 6 is an account by the Our New Future Self-advocacy Group from Flanders in Belgium. It continues Hreinsdøttir and Grétarsson's pro-active stance through their discussion of work they have undertaken to raise awareness of the UN Declaration of Human Rights. The need for this work is exemplified by accounts from three self-advocates trying to negotiate development of a close relationship whilst remaining dependent on support from services.

Chapter 7 is from a Japanese perspective, we learn how some people with intellectual disabilities and their allies are beginning to speak up about their sexual rights and oppression. Yet authors Eiji Tsuda and Takako Ueto emphasise that resistance to sex education remains strong, with many parents seeking to protect their children by keeping them away from sexual knowledge and behaviour. These authors draw upon self-advocate stories to explore how two people with intellectual disabilities have managed relationships with parents and the impact of this on their sexuality.

Chapter 8, written by Claire Azzopardi Lane from Malta, provides insight into the impact of Catholicism on attitudes to the sexuality of people with intellectual disabilities.

Chapter 9 presents a discussion from Australian authors Patsie Frawley and Christine Bigby with Janice Slattery. These researchers describe their innovative use of life stories and materials written and developed by women with intellectual disabilities in a sexuality programme delivered by people with intellectual disabilities as tutors.

Chapter 10, written by the Editors, concludes Part 1 of the book with an analysis of the main emergent themes 'from around the globe'.

Part 2 chapters of the book are introduced in Chapter 11. We do hope you enjoy this journey as much as we have.

References

Atkinson, D. and Williams, F. (1990) *Know Me As I Am: An Anthology of Prose, Poetry and Art by People with Learning Difficulties.* London: Hodder and Stoughton.

Buckingham County Council (1998) *Independent Longcare Enquiry.* Aylesbury: Buckinghamshire County Council.

Department of Health (2001) *Valuing People.* London: The Stationery Office.

Department of Health (2009) *Valuing People Now: A New Three-year Strategy for People with Learning Disabilities.* London: The Stationery Office.

Docherty, D. (2007) 'Good as you 2.' Paper presented at The Learning Disability, Relationships and Sexuality: Past and Present conference Open University, Milton Keynes, 5 July.

Family Planning Association (2013) Training course materials entitled 'Learning Disabilities, Sex Law and Policy.' Course date 12 November 2013.

UN (2006) *Convention on the Rights of Persons with Disabilities.* Available at www.un.org/disabilities/convention/conventionfull.shtml, accessed on 2 December 2008.

Kerr-Edwards, L. and Scott, L. (2003) *Talking Together… About Sex and Relationships: A Practical Resource for Schools and Parents of Children with Learning Disabilities.* London: FPA.

Kerr-Edwards, L. and Scott, L. (2007) *Talking Together… About Contraception: A Practical Resource for Staff and Parents Working with Young People with Learning Disabilities.* London: FPA.

Ledger, S. and Tilley, E. (2010) 'Reminiscence, identity and developing a living archive of learning disability history.' Paper given at LGTB Seminar, LM Archives, December.

McCarthy, M. and Thompson, D. (2010) 'Introduction.' In M. McCarthy and D. Thompson (eds) *Sexuality and Learning Disabilities.* Brighton: Pavillion.

Tuchman, G. (1994) 'Historical Social Science: Methodologies, Methods, and Meanings.' In Denzin, N. and Lincoln, Y. (eds) *Handbook of Qualitative Research*. California: Sage.

Walmsley, J. and Rolph, S. (2001) 'The development of community care for people with learning difficulties 1913 to 1945.' *Critical Social Policy 21*, 1, 59–80.

STORIES FROM AROUND THE GLOBE

Sue Ledger, Rohhss Chapman and Louise Townson

Overview ——————————————————————

- This chapter introduces Part 1: the international aspect of the book.

- The countries written about come from the networks of people we have worked with.

- This is because it is important to form relationships of trust with people when you are asking about personal topics.

- There are a lot of interesting stories to contrast and compare.

- The stories show how cultural background can affect relationships.

- There are often very big differences between policy and what actually happens.

- We include an international timeline to help people find out about the history of laws and policies in each of the countries written about.

The writing process

This chapter was written by Sue, Rohhss and Louise and has an introductory quote from Daniel Docherty. Daniel had been involved early on in our writing process when we talked a lot about the need for the book and the reason it should have an international perspective. His notes were recorded and later transcribed by Louise. Sue, Rohhss and Louise wrote their sections adding in Daniel's comments. We then revised the chapter together adding further material from all of us and making changes in responses to feedback from each other.

Introduction

There are lessons to be learned. Really, we need to be able to show other countries that we are all in the same boat. Yes of course some countries have their own customs, but at the end of the day we all need to go in the same direction. Things are still blocking it like the fear of parents and the fear of staff. There is a big lack of information. That's why the international part is important.

DANIEL DOCHERTY (20 JULY 2011)

Part 1 of this book opens up discussion on the subjects of sex, sexuality and relationships by bringing together the experiences of people with intellectual disabilities across a range of countries and cultures: the UK (through the editorial), Iceland, Ireland, Belgium, Japan, Malta and Australia.

What the chapters have in common
LOUISE

The global stories seem to have sections that are similar. Issues such as the lack of sex education and sterilisation, all of the things we might think we had got rid of, are still happening anyway. It seems to be ingrained in people not to talk about sex and relationships because it's 'not nice'. This applies to intellectually disabled people too. For example, even one of our friends in the Carlisle People First Research Team Ltd said, 'We don't want that sort of talk in here, thank you'!

In my experience when people with intellectual disabilities talk about relationships and sexuality they often get 'shushed' by staff and support workers. I wonder if this is because they themselves find the topic uncomfortable. I remember talking to Daniel and he told me a story about a woman he shared a house with. She used to carry a doll around with her and every time she talked about babies she got told to 'forget about that'. Daniel and I wondered if she had a child at one point that was taken away and that she maybe found the doll a comfort. I know this happened to some of the women I met at the institution in Cumbria who had been labelled 'moral defectives' at the time. They were rounded up, institutionalised, gave birth to their babies and were then cruelly separated from them. The babies went away for adoption and these women never ever saw their babies again.

Drawing upon networks where trust has been built
SUE AND ROHHSS

The stories and experiences shared through this book have been gathered using existing inclusive research networks of the Social History Research Group at The

Open University, the Carlisle People First Research Team and associated advocacy groups. As editors we were a team with experience of facilitating and supporting self-advocacy conferences on relationships, sex and sexuality in addition to the development of policy and practice within services. In working on the book we drew substantially upon networks we had established through this work.

Sex and relationships are for many people a more hidden area of life, an area where people with intellectual disabilities, families and staff can feel vulnerable and tentative about sharing their experiences, feelings, opinions and ideas. Writing about what are often deeply personal matters requires a considerable degree of trust: trust that the material will be treated sensitively and respectfully, that people's privacy and confidentiality will be honoured and trust in the sense of shared purpose in why we are publishing the stories and what we hope to achieve.

Clearly this selection is not globally representative. We would have liked to be able to include stories from Africa, Asia and South America but we are still in the process of building the relationships and networks to achieve this. Whilst we fully accept these limitations, the chapters that follow powerfully bring to life various ways in which culture can influence the relationships and sexuality of people with intellectual disabilities.

In the chapters, many contributors have been courageous in coming forward and sharing their experiences in the hope that their lives and reflections will in turn support others to understand that they are not alone in the issues they face and that there are positive ways forward. The countries represented are sufficiently diverse to allow recurrent themes to be identified and it is these themes, present across a range of cultural contexts, which make the material so fascinating. We hope that these pioneering accounts will serve as an invitation for others from different parts of the world, with differing religious and cultural backgrounds, to share their experiences, and, if they wish, participate in an expanding advocacy and inclusive research network.

The benefits of an international perspective
ROHHSS

As Daniel pointed out, gathering an international perspective was really important to us. We had never heard of a book that covered stories about sexuality and relationships from the perspectives of people with intellectual disabilities.

Due to extensive past involvement in the development of the self-advocacy movement, I have been fortunate enough to travel to several cities and countries talking to people with intellectual disabilities and their allies about their lives. I have attended conferences alongside Louise as a supporter, ally and later as a friend in Canada, USA, Australia, Belgium, Iceland, Ireland and Germany amongst other places. I have also visited Bali and Japan. In Japan I worked with one of the authors, Eiji Tsuda, whom I had met at an SHLD conference. Alongside a Korean speaker, I was invited to present my work at an educational conference on community inclusion at Kobe University where students were establishing exciting and innovative programmes with young children and their parents. I then travelled to speak at a meeting of parents from 'Inclusion International' in Tokyo. The exchange of their experiences and ideas was enlightening. I visited a local Kobe self-advocacy group and was later taken to visit an institution. The learning I undertook in those few precious days will stay with me forever and has instilled in me different ideas about community spiritedness and interdependence (Tsuda 2006). Some aspects of how organisations and groups function and people's experiences within them were very familiar, particularly in the self-advocacy groups; yet there were also important cultural differences.

The self-advocacy movement of People First is an international movement where people are remarkably hospitable and keen to share their experiences with each other. Through attending presentations and, more importantly, social events, I have had the pleasure to make contacts and form relationships, many of which have been sustained over a long period of time. People I met in Alaska in 2002 are still in touch and friends from Iceland made through the Grundtvig network at the Open University are continuing to co-work and visit, 12 years later. The feeling that we are all part of the same planet and striving for similar lifestyles with shared values is enormously empowering for all of us, whatever our roles. The opportunity to have such meetings is of course limited through access to resources, but is essentially life changing. In my view, it is imperative for people to know that others have similar experiences, and that barriers to choice and fulfilment are often similar, no matter which part of the world you are from.

LOUISE

I have also been lucky enough to travel to these countries around the world and present my views at conferences either individually, by co-presenting, or as part of a team. One of the things I have found interesting was a question from a Japanese group about how to get started in self-advocacy. I found this rather surprising as I had just assumed that all People First groups were at the same stage of development. It has also been really satisfying because when you go to these conferences you may meet the same groups of people with intellectual disabilities and their supporters, as well as meeting and making new connections. It gives the opportunity to catch up with people you don't see very often.

Exploring gaps between policy and practice

SUE

Like everyone else, people with intellectual disabilities tell us that relationships are important. Yet the evidence is that people with intellectual disabilities often have very few relationships and limited opportunities to form or sustain them. Significantly, they are often lonely. One of the reasons for this is their exclusion from the kinds of places where other people form and maintain relationships, such as work, college, clubs, places of worship and leisure centres. But importantly, there are other reasons for this too, some of which are based on limiting assumptions about people with intellectual abilities.

Welshman and Walmsley (2006) argue that *insider accounts* from people with intellectual disabilities and others closely involved in their support (Rolph *et al.* 2005) shed light on areas of social care where gaps exist between official policy and practice. By incorporating insider accounts from people with intellectual disabilities and their allies across a range of cultures, we set out to shed light on gaps that may exist between rights to relationships expounded in (for example) Human Rights legislation and United Nations conventions, and the actual circumstances and attitudes encountered in people's everyday lives.

In the UK research has shown that people with intellectual disabilities have very little knowledge of the law in relation to sexual relationships, marriage, consent and abuse (see for example O'Callaghan and Murphy 2007). In preparation for co-writing Chapter 15 (about the experiences of gay women with intellectual disabilities), I carried out a series of interviews with people with intellectual disabilities, their families and staff within services. Not only did people with intellectual disabilities describe themselves as 'in the dark about the law', but families, front line staff, and managers also reported a considerable degree of confusion and concern about 'what was allowed'.

The accounts in the following chapters, however, highlight that the law is not the only set of 'rules' that people sometimes struggle to understand and abide by (Fanstore and Andrews 2009). With regard to sex and relationships, people with intellectual disabilities raise issues about family rules and values; what is appropriate in their local neighbourhood or in the house or group home where they live; what is deemed acceptable within their cultural and religious groups; and how to act on a wish to seek out sexual relationships with non-disabled people. In addition, there are often staff rules, house rules and safeguarding rules to contend with alongside the practicalities of getting out to meet people or trying to date using the internet. We return to these subjects in Chapter 10 as we bring together emerging themes from Part 1 stories and in Chapter 11 when we discuss the UK legal and policy framework in more depth.

LOUISE

This is a topic myself and my friend/support worker have discussed. Sometimes people with intellectual disabilities have to comply with the needs of the service and its staff rather than the service putting the needs of the people who use it first. As an example, when people from a group home meet their partners or friends at a disco they invariably have to leave early to return home because of staff changeovers. My friend and I feel this is wrong. There needs to be more flexibility and if a staff member has to work until 10.30 pm instead of 10.00 pm, then what is the problem?

SUE

A woman I have known for a long time recently met a man she really liked through a local music group. When she asked the staff if they could help her arrange to meet him again they said that as he was supported by a different service it would be complicated. Her support team are generally very helpful but this situation highlights how service-based systems can present barriers that staff find hard to navigate.

Across a range of cultures, the stories in Part 1 reveal gaps between policy intention and actual experience. Life stories show how family views and cultural norms have impacted upon sexuality and sexual expression. The stories give examples of how practical barriers such as transport, money and staff support sometimes impede the development of relationships and also provide examples of how such challenges have been overcome. A number of stories provide insight into the ways in which national policy and guidance are interpreted by support staff at local level. As Louise insightfully observed 'staff interpretation leaves a lot of room for gaps'.

International timeline as a teaching and learning aid

SUE AND ROHHSS

This chapter includes an international timeline (Table 2.1) of the key milestones in terms of legal, policy and service approaches to sex and relationships, identified by the authors from each culture. This enables the UK experience to be presented and understood in an international context. Our aim is that *these can be read by or shared with people with intellectual disabilities*, affording people the opportunity to view their own story and experiences in a wider context (see Chapter 21). Ideally we would have included a global overview, but space is limited so we chose to concentrate on events that would provide context for the stories to follow.

We want to help the reader understand changes that have happened in the countries represented in the book. Looking at the pictorial timetable it is possible to distinguish similarities and differences at a glance and this will be particularly helped by reading the international overview from Lee-Ann Monk (Chapter 3).

When we were developing our timeline Sue met with a group of self-advocates to review the proposed content. Whilst people with intellectual disabilities within the group found it useful they also suggested that we added some visual imagery to make it more accessible. Once we had inserted appropriate graphics it also became more helpful to us. We suggest that readers use it in their work supporting people with intellectual difficulties or with their students. In this way the timeline can be used as a base from which to add developments in other countries/cultures which may be of particular significance.

The group Sue was working with said they were surprised that eugenics had been a worldwide phenomenon, not confined solely to the Nazi regime. Many people, because of a limiting education, have had little chance to uncover the history of people with intellectual disabilities. Yet this linking up of events and experiences can be very empowering for people. It could be argued that any social movement, including the intellectual disability self-advocacy movement, has a fundamental need for its members, and those it is seeking to influence, to understand its roots and history (Bersani 1998).

How the past informs the present
SUE
Reflections from people with learning disabilities underline the value to individuals of improved historical understanding. In Chapter 4 Ebba from Iceland comments that the anger she felt when she discovered that she had been sterilised decreased when she was able to share this experience and understand the wider historical context in which it took place.

Similarly Anne Lewthwaite, an intellectually disabled woman from England who participated in research to document the history of the long-stay hospitals, said that it helped her understand that what had happened to her (her admission to hospital at the age of three) had happened to thousands of other children all over Britain. Lewthwaite said that listening to the life stories of others admitted to institutions as young children enabled her to see that it wasn't that her parents had 'put her away' but rather that this was 'normal' in that period for many children with intellectual disabilities (Hreinsdøttir *et al.* 2006).

LOUISE
I think it is important that a timeline has been put in. So many people with intellectual disabilities don't know about what happened to them in the past. Younger people might not know about how people used to be put away in the big institutions.

I've worked in the self-advocacy movement for a long time but some of the things in this timeline I didn't know, such as thousands of people being sterilised and being made to be sterilised before they could live in the community. This is terrible…it definitely taught me some things.

Summary

As mentioned in Chapter 1, the book has its origins in the International 2007 Social History of Learning Disability conference, 'Learning Disability, Relationships and Sexuality: Past and Present'. From the outset, using an historical perspective as a foundation to consider the future was a fundamental premise of our approach. Informed by discussions at that conference we argue that contemporary attitudes towards sex and relationships of people with intellectual disabilities are substantially influenced by the legacy of the past. It follows from this that developing a deeper understanding of the treatment of people with intellectual disabilities today is reliant on knowledge of its origins, its historical and (importantly) its geographical context (North 2011).

TABLE 2.1 SEXUALITY AND RELATIONSHIPS RIGHTS, PROTECTION AND CONTROL TIMELINE: THE UK IN
INTERNATIONAL PERSPECTIVE

Time Period	Key legislation, major policy developments and milestones	Publications	Campaigning groups	World Events
1900–1910	1907: Indiana, USA. first state to legalise involuntary sterilisation of 'insane, epileptics and idiots'. Sterilisation of 'mental defectives' pioneered in USA. By 1939 almost 31,000 in 30 states sterilised. Report 2 1 UK: 1908 'Report of the Royal Commission on the Care and Control of the Feeble Minded' – recommended institutional care to prevent 'procreation'.	Dendy, M. (1903) *The Feeble-Minded* Tredgold, A.F (1908) 'Mental Deficiency'		UK: 1903 Women's Social and Political Union was formed to campaign for women's suffrage. 3  The advent of cars. 4
1910s	1913: UK Mental Deficiency Act created a Board of Control responsible to the Home Secretary, and required councils to provide institutional care. Concerns over sexual control probably contributed to a higher notification of 'female defectives' under the Act. 1912 UK: First International Eugenics Conference organised by the British Eugenics Education Society. 1915–1922: Marriage made illegal for 'mental defectives' in many USA states, Switzerland, Denmark, Finland, Norway, Sweden. 	Dendy, M. (1911) M. 'Mental Deficiency Section' in Report of the Proceedings of the National Conference on the Prevention of Destitution. MacKellar, C. and Welsh, D.(1917)*Mental Deficiency: A Medico-Sociological Study of Feeble-Mindedness.*	1913 UK: Central Association for the Care of the Mentally Defective formed (from 1921 re-named the Central Association for Mental Welfare, CAMW).	1912 The liner *Titanic* sank on her maiden voyage from Southampton, UK. 1914–1918: First World War. 1916: Easter Uprising in Ireland. 1917: Russian Revolution. 5

1920s	1920: Tasmania, Australia, Mental Deficiency Act.	1921: UK CAMW constitution committed to 'influencing public opinion and promoting the well-being of the mentally defective'.	1922: Partition of Ireland (Irish Free State).
	1927: UK Mental Deficiency (Amendment) Act enabled compulsory institutionalisation of women giving birth to an illegitimate child.	
1923: Great Kanto earthquake kills 105,000 in Japan.
	1929, Australia Report on Mental Deficiency in the Commonwealth of Australia.		6
	1920s–1940s: UK, Scandinavia, USA, Australia rapid growth of institutionalisation for people with learning disabilities.		1927: World population reaches 2 billion.
	1923: USA 43,000 institutionalised.		1929: Wall Street Crash leading to Great Depression.
7 |

1930s	UK: Campaign to legalise involuntary sterilisation of intellectually disabled women Eugenicist Movement at its height. First institution established in Iceland, 1930. UK: New institutions opened to accommodate large numbers (typically 1000–2000 'patients' per institution) People separated from society and sexes often segregated to limit contact. 1933: Nazi Government introduced programme of sterilisation for mental defectives – Aktion T4 programme. 1938: sterilisation of and abortion for women with intellectual disabilities legalised in Iceland. 1938–1976: approximately 60,000 people subjected to eugenic sterilisation in Sweden (Rolph *et al.* 2005).	The Brock Committee Report (1934) argued there was no case for compulsory sterilisation yet advised voluntary sterilisation may be warranted with genetic disorders. Myrdal, A. and Myrdal G. (1934) *Crisis in the population?* In response to a rapid fall in birth rate this book advocated 'intelligent natalism' and improved family welfare.	1930 onwards: The Great Depression. 1932: BBC World Service begins. 1936: The Spanish Civil War begins. 1939: Second World War begins.
1940s	1944: UK Education Act – introduced the practice of certifying children with severe intellectual disabilities as 'ineducable'. Eugenics discredited after Second World War, but eugenicist ideas continued to influence local and national polices in many countries.		1946: UK National Association of Parents of Backward Children (NAPBC) founded – parents spoke out for their children to remain in local communities rather than be sent to institutions. UK: Local Mencap societies Founded. 	1940: Nazis invade France, Netherlands, Denmark and Norway. 1940: John Lennon born. 1945: Atomic bombing of Hiroshima and Nagasaki. 1945: Second World war Ends and Holocaust ends after 12 million deaths including 6 million Jews. 1945: Occupation of Japan. 1948: State of Israel formed and Apartheid in South Africa. 1949: Creation of NATO.

| 1950s | UK: Royal Commission on the Law relating to Mental Illness and Deficiency(1954–1957) examined the circumstances of people with intellectual disabilities detailed within long-stay hospitals.

1959: UK Mental Health Act repealed the 1913 and 1927 Mental Deficiency Acts and advocated community-based care as a positive alternative to institutional provision.

UK: Policy shift away from institutional models of care to community based provision.

Concerns about the cost of institutions were a factor in exploring community care alternatives.

 | 1951: National Council for Civil Liberties (NCCL) *50,000 Outside the Law* drew attention to the civil rights breaches of people detained in long-stay hospitals, the abuse suffered by some and hospital scandals.

1956: Tizard, J, and O'Connor, N. *The Social Problem of Mental Deficiency* Advocated the right of people with intellectual disabilities to the fullest life possible. | 1954: UK Families lobbied the Royal Commission (see Column 1) for improved education and community provision. | 1951: Occupation of Japan ends, Korean War starts.

1954: USA calls for end to racial segregation in schools.

1954–1975: Vietnam War.

1958: Campaign for Nuclear Disarmament formed.

10

1958: Alaska and Hawaii join United States.

1959–1975: Vietnam War.

1959: World population 3 billion. |

8   Image courtesy of Tom Curtis at FreeDigitalPhotos.net
9   Reproduced with kind permission from Mencap
10 Image courtesy of Victor Habbick at FreeDigitalPhotos.net

1960s				
1967: England, Wales and Scotland abortion legalised. 1965–1975: Iceland – sterilisation for intellectually disabled people became more widely practised.  1967–1977: Denmark, Sweden and Norway repealed sterilisation laws replacing them with laws based on voluntary consent. Advances in contraception meant that the idea of sexual relationships without children could be more widely promoted. Medication could be used to manage fertility outside institutional settings. UK: series of hospital scandals and evidence of ill treatment resulted in increased pressure to develop community service.	Goffman, E. (1961) *Asylums*: critique of institutional regimes. Tizard, J (1964) *Community Services for the Mentally Handicapped* – argued for the development of small communitybased residential units. Segal, S. (1966) *No Child is Ineducable* paved the way for education for all . Edgerton,R (1967) *The Cloak of Competence* – the right to marry and have children noted to be important to people leaving American institutions. Nirje, B. (1969) *The Normalization Principle and its Human Management Implications*.	1966: UK First Gateway Club opened for adults with intellectual disabilities to meet and socialise. 	Swinging 60s. Concorde made its maiden flight. 1960: Beatles formed in Liverpool. 1963: USA President John F Kennedy assassinated. Civil Rights Movement gained momentum. 11	1964: Civil Rights Act – abolishes racial segregation in USA. 1968: Martin Luther King and Robert F Kennedy assassinated. 1968: The 'Troubles' begin in Northern Ireland. 12

1970s			
1970: UK Education (Handicapped Children) Act extended education to all children with intellectual disabilities. 1971: UN Declaration of the Rights of Mentally Retarded Persons. Denmark and Sweden change laws restricting marriage. 1977: Victoria, Australia, *The Report of the Victorian Committee on Mental Retardation*, recognised the sexual rights of people with learning disabilities Influence of normalisation – emphasis on enabling people to experience a lifestyle as close as possible to the norms and patterns of mainstream society including sexual relationships and marriage (but not children). 1979: New legislation on assistance of people with intellectual disabilities enacted in Iceland. Reflected the spirit of normalisation and was the first to state the right of disabled people to live an ordinary life and participate in society. 1979: UK Jay Report: argued that people with intellectual disabilities could be successfully supported to live as married couples in their local communities.	Wolfensberger, W. (1972) '*The Principle of Normalisation in Human Services*'. Yokotsuka, H. (1975) '*Mother! Don't Kill Us!* Sususawa-shoten Japan – mothers who killed their own disabled children accused by Disability Movement. Craft, M. and Craft, A. (1978) *Sex and the Mentally Handicapped*. Craft M. and Craft A. (1979) *Handicapped Married Couples*. Evidence of positive impact of marriage on intellectually disabled people. 	1970: Campaign for 'People with a Mental Handicap' established (later re-named Values Into Action). 1972: 'Our Life' – First National Conference of 'Mentally Handicapped' people in Britain organised by CMH(Campaign for the Mentally Handicapped). Relationships raised as an issue by people with intellectual disabilities at the conference.	 Influence of civil rights movement across many western countries began to influence disability policy. 1970: Jimi Hendrix and Janis Joplin die. 1971: Decimalisation in Britain and Internment begins in Northern Ireland. 1979: Margaret Thatcher became Britain's first female prime minister.

11 Image courtesy of Victor Habbick at FreeDigitalPhotos.net
12 Image courtesy of taesmileland at FreeDigitalPhotos.net

1980s				
	1981: Australia the 5th Strand Conference Australia's first self-advocacy conference was held in conjunction with the 2nd South Pacific Regional conference on Mental Retardation. 1984: UK Registered Homes Act: new regulatory framework incorporating residential homes advocated support with relationships and development of sexuality polices within care settings. 1988: UK Education Reform Act (Section 1) state that all pupils should be offered the opportunity of receiving a comprehensive programme of sex education. Established a national curriculum with exceptions allowed for intellectually disabled people. Iceland research findings indicated that sterilisation was continuing – often around times of transition (people moving from family to a group home or leaving institutions). UK: Accelerated shift to community care, including private care. Europe and USA: increased awareness of AIDS increased concerns about sexual relationships Rise of fear of sexual vulnerability of intellectually disabled people.	Williams, P. and Shoultz, B.(1982) *We Can Speak For Ourselves.* Independent Development Council for People with a Mental Handicap (1985) *Living like other people: next steps in day services for people with mental handicap.* Towell, D. (1988) *An Ordinary Life in Practice*, London, Kings Fund.	1981: At the 5th Strand Conference Australia's first self-advocacy group, Force 10 (later renamed Reinforce), developed a Code of Rights that included 'the right to information about marriage and relationships'. 1982: UK Speaking For Ourselves – First conference of the Mencap London Division Participation Forum. 1984: UK delegates with intellectual disabilities attended first international self advocacy leadership conference in Tacoma, USA. English delegates inspired to set up People First, London late 1980s: UK People First begin to campaign for 'information and training on sex, relationships' for adults.	1980: John Lennon assassinated. 1982: Falklands War.  13 1984–85: UK Miners Strike. 1987: World population reaches 5 billion. 1989: Fall of the Berlin War. 1989: World Wide Web invented.

1990s			
1990: Family Planning Association Intellectual Disability Unit established in Melbourne to provide education, training and resources for people with an intellectual disability and support staff.

1990: England NHS and Community Care Act introduced system of individual needs assessment with associated individual packages of care.

1992: Australia 'Marion's Case' Family Court of Australia –14-year-old girl with intellectual disability – parents were seeking an order to give consent for sterilisation. Court ruled that parents authority did not extend to treatment which was not in the child's best interests. Parents did not have the authority to consent on behalf of their child.

1993: Republic of Ireland Sexual Offences Act –made it illegal to have sex with a person known to have intellectual disabilities.

1995: Disability Discrimination Act – after a long campaign, introduction of a rights-based agenda including the right to relationships.

1998: Human Rights Act Article 8 – right to respect for private and family life, home and correspondence Article 12 Right to Marry Article 14 Prohibition of Discrimination.

1998: UK Longcare Scandal – residents sexually abused over extended period by home manager. Growing awareness of the high incidence of sexual abuse amongst people with intellectual disabilities.  | 1990: Atkinson, D and Williams, F. *Know Me as I Am.* First anthology of writing, art and poetry by people with intellectual disabilities raised issues of relationships and parenting.

1993: NAPSAC *It could Never Happen Here.* ARC, UK.

1996: Campbell and Oliver: '*Disability Politics: Understanding Our Past, Changing Our Future* - outlined the social model of disability adopting a rights-based approach that locates disability as barriers imposed by society as opposed to individual limitations.  | 1993: Iceland – Atak – first self-advocacy group set up in Iceland.

1997: Belgium Our New Future Self-advocacy group founded.

1999: Japan first self advocacy group called 'Friend' established by parents of people with intellectual disabilities. | 1990: German reunification.

1991: End of Soviet Union.

1992: European Union created.

1994: End of apartheid - Nelson Mandela elected President of South Africa.

1995: Bosnian War.

1998: UK Parliament established for Scotland.

1999: National Assembly started in Wales.

1999: Devolution for Northern Ireland.

1999: Euro launched and world population reaches 6 billion. |

13   Image courtesy of James Barker at FreeDigitalPhotos.net

2000s			
2000: Japan – Act on Welfare of Mentally Retarded. 2000: Malta – The Equal Opportunities (Persons with Disability) Act (EOA) was passed into law in order to recognise and safeguard the rights of persons with disability with a view to ending discrimination on the basis of disability. 2001: UK Department of Health No Secrets: Guidance on developing and implementing multi-agency policies and procedures to protect vulnerable adults from abuse. 2001: UK Special Needs and Disability Act (SENDA) made educational discrimination unlawful. 2001: DH Valuing People: right for all to choose where they live and for community inclusion to be fully supported. 2003, Belgium – Anti-Discrimination Law prohibited direct or indirect discrimination on all life domains (updated 2007). 2003: Japan Disciplinary Measures taken by Tokyo Board of Education against teachers using explicit sexual materials in classes with young people with learning disabilities. 2005: England and Wales Mental Capacity Act – presumption of capacity to make own decisions and legal duty to involve people with intellectual disabilities in decision-making. The act required information to support decision-making to be made accessible including information about the law, sex and contraception. 2006: UK Disability Equality Duty came into force United Nations. 2006: Convention of the Rights of Persons with Disabilities Article 23 made specific reference to sexual and personal relationships. 2007: England, HM Government Putting People First – transformation of adult social care to a personalised model. 2009 UK last long-stay hospital closed in England. 2009: DH Valuing People Now – strategy emphasised the importance of services enabling people with intellectual disabilities to meet new people, form all kinds of relationships *including the choice to become parents*. 	2001–2011: Australia Living Safer Sexual Lives Initiative – collaborative research and advocacy using life stories of people with an intellectual disability. Relationships (LSSL:RR) Frawley, P., Slattery, J., Stokoe, L, Houghton, D and O'Shea, A. Peer education programme developed in collaboration with women with intellectual disabilities trained people with intellectual disabilities to run across Australia UK (2008). Joint Committee on Human Rights *A Life Like Any Other?* Human Rights of Adults with Learning Disabilities. 	2003: Ireland, first landmark conference on 'Sexuality, Disability and Relationships' organised by Forum of People with Disabilities & Inclusion Ireland. R.E.S.PE.C.T. Organised by the National Federation of Voluntary Bodies and the Irish Sex Education Network 2008 UK People with Intellectual Disabilities gave evidence to the Joint Committee of Human Rights. Concerns about support with sex education and parenting acknowledged by committee. 2007: SHLD Conference, Learning Disability, Relationships and Sexuality: Past and Present, Open University (idea for this book came from discussion at this conference).	2001: Bombing of The World Trade Centre in New York. 2003: Iraq War Begins and human genome project completed. 14 2004: Boxing Day Tsunami in Indian Ocean. 2005: IRA ends military campaign in Northern Ireland and 7/7 attacks on London Underground. 2007: Start of global recession. 2008: Obama elected as President in United States. 15

2010–2013	2011: Belgium, first report on Committee of Rights of Persons with Disabilities included that services are to support sexuality of people with disabilities and actions to prevent sexual abuse and Task Force on prevention of HIV. 2011: UK Winterbourne View Private Hospital Scandal – undercover reporter produced film to show appalling abuse of 'patients'. 16 17 2012: Malta Guardianship Act – guardians appointed to safeguard and, if necessary, represent people with intellectual disabilities. The Act required freedom of choice and action to be respected. 2013: Australian government Senate Committee held inquiry into the involuntary or coerced sterilisation of people with disabilities in Australia. Whilst legal programmes of mass sterilisation formally ended in the 1970s, private, often family-initiated, sterilisation continued in community settings in many countries.	2010: research into contraceptive use by McCarthy,M. *Exercising choice and control- women with learning disabilities and contraception* - raised concern that chemical sterilisation in the form of long-term contraceptive use may be replacing surgical sterilisation. 2014: World Health Organisation *Eliminating forced, coercive and otherwise involuntary sterilization*	2010: Flanders Self Advocacy, 'Love is all around' Conference.	2010: Devastating Earthquake in Haiti. 2011: Earthquake and tsunami in Japan. 2011: Revolutions in Tunisia, Egypt and Libya. World population reaches 7 billion. 2014: West Africa Ebola outbreak. 2014: Scottish Independence Referendum.

14   Image courtesy of think4photop at FreeDigitalPhotos.net
15   Image courtesy of vitasamb2001 at FreeDigitalPhotos.net
16   Image courtesy of Mencap
17   Image courtesy of Mencap

References

Atkinson, D. and Williams, F. (1990) *Know Me As I Am: An Anthology of Prose, Poetry and Art by People with Learning Difficulties.* London: Hodder and Stoughton.

Bersani, H. Jnr (1998) 'From Social Clubs to Social Movement.' In L. Ward (ed.) *Innovations in Advocacy and Empowerment.* Lancashire: Lisieux Hall Publications.

Brock,L.G.(1934) Report of the Departmental Committee on Sterilisation London HMSO.

Campbell, J. and Oliver, M. (1996) *Disability Politics: Understanding Our Past, Changing Our Future,* Oxon, Routledge.

Craft, M. and Craft, A. (1978) *Sex and the Mentally Handicapped,* London, Routledge and Kagan Paul.

Craft, M. and Craft, A. (1979) *Handicapped Married Couples: a Welsh study of couples handicapped from birth by mental, physical or personality disorder.* London, Routledge and Kagan Paul.

Dendy, M. (1903) 'The Feeble Minded' in Economic Review, July 1903 (1)

Dendy, M. (1911) 'The Care of the Feeble Minded' in *Proceedings at a conference on the Care of the Feeble Minded,* Manchester and Salford Sanitary Association, London, Sherrat and Hughes.

Edgerton, R. (1967) *The Cloak of Competence: Stigma in the Lives of the Mentally Retarded.* Berkley, CA: University of California Press.

Fanstone, C. and Andrews, S. (2009) *Learning Disabilities, Sex and the Law.* London: FPA.

Frawley, P., Slattery, J., Stokoe, L., Houghton, D. and O'Shea, (2011) *Living Safer Sexual Lives: Respectful Relationships. Peer Educator and Co-Facilitator Manual.* Australian Research Centre in Sex, Health and Society, La Trobe University, Melbourne.

Goffman, E. (1961) *Asylums: Essays on the Social Situation of Mental Patients and other inmates.* Toronto: Anchor Books, Random House.

Hreinsdøttir, E.E., Stefánsdøttir, G., Lewthwaite, A., Ledger, S. & Shufflebotham, L. (2006). Is my story so different from yours? Comparing life stories: Experience of institutionalization and self-advocacy in England and Iceland. *British Journal of Learning Disabilities,* 34(3), 157–167.

Independent Development Council for People with a Mental Handicap (1985) *Living Like Other People: next steps in day services for people with mental handicap.* London: Independent Development Council for People with a Mental Handicap.

Joint committee on Human Rights (2008) *A life like any other?: human rights of adults with learning disabilities seventh report of session* 2007-08: Vol. 1 Report and formal minutes, House of Lords papers 40-I 2007-08. House of Commons papers 73-I 2007-08.

King's Fund Centre (1980) *An ordinary life: comprehensive, locally based, residential services for mentally handicapped people.* London: King's Fund Centre.

Mackellar, C. and Welsh, D.(1917) *Mental Deficiency: A Medico-sociological study of feeblemindedness.* Sydney, W.A: Gullick, Government Printer.

McCarthy, M. (2010a). Exercising choice and control - women with learning disabilities and contraception, *British Journal Of Learning Disabilities,* 38, 293–302.

McCarthy, M. (2010b). The sexual lives of women with learning disabilities, in *Learning Disability: a Lifecycle Approach,* edited by G. Grant, P. Ramcharan, M. Flynn and M. Richardson Maidenhead: Open University Press, 259–265.

Myrdal, A. and Myrdal G. (1934) *Crisis in the population?* Stockholm: Bonner.

NAPSAC (1993) *It could never happen here: the prevention and treatment of sexual abuse of adults with learning disabilities in residential settings.* UK, ARC/NAPSAC.

North, J. (2011) 'Making it happen' Paper given at *Housing Options and Challenging* Behaviour Foundation Conference: 'Keeping it Local', Birmingham, 4th November 2011.

O'Callaghan, A. and Murphy, G. (2007) 'Sexual relationships in adults with intellectual disabilities: Understanding the law.' *Journal of Intellectual Disability Research 51*, 3, 197–206.

Rolph, S., Atkinson, D., Nind, M. and Welshman, J. (eds) (2005) *Witnesses to Change: Families, Learning Difficulties and History*. Kidderminster: BILD.

Royal Commission on the Law Relating to Mental Illness and Mental Disability 1954–1957 (1957) (Cmnd. 169), London: HMSO.

Segal, S. (1966) *No Child is Ineducable*. Oxford: Pergamon Press.

Thompson, J. and Westwood, L. (2007) 'What is important to you?' *Association of Practitioners in Learning Disability 23*, 3, 8–14.

Tilley E, Earle S, Walmsley J, and Atkinson D (2012) *'The Silence is roaring': Sterilization, reproductive rights and women with intellectual disabilities, in* Disability and Society, 27(3) pp. 413–426

Tizard, J. and O'Connor, N. (1956) *The Social Problem of Mental Deficiency*, London and New York: Pergamon Press.

Tizard, J. (1964) *Community Services for the Mentally Handicapped*, London: Oxford University Press.

Tredgold, A. (1908) Mental Deficiency (Amentia), New York: William Wood and Company.

Tsuda, E. (2006) 'Japanese culture and the philosophy of self-advocacy: The importance of interdependence in community living.' *British Journal of Learning Disabilities 34*, 3, 151–156.

Welshman, J. and Walmsley, J. (eds) (2006) *Community Care in Perspective: Care, Control and Citizenship*. Basingstoke: Palgrave Macmillan.

Williams, P. and Shoultz, B. (1982) *We Can Speak For Ourselves*. London: Souvenir Press.

Wolfensberger, W. (1972) *The Principle of Normalisation in human services*. Toronto: National Institute on Mental Retardation.

Yokotsuka, H. (1975) *Hahayo! Mothers! Don't kill! Korosuna!*. Suzusawa Shoten (in Japanese). US.

CHAPTER 3

INTIMACY AND OPPRESSION

A Historical Perspective

Lee-Ann Monk with an introduction by Louise Townson

Overview

- This chapter looks at ideas about people with intellectual disabilities and sex from the early 1900s to the present.

- Because of these ideas, people with intellectual disabilities were put away in institutions, not allowed to marry or forced to have operations so they could not have children.

- They were not allowed to make their own decisions about sex and relationships.

- In the 1970s, these ideas began to change. People realised that people with intellectual disabilities should make their own decisions about sex and relationships.

- Even though people realised this, there were still problems. Many people with intellectual disabilities still did not have control over who they had sex or relationships with and whether they would have children.

- The chapter suggests that ideas and practices from the past continue to influence what happens today.

The writing process

As this chapter is an overview of the historical context of relationships and sexuality for intellectually disabled people across different countries, we asked an academic historian, Lee-Ann Monk, to write it. Lee-Ann comes from Australia and her preferred terminology is 'people with intellectual disabilities'. However, when necessary she also uses historical labels to maintain the authenticity of the account.

Louise Townson has written an introduction from her own perspective.

Introduction

LOUISE

For many years the subject of sexuality and relationships was taboo, particularly for people with intellectual disabilities. It was assumed that 'they don't need to know about things like that'.

I agree that people need to be protected from harm, but people were told that talk about sex is 'dirty and not nice', it was drummed into them. If people wanted to go off and have sex together then they did it anyway. A friend of mine who was in a long-stay institution always talked about the segregation between the men and women and how they got together.

One night a man and a woman went off together to have sex and were caught by a member of staff. They were disciplined by the doctor who ordered them to be sent to their (separate) beds for a month. When the punishment was over, then they did exactly the same thing again. If people want to do something like that, they will always find a way to do it.

Introduction

LEE-ANN MONK

That sexuality and intimate relationships are complex issues for people with intellectual disabilities is in part the legacy of the past. For much of the twentieth century, overlapping and contradictory ideas about people with intellectual disabilities saw the implementation of polices – institutional segregation, coercive sterilisation and legal restrictions to marry among them – that denied their sexual rights in the name of their protection or that of society. The purpose of this chapter is to provide a broad overview of the history of the treatment of people with intellectual disabilities in relation to sexuality across the twentieth and early twenty-first centuries and an international perspective, to provide context for the chapters that follow.

The many names used to refer to people with intellectual disabilities in the past are highly offensive and for that reason their use presents a dilemma to the historian. I have chosen to retain the use of contemporary terms in this chapter because they are revealing of past attitudes to and changing understandings of intellectual disabilities. However, I emphasise that I do not share the assumptions this contemporary language expresses. Terms generally considered to be derogatory are placed in inverted commas, unless they are integral to a quotation.

The menace of the 'feebleminded'

In the late nineteenth and early twentieth centuries, a confluence of social and racial anxieties saw the conviction take hold in many western countries that the so-called 'feebleminded' were the cause of a multitude of social problems (Jackson 1996, pp.165–6, 168–9; Simmons 1978, pp.388–91; Strange and Stephen 2010, pp.525–7; Trent 1994, pp.141, 160–5, 178). 'Feeblemindedness' was, in the words of English social reformer Mary Dendy, 'an evil which brings all other evils in its train' (Dendy, *The Importance of Permanence in the Care of the Feeble-Minded*, n.d., p.2, quoted in Jackson 1996, p.169). Contemporaries like Dendy, convinced of the 'menace of the feebleminded', assumed that 'mental deficiency' was a hereditary defect passed from one generation of the feebleminded to the next, which rendered them 'constitutionally inclined' to immorality. This moral debility led in turn to 'profligate breeding' and an ever-increasing number of the feebleminded, threatening an eventual decline in the 'overall fitness of the population' (Thomson 2010, p.119). To prevent social and racial disaster, then, contemporaries like Dendy considered it imperative to impose control where they assumed none existed. Moreover, because 'feeblemindedness' was an inherited and incurable defect, no resort to 'education, exhortation or example' could be effective (Jackson 1996, p.171; Simmons 1978, p.395). In the words of the 1908 Report of the Royal Commission on the Care and Control of the Feeble-Minded, 'the only remedy is to place persons so suffering under such restrictions as to make procreation impossible' (Sixty-Third Report of the Commissioners in Lunacy 1909, pp.4–5, quoted in May and Simpson 2003, p.29).

The first decades of the twentieth century consequently witnessed the introduction in many western countries of social policies intended to impose the necessary control by various means. The English Mental Deficiency Act of 1913 was 'the first comprehensive legislation of its kind' enacted in the western world (Simmons 1978, p.388). The Act required local authorities to 'ascertain, certify and make provision for mental defectives in their areas', primarily through the development of institutions (Walmsley, Atkinson and Rolph 1999, pp.184–5). While it did not provide unfettered power to intervene in the lives of people certified 'mentally defective', the Act did provide for their compulsory institutionalisation in certain circumstances, notably including women 'in receipt of poor relief when pregnant with, or while giving birth to, an illegitimate child' (Jackson 2000, p.219).

Historian Jan Walmsley has concluded from her research into the implementation of the Act that 'sexual control' was 'paramount' in decisions to institutionalise, 'particularly early in the period of the Mental Deficiency Act, when institutional places were at a premium'. At the height of its effect, '65,000 people were placed in colonies, hospitals or other institutions, in some cases for many years, with no legal right to petition against continued detention' (Walmsley 2005, pp.58–9; 2000, p.65).

The United States did not pass similarly comprehensive legislation. However, the first decades of the twentieth century witnessed a 'dramatic increase' in the number of people admitted to American institutions for the mentally defective, from 14,347 in 1904 to 43,000 in 1923. By the latter year, only six states were without a public institution for 'mental defectives'. Several had more than one: New York state had six. Private institutions multiplied even faster, from about ten in 1900 to eighty by 1923 (Simmons 1978, p.388; Trent 1994, pp.185, 188).

Those in charge of such institutions strove through strict segregation and supervision to limit contact between the sexes. Attempts by inmates to circumvent these restrictions met with repression and punishment (Potts and Fido 1991, pp.110–12). When 21-year-old Louisa Thomson, an inmate of an institution for 'mental defectives' in Australia, began showing what the doctor called 'amatory tendencies, wandering up to' the fence dividing the male and female divisions of the institution and 'refusing to come away', the staff dragged her away by force (PROV, VPRS 7448, Unit 1, p.84).

Institutionalisation was not the only measure employed in western countries in an attempt to prevent 'mental defectives' reproducing. In 1895, the US state of Connecticut introduced a law prohibiting 'defectives' from marrying. In a little under two decades, more than half of American states had legislated to restrict marriage. Switzerland prohibited the marriage of the 'mentally deficient' in its Civil Code of 1907. Between 1915 and 1922, Denmark, Norway and Sweden all enacted laws which made mental deficiency an impediment to marriage (Broberg and Tydén 1996, p.100; Gerodetti 2006, pp.68, 79; Hansen 1996, p.31; Thomson 2010, p.120; Trent 1994, p.165).

The United States was also a pioneer in the sexual sterilisation of 'mental defectives' (Thomson 2010, p.120). In the 1890s, the superintendents of some American institutions for the 'feebleminded' were using sterilisation, mostly in the form of castration, to control sexual behaviours such as masturbation, considered detrimental to the inmates' well-being or offensive to 'social sensibilities' (Trent 1994, pp.193–5). In the first decade of the twentieth century, fear of the 'feebleminded' saw sterilisation find a new purpose, succinctly summarised by the Superintendent of the Pennsylvania Training School, Martin W. Barr, as 'preventing increase'

(Barr, The Imbecile and the Epileptic versus the Tax-Payer and the Community, *Proceedings of the National Conference of Charities and Correction* 1902, pp.161–5, quoted in Trent 1994, p.196). In 1907, Indiana became the first state to legalise the compulsory sterilisation of people confined in its state institutions. While the law focused on 'habitual criminals and rapists', it also provided for 'the involuntary sterilization of the insane, epileptics and idiots'. By 1917, eleven more states had followed Indiana's lead. These laws did not stand unchallenged, however, many being struck down by the courts as unconstitutional. Two decades after Indiana passed its law, in the landmark case *Buck v. Bell*, the Supreme Court declared involuntary sterilisation constitutional, the presiding judge, Justice Oliver Wendell Holmes, famously proclaiming, 'Three generations of imbeciles are enough'. In the wake of the decision, there was a rush by many states to legalise sterilisation (Keely 2004, p.208; Trent 1994, pp.197, 199). By 1939, almost 31,000 people in thirty states had been sterilised, many on the assumption that they were mentally defective (Park and Radford 1998, p.318).

Laws sanctioning sterilisation of the 'unfit' were also adopted elsewhere. In Canada, for example, the provinces of Alberta and British Columbia passed sterilisation laws in 1926 and 1933 respectively. In Europe, the Swiss canton of Vaud legislated to regulate sterilisation in 1928 (Gerodetti 2006, p.69). The following year Denmark passed its first sterilisation law, sanctioning sterilisation of people confined to institutions. Norway and Sweden followed suit in 1934, Finland in 1935 (Broberg and Tydén 1996, pp.98, 102–3; Hansen 1996, pp.36, 37, 39; Hietala 1996, p.195). Wherever governments legalised sterilisation in this period, the main target was the 'mental defective'. In Germany, for example, of the 375,000 people sterilised under the provisions of the 1933 Nazi Law for the Prevention of Hereditarily Afflicted Progeny, more than half were so-called 'mental defectives' (Thomson 2010, p.120).

In the United States, where laws allowed sterilisation without the consent of those subjected to it, it was manifestly coercive. Even where sterilisation was ostensibly voluntary, provisions which made it a condition for institutional release or allowed others to consent to the procedure without regard to the individual's wishes made the difference more illusory than real (Strange and Stephen 2010, p.532). In 1942, a Swedish woman deemed mentally deficient who had signed an application for sterilisation wrote to the Board of Health to ask that she not be made to have the operation, explaining that when she was in hospital 'they kept on at me so as to get me to sign the papers that I don't even know if I even read what I signed' (Broberg and Tydén 1996, pp.117–18). However the absence of sterilisations laws did not prevent sterilisation: evidence survives of doctors performing operations without legal sanction (Broberg and Tydén 1996, pp.98, 103; Largent 2008, p.32).

Nonetheless, laws which restrained the power of doctors to sterilise on their own initiative may have limited the number of procedures that might otherwise have been performed, as historian Natalia Gerodetti (2006, pp.71, 76–7) argues was the case in the Swiss canton of Vaud.

Acute anxieties about 'feebleminded' women meant that policies intended to protect against the menace of the 'feebleminded' affected women disproportionately. For contemporaries, the 'reckless promiscuity' (Stern 2010, p.177) of the 'feebleminded' woman made her 'a potent factor in the increase of the unfit and a menace to public morals' (Tenth Biennial Report of the Wisconsin Home for the Feeble-Minded, Madison 1916, p.274, quoted in Tyor 1977, p.477). Because contemporaries considered 'feeblemindedness' a hereditary defect and the 'feebleminded' woman more fecund than her 'normal' sisters, her 'unbridled sexuality' must result in ever more 'feebleminded' children (Digby 1996, p.11; Simmons 1978, pp.393–4). Moreover, because her defect left her 'prone to licentious behaviour' and particularly susceptible to sexual exploitation by unscrupulous men, she represented a 'sexual threat to respectability and normal family life' (Digby 1996, p.11; Stern 2010, p.177; Trent 1994, p.212). She should be controlled both to protect society but, by the same reasoning, also for her own protection (Tyor 1977, p.482). Consequently, women were more likely to be institutionalised than men and for longer periods, and more likely to be sterilised (Gerodetti 2006, pp.71, 76; Park and Radford 1998, p.322; Thomson 1996, pp.208, 211; Tydén 2010, p.370).

Advocates of policies intended to defend against the menace of the 'feebleminded' did not always succeed in having them implemented. Nor was their impact always as far-reaching as their supporters had hoped (Dale 2003, p.405; Simmons 1978, pp.388, 399–400). Nonetheless, policies and practices instituted to guard against that danger denied many tens of thousands of people so labelled their sexual rights.

'Forever children'

In 1950, American author Pearl S. Buck publicly recounted the story of her life as the parent of a 'mentally retarded' daughter. In *The Child Who Never Grew*, Buck wrote of her gradual realisation that her daughter, Carol, was 'different from other children' and her subsequent desperate search for a cure, a search that ended with her final acceptance that Carol could 'never be normal'. Having admitted Carol, aged nine, to the Vineland Training School in New Jersey, Buck was partly motivated to tell her story by the many letters she received from other parents of mentally retarded children. To them she explained that the 'mentally retarded' were 'forever children', destined because of their 'arrested' mental development to remain children in mind despite having grown physically into adulthood (Buck 1992 [1950]; Trent 1994, pp.230–2).

Fifty years before Buck told her story, doctors interested in mental deficiency, drawing on contemporary theories of child development, had argued that 'feeblemindedness' was the result of diseased inheritance that made normal development impossible. Their development permanently 'arrested', the 'feebleminded' were left, in American psychologist Henry H. Goddard's words, 'perpetual children' (Goddard, *Feeble-Mindedness: Its Causes and Consequences*, 1914, p.585, quoted in Brockley 2001, p.40; Jackson 2003, pp.151–3). As such, and lacking the capacities of adulthood, they were deemed in need of 'permanent care and supervision' and denied the rights of full citizenship. For those, like Mary Dendy and Goddard, convinced of the menace of the 'feebleminded', the infantilisation of the 'feebleminded' as 'grown-up children' provided a paternalist rationale for the policies, such as permanent institutionalisation, they favoured (Brockley 2001, pp.40–1; Jackson 2003, pp.153–4).

The idea that people with intellectual disabilities were 'forever children' also gave parents a way to understand their responsibilities toward their children (Brockley 2001, pp.1, 10). In 1950, Buck wrote that, having accepted the 'inevitable knowledge that my child would never be as other children', she found herself confronted with the question of how to 'safeguard a child who may live to be physically very old and will always be helpless', one never able to take responsibility for herself (Buck 1992 [1950], p.48). For Buck, the answer was permanent institutionalisation. As her remarks suggest, 'eternal childhood' implied eternal dependence. Because their children would 'never grow', it fell to the parents of children with intellectual disabilities to make decisions about their lives on their behalf, including decisions about sexuality and intimate relationships (Brockley 2001, pp.11–12).

For much of the century, such decisions were likely shaped by the belief that as 'eternal children' people with intellectual disabilities were asexual, as all children were assumed to be (Kempton and Kahn 1991, p.97; McCarthy 1999, p.53). In 1950, Buck wrote of Carol that she was 'one who has never grown mentally beyond her early childhood…although in years she is old enough now to have been married and to have children of her own – my grandchildren who will never be'. To Buck's mind, as to others, the 'mentally retarded' were innocent children and, as such, should be 'innocent of sex' (Brockley 2001, pp.143–4; Buck 1992 [1950], pp.25, 28, 51). According to Michelle McCarthy (1999, p.53):

> Just as it was unthinkable to talk to young children about sex, so it was unthinkable to talk to adults with learning disabilities about sex – protecting their natural innocence was the priority and this fitted into an 'ignorance is bliss' philosophy.

As historian Mathew Thomson suggests, associating 'mental deficiency with a child-like state made the development of defectives' sexual interests a shock to parents'

(1996, p.221). Thomson suggests that, 'Concerns over sexual control of adolescent daughters probably contributed to a higher familial notification of female, than male, defectives' (p.221) under the 1913 Mental Deficiency Act. He argues, however, that to see such 'familial use of statutory control as simply a negative restrictive action' (p.221) would be misleading. Such actions, he suggests, were likely motivated as much by care as control (p.221). Nonetheless, such beliefs denied people with intellectual disabilities the right to make decisions about their sexual lives and restricted their opportunities for sexual expression and intimate relationships for much of the century.

'The right to sexuality is a fundamental human right'[1]

Beginning in the 1950s, institutions for people with intellectual disabilities came under increasing criticism. Media exposés, social research and official investigations uncovered the 'abusive and dehumanizing conditions' (Taylor 2006, p.145) their inmates experienced. Parent organisations and civil liberties groups campaigned for change. The criticisms, combined with the desire of governments to cut costs, resulted in decisions to close institutions and substitute community care in their place (Bank-Mikkelsen 1976, p.242; McCarthy 1999, pp.50–1; Taylor 2006; Trent 1994, pp.252–9, 261–2).

While de-institutionalisation removed the constraint on sexual expression that institutional segregation had formerly imposed, institutional life, with its strict limits on sexual expression and intimate relationships, left many patients unprepared for sex and marriage. As one participant in sociologist Robert Edgerton's study of the lives of patients discharged from the Pacific State Hospital in California between 1949 and 1958 explained, he and his wife, also a former inmate, had 'had to learn "the hard way"', the hospital having taught them nothing about sex. Believing that sexual behaviour was particularly important if ex-patients were to live successfully 'on the outs', Edgerton argued that 'skill in the management of sexual conduct must be developed if the ex-patient is to avoid serious difficulty in life outside the hospital' (Edgerton and Dingman 1964, pp.228–32; Edgerton 1967, pp.31, 111). While Edgerton and Dingman argued based on need, a new philosophy – normalisation – would recast sexual expression as a right to which people with intellectual disabilities were entitled.

Normalisation originated in Denmark. In 1959, a new Mental Retardation Act set out as the objective for services the creation of 'an existence for the mentally retarded as close to normal living conditions as possible'. In 1976, Niels Erik Bank-Mikkelsen, formerly director of the Danish Service for the Mentally Retarded,

---

1   Bank-Mikkelson (1976) p. 247

elaborated on the meaning of the concept. Normalisation did not mean making people with intellectual disabilities normal. Rather, he explained, normalisation 'means making normal, mentally retarded people's housing, education, working, and leisure conditions. It means bringing them the legal and human rights of other citizens' (Bank-Mikkelsen 1976, p.243). Normalisation had considerable influence in both Denmark and Sweden (Emerson 1992, p.2). In 1969, Bengt Nirje, the executive director of the Swedish Association for Retarded Children, defined the normalisation principle as 'making available to the mentally retarded patterns and conditions of everyday life which are as close as possible to the norms and patterns of the mainstream society'. This, Nirje explained, meant that services must be organised to allow 'mentally retarded' people to experience the rhythms and routines of normal life, including the 'normal developmental experiences of the life cycle' such as the 'coming of adulthood'. It also meant living in a 'bisexual world': the desegregation of services to allow the 'mixing of the sexes according to the normal patterns of everyday society' (Nirje 1969, pp.182–5).

Normalisation, as conceived by Nirje and Bank-Mikkelsen, emphasised the equality and civil rights of people with intellectual disabilities, its aim being to 'ensure that people with learning difficulties enjoyed their rights to the same quality of life as non-disabled members of society'. In this emphasis, normalisation reflected the civil rights movements then occurring in many western countries, which eventually came to include people with disabilities (Brockley 2001, pp.10–11; Emerson 1992, p.3). It also reflected a reconceptualisation of mental retardation as 'a dynamic condition which', in Bank-Mikkelsen's words, could 'be influenced by treatment, education and training', undermining the idea of the 'mentally retarded' as eternal children (Bank-Mikkelsen 1976, p.243; Lewis 1988, p.161).

In 1972, North American sociologist Wolf Wolfensberger redefined normalisation in his influential book *The Principle of Normalization in Human Services*. Influenced by contemporary sociological theory, he argued that existing services for the mentally retarded – special institutions and school programmes, sheltered workshops – merely 'drew attention to the uniquely devalued qualities of retarded people'. To overcome this labelling, Wolfensberger argued, service providers must 'work with mentally retarded people to help them assume socially valued behaviours and integrate them into culturally normative settings' (Trent 1994, pp.262–3). As Wolfensberger defined it, normalisation was the 'utilisation of means which are as culturally normative as possible, in order to establish and/or maintain personal behaviors and characteristics which are as culturally normative as possible' (Wolfensberger 1972, p.28). In contrast to the Scandinavians, Wolfensberger insisted that achieving the aims of normalisation was impossible while people with intellectual disabilities remained congregated and segregated in institutions that called attention to their 'deviance'; normalisation was possible only through their integration into wider society (Stella 1996, p.94).

The principle of normalisation was immensely influential and adopted in services across the western world. This philosophy advocated the need for a significant shift in attitude toward the sexuality of people with intellectual disabilities. The emphasis in normalisation on the right to a 'normal' life implied, at least theoretically, the 'right to a sexual life' (Bank-Mikkelsen 1975, p.188; McCarthy 1999, pp.55, 56). In 1976, Nirje acknowledged this when he listed sex education as one of the necessary preparations services should provide to facilitate people's development into adulthood. In the same volume, Bank-Mikkelsen declared 'the right to sexuality a fundamental human right' (Bank-Mikkelsen 1976, p.247; Nirje 1976, p.236). However, as he conceded, this idea did not meet with immediate or universal acceptance. Public discussion about what mentally retarded people should be taught about sex revealed differing opinions, with some participants expressing what Bank-Mikkelsen termed 'old protectionist views…as well as fears about exploitation and abuse of retarded people' (Bank-Mikkelsen 1976, p.247). His remarks reflect the controversies and anxieties the new ideas about sexuality caused many parents and services staff (Lewis 1988, pp.161–2).

In 1969, Nirje (p.185) had argued that 'the mildly retarded sometimes suffer in a loneliness that has no sense, and as others, they may be better off married'. Edgerton had shown that the right to marry (and have children) was important to the participants in his study, dramatically emphasising 'their newly won status as free and full members of the outside world' (Edgerton 1967, pp.111, 154). In the 1970s, some authors and activists began to advocate for 'the right of people with learning disabilities to date the opposite sex and marry'. In 'pioneering and influential' research on marriages of people with intellectual disabilities, Janet Mattinson and Michael and Ann Craft 'both depicted marriage as a predominantly positive choice and lifestyle for the couples they researched' (May and Simpson 2003, p.32; McCarthy 1999, pp.57, 59). In Denmark, belief in the equality of the mentally retarded inspired a campaign to amend the law restricting marriage. Sweden, too, liberalised its law (Bank-Mikkelsen 1975, pp.184–5; Grunewald 1976, p.263).

However, the anxieties that had seen restrictive marriage laws first enacted had not disappeared. Marriage, as advocated by the Crafts and others in the 1970s was, significantly, marriage without children (May and Simpson 2003, pp.32–3). While Wolfensberger considered 'social-sexual fulfilment' a right, he insisted that at least in North America it must be achieved via childless marriage, 'because the North American public will not now approve, and probably never will, child-bearing by those unlikely to be capable of children rearing'. The necessary 'sterility' of such unions could be 'assured either by sterilization or contraception' though the former, he added, should be voluntary (Wolfensberger 1972, pp.171, 172). Similarly, in a 1974 pamphlet on the 'Sexual Rights of the Retarded' published by the National Society for Mentally Handicapped Children, George W. Lee argued that the 'rights of the mentally retarded…must include the right of sexual expression'. However, like Wolfensberger, he was unwilling to countenance their becoming parents. Respect for the rights and welfare of the potential children required that 'the mentally retarded should not be persuaded of their right to procreate' (Lee 1974, pp.7–9).

Such assumptions about the incompetence of people with intellectual disabilities to parent had long justified denying their right to marry (Carey 2009, p.87; May and Simpson 2003, p.31). In 1926, for example, the Board of Control argued against allowing 'mental defectives' to marry because any resulting children must remain 'under the control of persons…incapable of taking care of them' and so be 'exposed to the hardships, neglect and ill treatment that the mental condition of their parents renders inevitable' (Board of Control Annual Report 1926, quoted in Walmsley *et al.* 1999, p.192). Arguably, the advent of effective contraception allowed Wolfensberger, Lee and others to contemplate heterosexual sex and marriage for people with intellectual disabilities. Contraception decoupled 'sex from procreation, thus removing one of the principal objections to the marriage of people with intellectual disabilities'. Contraception thus provided a means both of liberation and of continuing regulation. In Lee's words, 'modern techniques of birth control' had rendered the earlier policies of institutional incarceration of young women 'not only effete but also indefensible' (Lee 1974, p.7; May and Simpson 2003, pp.32, 36; McCarthy 1999, pp.56–7).

This assumed incompetence had also provided a rationale for involuntary sterilisation. In the United States and the Nordic countries, for example, advocates of sterilisation argued for it as a protection against the social harm of allowing mental defectives to raise children (Tilley *et al.* 2012b, pp.415–16). Despite the revelations of Nazi atrocities, sterilisations continued into the post-war era. In the Canadian province of Alberta, numbers actually peaked in the 1950s and 1960s. By contrast, in Scandinavia sterilisations of the 'mentally retarded' fell rapidly from the mid-1940s through the 1950s. In the United States, while the number declined from a high point in the 1930s, several states continued to sterilise 'several hundred retarded persons' a year into the mid-1960s (Park and Radford 1998, p.318; Reilly 1991, pp.128–9; Roll-Hansen 1996, p.264).

In the US no new laws were enacted after 1937, but neither were any repealed; in 1961 26 states still had laws sanctioning involuntary sterilisation. Two decades later, however, many had repealed their laws (Carey 2010, p.85; Elkins and Anderson 1992, p.20; Reilly 1991, p.136, 148). This was partly a consequence of changing attitudes toward reproductive rights generally. A series of legal cases, prompted by the civil rights movements of the era, had affirmed that it was the right of the individual, not the state, to control their reproduction (Diekema 2003, p.22; Largent 2008, p.140). A similar emphasis on the recognition of individual reproductive rights was also important elsewhere (Broberg and Tydén 1996, pp.133–4). Between 1967 and 1977, Denmark, Sweden and Norway repealed their earlier sterilisation laws, replacing them with 'laws based on voluntary consent'. Alberta and British Columbia repealed their laws in 1972 (Thomson 2010, p.125; Tydén 2010, p.372).

'An ordinary sexual life?'[2]

In 1987, a decade after Bank-Mikkelsen declared 'the right to sexuality a fundamental human right', Ann Craft remarked on the discomfort still felt toward the sexuality of people with intellectual disabilities. She located its origin partly in contemporary expectations of people with intellectual disabilities, expectations deeply rooted in the enduring perceptions of them as a sexual threat or, conversely, as asexual 'eternal children'. Craft argued that these beliefs continued to 'exert a powerful influence, colouring attitudes towards and expectations of people with mental handicaps' (Craft 1987, pp.13–15).

Their continuing influence was certainly visible in the area of reproductive rights. In 1974, as noted above, Lee had observed that modern birth control had rendered institutional incarceration of women with intellectual disabilities obsolete. His remark implies that contraception represented a new, more effective method to prevent women with intellectual disabilities becoming mothers. As institutionalisation had earlier denied women with intellectual disabilities control of their reproductive lives, so approaches to contraception in the 1980s continued to do so. Michelle McCarthy argues that doctors prescribed 'certain methods of contraception…precisely because they require[d] little or no "active user participation"', notable among them Depo-Provera. Despite challenges to its over-use in the 1990s, disproportionate prescription of Depo-Provera[3] to women with intellectual disabilities continues (McCarthy 2009, 1999, p.61).

The repeal of laws sanctioning involuntary sterilisation did little to end the sterilisation of women with intellectual disabilities. As legislatures in the United States began to repeal compulsory sterilisation laws, a new kind of sterilisation lawsuit emerged in which the petitioners sought court approval to sterilise non-

---

2   Brown (1994), p.123.

3   Depo-Provera is a long lasting (usually 12 weeks) form of contraception usually delivered by injection. The injection contains progestogen. This thickens the mucus in the cervix, stopping sperm reaching an egg. It also thins the womb lining and, in some, prevents the release of an egg (www.nhs.uk/Conditions/contraception-guide/Pages/contraceptive-injection.aspx, accessed on 3 January 2014).

institutionalised women with intellectual disabilities (Reilly 1991, p.149). Tilley *et al.* (2012b, p.417) argue these suits hint at a 'hidden history' of sterilisation outside institutions. While legal programmes of mass sterilisation formally ended in the 1970s, private, often family-initiated, sterilisation in the community continued. In England, for example, surveys of family intentions and applications to the Official Solicitor suggest that such sterilisations 'may have been quite common until relatively recently'. Other evidence suggests this was also the case elsewhere (Tilley *et al.* 2012a, pp.27–8).

As with contraception, the enduring belief that women with intellectual disabilities should not conceive or raise children often motivated the decision to seek sterilisation (Tilley *et al.* 2012b, p.419). The lower standard of evidence applied in legal decisions to remove children from mothers with intellectual disabilities compared with parents without disabilities in this period is another example of the persistence of these beliefs. For mothers with intellectual disabilities, their disability alone constituted sufficient cause for removal; no proof of abuse or neglect was necessary (Carey 2009, p.174).

In the 1970s and 1980s, approaches to sexuality had emphasised civil rights and the importance of knowledge as a way for people with intellectual disabilities to have 'the same kinds of sexual lives as other people'. By the early 1990s, this approach was under question as awareness of the sexual abuse and exploitation of people with intellectual disabilities, the risks of HIV/AIDs and difficult sexual behaviours grew. These issues suggested that the earlier approach had failed to take account of the different experiences of people with intellectual disabilities, experiences that disadvantaged and endangered them in their sexual lives. An approach based on securing the sexual rights of people with intellectual disabilities, while necessary, now seemed inadequate. A new paradigm emerged, one that emphasised the need to confront the real circumstances of people's sexual lives (Brown 1993, pp.623, 627; McCarthy 1999, pp.61, 63–4).

Arguably, this new emphasis resulted in part from the advent of self-advocacy, which encouraged people with intellectual disabilities to 'speak up' about their sexual experiences, both good and bad (Brown 1993, p.623; McCarthy 1999, p.68). While people with intellectual disabilities have long 'stuck up' for themselves (Buchanan and Walmsley 2006, p.134; Mitchell *et al.* 2006), histories of the formal self-advocacy movement trace its origins to the late 1960s. In 1968, the Swedish Parents Association organised 'the very first national conference of persons with intellectual disability' (McKenna 1996, p.82), the Swedish National Conference of Retarded Adults. A second conference followed two years later. Both 'reflected a social climate, inside and outside of services, wherein the views of people with learning difficulties were starting to be formally recognized'. That climate was in turn the consequence of the civil rights movements of the era and changing attitudes towards people with disabilities (Goodley 2000, p.10; Traustadóttir 2006, p.176). In the decades that followed, the self-advocacy movement spread to North America, Britain, Australia and Europe, people with intellectual disabilities setting up a variety of groups and organisations through which they gained the confidence and skills to speak for themselves and collectively work for change (Buchanan and Walmsley 2006; Dybwad and Bersani 1996; Goodley 2000).

Self-advocacy has empowered people with intellectual disabilities to speak up about sexuality and relationships and campaign for their sexual rights. In 1970, for example, the Second Swedish National Conference of Retarded Adults included in its recommendations that: 'We want the right to move together with a member of the opposite sex when we feel ready for it, and we do want the right to marry when we ourselves find the time is right' (McKenna 1996, p.83). In 1981, when Canadian self-advocates became aware of a legal case in which the mother of a young woman with intellectual disabilities was seeking court approval to have her daughter 'Eve' involuntarily sterilised, they decided to fight for Eve's right not to be sterilised without her consent. The Canadian Supreme Court granted their request to appear before it to speak against the sterilisation (Dybwad 1996, p.10; Kappel 1996, pp.105–7). One of the self-advocates, Barb Goode (Goode, quoted in Kappel 1996, p.107), subsequently described the importance of the Court's decision:

> Before, people were just given the operation. We were not always given the choice. Now it is against the law to be sterilized without you saying you want it or not…

> It was a great day for all of us. It tells everyone that people with mental handicaps can make up their minds given the proper information, and the information is explained to them.

In the 1990s, the influence of self-advocacy saw people with intellectual disabilities become involved in educating others about sex (McCarthy 1999, p.67). The sexual politics of the period, with its emphasis on social inequalities and the social construction of sexuality, was also influential in the shift toward the 'new realism' (McCarthy and Thompson, 1995). In 1994, for example, Hilary Brown argued that in assuming the naturalness of sexuality, normalisation had failed to take account of the ways in which 'normal' sexuality is socially defined and regulated in the interests of the powerful (Brown 1994). New strands in 'sexuality work' developed. Same-sex sexual expression, previously ignored or dismissed as a perversion of 'natural' heterosexuality caused by enforced sex-segregation, began to be represented more positively in the literature on sexuality and in sex education materials, though homophobia and marginalisation continued. Feminist researchers pointed to the risks for women with intellectual disabilities of encouraging heterosexual relationships in a society where men dominate women, whilst also acknowledging that women with intellectual disabilities often value such relationships. Researchers also sought a greater understanding of the nature, extent and circumstances of sexual abuse, in part because people with intellectual disabilities were themselves speaking out about the abuse they had experienced, and ways to safeguard people in their sexual lives (McCarthy 1999, pp.68–74).

Summary

At the beginning of the twentieth century, fear of the so-called 'feebleminded' saw the sexual rights of people with intellectual disabilities denied in the name of protecting society. In this way people labelled as 'feebleminded' were confined to sex-segregated institutions, subjected to coercive sterilisation and legally prevented from marrying. By the last decades of the century, the outright 'denial and repression' of the earlier era was at an end. The right of people with intellectual disabilities to a sexual life had been articulated, former residents of institutions were living in the community and many of the laws restricting marriage or involuntary sterilisation had been repealed or amended. Yet, by the century's end, most people with intellectual disabilities still did 'not marry, have children or enjoy intimate relationships' (May and Simpson 2003, pp.36, 38; McCarthy 1999, pp.56, 59). Despite the formal recognition that sexuality is a fundamental human right shared by people with intellectual disabilities, 'an ordinary sexual life continues to elude people' (Brown 1994, p.123). Older ideas about the sexuality of people with intellectual disabilities continue to reverberate (Block 2000).

This chapter has considered how the sexuality of people with intellectual disabilities has been viewed and addressed by earlier generations across a range of countries.

In doing so it seeks to enable understanding of how the legacy of the past continues to impact on the lives of people with intellectual disabilities today. It also underlines the substantial time-lags that can occur between changes in policy and ideology. The reasons why this is so often the case are further explored in the chapters to follow.

References

Bank-Mikkelsen, N.E. (1975) 'Marriage and Mental Retardation in Denmark: Legal and Medical Aspects.' In D.A.A. Primrose (ed.) *Proceedings of the Third Congress of the International Association for the Scientific Study of Mental Deficiency*. Warsaw: Polish Medical Publishers.

Bank-Mikkelsen, N.E. (1976) 'Denmark.' In R.B. Kugel and A. Shearer (eds) *Changing Patterns in Residential Services for the Mentally Retarded*. Washington: President's Committee on Mental Retardation.

Block, P. (2000) 'Sexuality, fertility and danger: Twentieth-century images of women with cognitive disabilities.' *Sexuality and Disability 18*, 4, 239–254.

Broberg, G. and Tydén, M. (1996) 'Eugenics in Sweden: Efficient Care.' In G. Broberg and N. Roll-Hansen (eds) *Eugenics and the Welfare State: Sterilization Policy in Denmark, Sweden, Norway and Finland.* East Lansing, MI: Michigan State University Press.

Brockley, J.A. (2001) 'Rearing the child who never grew: Parents, professionals, and children with intellectual disabilities, 1910–1965.' Unpublished PhD dissertation, New Brunswick: Rutgers University.

Brown, H. J (1993) 'Sexuality and intellectual disability: The new realism.' *Current Opinion in Psychiatry 6*, 5, 623–628.

Brown, H. (1994) 'An ordinary sexual life: A review of the normalisation principle as it applies to the sexual options of people with learning disabilities.' *Disability and Society 9*, 123–144.

Buchanan I. and Walmsley, J. (2006), 'Self-advocacy in historical perspective.' *British Journal of Learning Disabilities 34*, 3, 133–138.

Buck, P.S. (1992) *The Child Who Never Grew*, 2nd edn. Rockville, MD: Woodbine House.

Carey, A.C. (2010) *On the Margins of Citizenship: Intellectual Disability and Civil Rights in Twentieth-Century America.* Philadelphia, PA: Temple University Press.

Craft, A. (1987) 'Mental Handicap and Sexuality: Issues for Individuals with a Mental Handicap, their Parents and Professionals.' In A. Craft (ed.) *Mental Handicap and Sexuality: Issues and Perspectives.* Tunbridge Wells: Costello.

Dale, P. (2003) 'Implementing the Mental Deficiency Act: Competing priorities and resource constraint evident in the south west of England before 1948.' *Social History of Medicine 16*, 3, 403–418.

Diekema, D.S. (2003) 'Involuntary sterilization of persons with mental retardation: An ethical analysis.' *Mental Retardation and Developmental Disabilities Research Reviews 9*, 21–26.

Digby, A. (1996) 'Contexts and Perspectives.' In D. Wright and A. Digby (eds) *From Idiocy to Mental Deficiency: Historical Perspectives on People with Learning Disabilities.* London and New York: Routledge.

Dybwad, G. (1996) 'Setting the Stage Historically.' In G. Dybwad and H. Bersani (eds) *New Voices: Self-Advocacy by People with Disabilities.* Cambridge, MA: Brookline Books.

Dybwad, G. and Bersani, H. (eds) (1996) *New Voices: Self-Advocacy by People with Disabilities.* Cambridge, MA: Brookline Books.

Edgerton, R.B. and Dingman, H.F. (1964) 'Good reasons for bad supervision: "Dating" in a hospital for the mentally retarded.' *The Psychiatric Quarterly Supplement 38*, 221–233.

Edgerton, R. (1967) *The Cloak of Competence: Stigma in the Lives of the Mentally Retarded.* Berkeley and Los Angeles, CA: University of California Press.

Elkins, T.E. and Andersen, H.F. (1992) 'Sterilization of persons with mental retardation.' *Journal of the Association for Persons with Severe Handicaps 17*, 1, 19–26.

Emerson, E. (1992) 'What is Normalisation?' In H. Brown and H. Smith (eds) *Normalisation: A Reader for the Nineties.* London: Routledge.

Gerodetti, N. (2006) 'From science to social technology: Eugenics and politics in twentieth-century Switzerland.' *Social Politics 13*, 1, 55–88.

Goodley, D. (2000) *Self-Advocacy in the Lives of People with Learning Difficulties.* Buckingham: Open University Press.

Grunewald, K. (1976) 'Sweden.' In R.B. Kugel and A. Shearer (eds) *Changing Patterns in Residential Services for the Mentally Retarded.* Washington, DC: President's Committee on Mental Retardation.

Hansen, B.S. (1996) 'Something Rotten in the State of Denmark: Eugenics and the Ascent of the Welfare State.' In G. Broberg, and N. Roll-Hansen (eds) *Eugenics and the Welfare State: Sterilization Policy in Denmark, Sweden, Norway and Finland.* East Lansing, MI: Michigan State University Press.

Hietala, M. (1996) 'From Race Hygiene to Sterilization: The Eugenics Movement in Finland.' In G. Broberg, and N. Roll-Hansen (eds) *Eugenics and the Welfare State: Sterilization Policy in Denmark, Sweden, Norway and Finland.* East Lansing, MI: Michigan State University Press.

Jackson, M. (1996) 'Institutional Provision for the Feeble-Minded in Edwardian England: Sandlebridge and the Scientific Morality of Permanent Care.' In D. Wright and A. Digby (eds) *From Idiocy to Mental Deficiency: Historical Perspectives on People with Learning Disabilities.* London and New York: Routledge.

Jackson, M. (2000) *The Borderland of Imbecility: Medicine, Society and the Fabrication of the Feeble Mind in Late Victorian and Edwardian England.* Manchester and New York: Manchester University Press.

Jackson, M. (2003) '"Grown-up Children": Understandings of Health and Mental Deficiency in Edwardian England.' In M. Gijswijt-Hofstra and H. Marland (eds) *Cultures of Child-Health in Britain and the Netherlands in the Twentieth Century.* Amsterdam and New York: Rodopi.

Kappel, B. (1996) 'A History of People First in Canada.' In G. Dybwad and H. Besani (eds) *New Voices: Self-Advocacy by People with Disabilities.* Cambridge, MA: Brookline Books.

Keely, K. (2004) 'Sexuality and Storytelling: Literary Representations of the "Feebleminded" in the Age of Sterilization.' In S. Noll and J.W. Trent (eds) *Mental Retardation in America: A Historical Reader.* New York and London: New York University Press.

Kempton, W. and Kahn, E. (1991) 'Sexuality and people with intellectual disabilities: A historical perspective.' *Sexuality and Disability 9,* 2, 3–11.

Largent, M. A. (2008) *Breeding Contempt: The History of Coerced Sterilization in the United States.* New Brunswick, New Jersey and London: Rutgers University Press.

Lee, G.W. and Katz, G. (1974) 'An international point of view.' *Sexual Rights of the Retarded: Two Papers Reflecting the International Point of View.* London: National Society for Mentally Handicapped Children, 3–9.

Lewis, M. (1988) *Managing Madness: Psychiatry and Society in Australia, 1788–1980.* Canberra: AGPS Press.

May, D. and Simpson, K. (2003) 'The parent trap: Marriage, parenthood and adulthood for people with intellectual disabilities.' *Critical Social Policy 23,* 1, 25–43.

McCarthy, M. (1999) *Sexuality and Women with Learning Disabilities.* London: Jessica Kingsley Publishers.

McCarthy, M. (2009) '"I have the jab so I can't be blamed for getting pregnant": Contraception and women with learning disabilities.' *Women's Studies International Forum 32,* 3, 198–208.

McCarthy, M. and Thompson, D. (1995) 'No More Double Standards: Sexuality and People with Learning Disabilities.' In T. Philpot and L. Ward (eds) *Values and Visions: Changing Ideas in Services for People with Learning Difficulties.* Oxford: Butterworth-Heineman.

McKenna, P. (1996) 'The Right to Self-Determination in Sweden.' In G. Dwybad and H. Besani (eds) *New Voices: Self-Advocacy by People with Disabilities.* Cambridge, MA: Brookline Books.

Mitchell, D., Traustadóttir, R., Chapman, R., Townson, L., Ingham, N. and Ledger, S. (eds) (2006) *Exploring Experiences of Advocacy by People with Learning Disabilities: Testimonies of Resistance.* London: Jessica Kingsley Publishers.

Nirje, B. (1969) 'The Normalization Principle and its Human Management Implications.' In R.B. Kugel and W. Wolfensberger (eds) *Changing Patterns in Residential Services for the Mentally Retarded.* Washington, DC: President's Committee on Mental Retardation.

Nirje, B. (1976) 'The Normalization Principle.' In R.B. Kugel and A. Shearer (eds) *Changing Patterns in Residential Services for the Mentally Retarded.* Washington, DC: President's Committee on Mental Retardation.

Park, D.C. and Radford J.P. (1998) 'From the case files: Reconstructing a history of involuntary sterilization.' *Disability and Society 13*, 3, 317–342.

Potts, M. and Fido, R. (1991) *'A Fit Person to Be Removed': Personal Accounts of Life in a Mental Deficiency Institution.* Plymouth: Northcote House.

Public Record Office Victoria (PROV), VPRS 7448/P1, Clinical Notes of Female Patients 1912–1921, Unit 1, p.84.

Reilly, P.R. (1991) *The Surgical Solution: A History of Involuntary Sterilization in the United States.* Baltimore, MD and London: Johns Hopkins University Press.

Roll-Hansen, Nils (1996) 'Conclusion: Scandinavian Eugenics in the International Context.' In G. Borberg and N. Roll-Hansen (eds) *Eugenics and the Welfare State: Sterilization Policy in Denmark, Sweden, Norway and Finland.* East Lansing, MI: Michigan State University Press.

Simmons, H.G. (1978) 'Explaining social policy: The English Mental Deficiency Act of 1913.' *Journal of Social History 11*, 3, 387–403.

Stella, L. (1996) 'Normalisation and Beyond: Public Sector Residential Care 1965–1990'. In E. Cocks, C. Fox, M. Brogan and M. Lee (eds) *Under Blue Skies: The Social Construction of Intellectual Disability in Western Australia.* Perth: Centre for Disability Research and Development, Faculty of Health and Human Services, Edith Cowan University.

Stern, A.M. (2010) 'Gender and Sexuality: A Global Tour and Compass.' In A. Bashford and P. Levine (eds) *The Oxford Handbook of The History of Eugenics.* Oxford and New York: Oxford University Press.

Strange, C. and Stephen, J.A. (2010) 'Eugenics in Canada: A Checkered History, 1850s–1990s.' In A. Bashford and P. Levine (eds) *The Oxford Handbook of The History of Eugenics.* Oxford and New York: Oxford University Press.

Taylor, S.J. (2006) 'Christmas in Purgatory: A retrospective look.' *Mental Retardation 44*, 2, 145–149.

Thomson, M. (1996) 'Family, Community and State: The Micro-Politics of Mental Deficiency.' In D. Wright and A. Digby (eds) *From Idiocy to Mental Deficiency: Historical Perspectives on People with Learning Disabilities.* London and New York: Routledge.

Thomson, M. (2010) 'Disability, Psychiatry and Eugenics.' In A. Bashford and P. Levine (eds) *The Oxford Handbook of The History of Eugenics.* Oxford and New York: Oxford University Press.

Tilley, E., Walmsley, J., Earle, S. and Atkinson, D. (2012a), 'International Perspectives on the Sterilization of Women with Intellectual Disabilities.' In S. Earle, C. Komaromy and L. Layne (eds) *Understanding Reproductive Loss: Perspectives on Life, Death and Fertility.* Farnham: Ashgate.

Tilley, E., Walmsley, J., Earle, S. and Atkinson, D. (2012b) '"The silence is roaring": Sterilization, reproductive rights and women with intellectual disabilities.' *Disability and Society 27*, 3, 413–426.

Traustadóttir, R. (2006) 'Learning about self-advocacy from life history: A case study from the United States.' *British Journal of Learning Disabilities 34*, 3, 175–180.

Trent, J.W. (1994) *Inventing the Feeble Mind: A History of Mental Retardation in the United States.* Berkley, CA: University of California Press.

Tydén, M. (2010) 'The Scandinavian States: Reformed Eugenics Applied.' In A. Bashford and P. Levine (eds) *The Oxford Handbook of The History of Eugenics.* Oxford and New York: Oxford University Press.

Tyor, P. (1977) '"Denied the power to choose the good": Sexuality and mental defect in American medical practice, 1850–1920.' *Journal of Social History 10*, 4, 472–489.

Walmsley, J. (2000) 'Women and the Mental Deficiency Act of 1913: Citizenship, sexuality and regulation.' *British Journal of Learning Disabilities 28*, 65–70.

Walmsley, J. (2005) 'Institutionalization: A Historical Perspective.' In K. Johnson, and R. Traustadóttir (eds) *Deinstitutionalization and People with Intellectual Disabilities: In and Out of Institutions.* London: Jessica Kingsley Publishers.

Walmsley, J., Atkinson, D. and Rolph, S. (1999) 'Community Care and Mental Deficiency 1913 to 1945.' In P. Bartlett and D. Wright (eds) *Outside the Walls of the Asylum: The History of Care in the Community 1750–2000.* London and New Brunswick, NJ: Athlone Press.

Wolfensberger, W. (1972) *The Principle of Normalization in Human Services.* Toronto: National Institute on Mental Retardation.

EBBA AND JONNI

This is Our Story

Eyglø Ebba Hreinsdøttir and Sigurjøn Grétarsson (Jonni) with Guðrún V. Stefánsdøttir

Overview ——————————————————————

- Eyglø *Ebba* Hreinsdøttir (*Ebba*) and Sigurjøn Grétarsson (*Jonni*) met in Reykjavík in 1990 and got married in 1993.

- This chapter is built on their life stories and supported by Guðrún Stefánsdøttir.

- It highlights the barriers they have faced and overcome in their lives, separately and together.

- Ebba and Jonni had different backgrounds before they met each other.

- Ebba lived at an institution for people with intellectual disabilities for many years, and after that in a group home.

- Jonni lived with his parents and siblings before he met Ebba.

- Meeting each other and getting married have been the biggest events in their lives.

- Today they live together in a flat they rent from a disabled people's organisation. She is a researcher and he is a photographer.

- They are happy together; even though they do not always agree, they are still best friends. They both think life history work is very important and that people should be in control of their own lives.

The writing process

Ebba and Jonni wrote this chapter with Guðrún, who they know quite well. We will start by talking briefly about our cooperation and how we wrote this chapter. After that Ebba and Jonni will tell their stories separately and together and, finally, they will point out what others can learn from their stories. This chapter uses the term 'people with intellectual disabilities'.

Introduction

GUÐRÚN

Ebba and I first met in the 1970s when I was working at an institution for people with intellectual disabilities in Iceland during the summertime. Ebba moved to the institution in 1969 and lived there for some years. She was 19 years old at the time we met and I was 16. After Ebba moved from the institution we didn't have contact for many years, but since 2003 we have worked closely together on an inclusive life history project (Hreinsdøttir and Stefánsdøttir 2010; Stefánsdøttir and Hreinsdøttir 2013). I first met Jonni after Ebba and I started to work together in 2003. Ebba and I have also participated in international life history work (Hreinsdøttir et al. 2006) and travelled a lot together. Although Ebba is an experienced researcher this is the first time that Jonni has taken part in research; however he has travelled with us many times to conferences and research meetings. Today the three of us all know each other quite well and are good friends. We have often talked about how it would be interesting to write Jonni's life story and the story of Ebba and Jonni together. When we were asked to write a chapter in this book we thought it would be a good opportunity to do so.

EBBA

We wrote this chapter, the three of us together. I and Guðrún have worked together for a long time and in the year 2010 we published my life history in Icelandic (Hreinsdøttir with Stefánsdøttir 2010). We decided that Guðrún would translate part of my story into English for this chapter. Then we met several times at our home and at Guðrún's office. We told our stories and she tape-recorded what Jonni and I had to say. First she had conversations with Jonni and then with us together. After each conversation Guðrún read the transcript for us and we took some bits out and put bits in. Our stories are told with our own words and I think that is very important. This is our story. I really like to tell my story to others. It has changed my life, I have learned a lot about myself. I think it is so important that people with intellectual disabilities from all over the world tell our stories together and learn from each other.

JONNI

When Ebba started to work with Guðrún in research I wasn't interested in participating, not at all. In the beginning I was suspicious. I am not used to telling people about my life. I rather like to keep it to myself. It was enough for me to travel with Ebba to conferences and meetings and take photos of our trips. I didn't know what all this research work was about in the beginning and you have to know what you are doing. It often takes time to make important decisions and you have to be safe. I would say I am a careful man. During the years I have seen that the research work has been good for Ebba and we have made friends from all over the world. I have also learned to trust Guðrún. Now I am ready and I have a story to tell.

Ebba's story

EBBA

I was born in Reykjavík on the 19th of December, 1950. I am the oldest of my siblings. I did everything with the other children and like the other children. I have a very good family and they have always supported me. I went to a normal school and learned to read and write when I was a little girl. I lived with my family until my mother died when I was 19. She couldn't die until she knew that I was safe and she thought I was safe at the institution. She was a nice person and I love her deeply but she was like other people at this time. Everyone thought that it was best for people like me to live in institutions. It was the same old story; if you have an intellectual disability people often treat you like you are in the third drawer. In the first drawer are these normal people. In the second drawer you have physically disabled people and in the third drawer you have people with intellectual disability.

I wish I could have been at home with my father and siblings when my mother died, but things were like they were and I couldn't have any influence on it. At the institution I decided that I couldn't be myself so I pretended that I was someone else. I have two names, Eygló Ebba, and my first name Eygló is generally not used. I used that name for the girl at the institution. When I went to my father's house during weekends I could be myself, Ebba. I did this all the years at the institution. I was so sad and angry those years and if I wasn't angry then I cried, so it was better to be angry. I am still angry but I have learned to live with it. But it wasn't all right and a person should not forget it either. I am still angry at the government that decided to send me and other people with intellectual disabilities to institutions. Worst of all was the label 'mentally retarded'. I didn't know that person who was labelled. It was not me.

FIGURE 4.1 EBBA AGED TWO YEARS OLD

I was sterilised when I was 14. At that time I lived with my parents and siblings. I didn't know about it until I was 27 years old. At that time I lived at the institution. The reason I learned about my sterilisation was because some of the other women at the institution were being prepared to undergo sterilisation. I asked: 'Why not me?' And then the woman in charge of the institution had to tell me.

At that time my mother had passed away and it was difficult because I was so angry with her. It is difficult to be angry with someone you love deeply who has passed away. When I was growing up I always felt like I was not any different from my siblings and I was sad to find out they thought I was different after all. I was not angry that I couldn't have children. I have never wanted to have a child, but I was angry because I didn't get the opportunity to decide for myself. I thought it was so humiliating to be sent to surgery, lied to and told your appendix was removed. I didn't want to have children even after I got married. After I started to talk about the institution and the sterilisation openly, I have learned to accept these incidents and I have forgiven my mother and father. They were only doing what they thought was best for me at that time. They thought they were protecting me by sending me to an institution and sterilising me. I understand now that this was a historical phase, or I hope so. I also understand that this was not my fault; it was the government that decided to do such things to people. I don't think of it every day. I am over that now, but I think it is important to talk openly about sterilisation and how women with intellectual disabilities have been treated. It shouldn't be a secret.

In 1976 I moved to the first group home in Iceland; we were six there in the beginning. My girlfriend Halla and I were the first to move, we were the pioneers. I think so, and I don't like it when people are talking about all the pioneers and mean the staff and the people from the organisation. They forget us. If we didn't exist they wouldn't have been pioneers. It was much better at the group home than the institution. I got my own money but the staff did not understand us so well and we didn't get many opportunities there. I could never decide anything or have any control. I was never asked and I hate it when I am not asked, I just get so angry.

In the beginning I wasn't going to talk about all the bad things that happened to me. The reason I didn't want to talk about the sterilisation and other bad things that have happened to me was because of the shame. I was always ashamed and it is difficult to live with shame. I thought it was my fault because I was so stupid. After I started to tell my story and talk about the past, I realised it was not my fault and I should not be ashamed. It was not our fault we had to live at institutions or undergo sterilisation. It was the government that decided how people with intellectual disabilities were treated. They should be ashamed. People should know that.

When people experience bad things in life like I have, it is sometimes difficult to remember the good things. Of course I have also had lot of good things in my life, like having friends, spending time with my family, travelling and so on. But the best thing that happened in my life was that I met Jonni and we got married. That changed everything.

Jonni's story
JONNI

I was born in Reykjavík on the 29th of October, 1953. I have two older sisters; they looked after me when I was a child. We have always been very good friends and they have supported me all the time. After they moved out from our parental home I lived there until I met Ebba. My parents and I were very close, we did everything together. We travelled abroad and in Iceland, we went to the theatre and cinema and so on. I often went with my father and visited his friends. I really liked that and they were nice to me. My first trip abroad was to Copenhagen. My aunt lived there. I was five years old at that time. I remember I really liked it there. We have nice photos from the trip. My father took a lot of photos. Later on we travelled to Germany, Yugoslavia, Spain and often to Copenhagen.

When I was a little boy I used to be like other little boys. I really liked to play with cars and I know all kinds of car types from all over the world. That used to be one of my hobbies and still is. I was a quiet boy but I really liked to tease my sisters and other children and I still like to joke and tease, but in a good way. My dad was like that as well. When I was seven years old I went to a normal school in Reykjavík. I was there for five years. I think I was 11 when I was moved to a special school. I really don't know why. I had friends at the normal school and I missed them after I was moved to the special school. There was no mobbing or anything like that, but I didn't get any extra support at the school and I am sure it took a longer time for me to learn than the other children. Now disabled children have much more support in normal schools than there used to be in those days. I finished the special school when I was 16 years old. I don't think I learned much there. I have often wondered why I didn't learn English like in ordinary school. When we travel it is important to be able to speak English. I wish I had learned English but I have taken some courses in the lifelong learning centre and now I can speak a little bit. I had good friends at the special school and some of them are still my friends. Some of the teachers were all right but others not. I remember one of the teachers used to beat us with a stick. I hated him. I protested and after some years he was fired.

After I finished the school my father found a job for me in a hardware store, as he knew the owners. I think that was in 1971. I worked there for several years and then I was fired. After that I got a job in a factory and worked there for 19 years. Two of my uncles owned the factory and I talked to them and I got the job. I liked it very much to work there and I still go there now and then for a coffee with the staff. I had to quit there because of my arthritis.

Even though I don't work anymore I have a lot of things to do. I take care of our money and I often have to go to the bank for me and Ebba. I am a photographer and that is what I do today. I got my first camera when I was confirmed. Then I was 13 years old. I have taken photos ever since. I take lot of landscapes photos. I really like to take photos of trees in the autumn or in the snow during wintertime and of waterfalls and mountains in Iceland. I also take photos of people and I have taken a lot of photos on our trips to different countries. I have had at least three exhibitions where many people came and looked at my photos. I have also given some of them away and some of them are for sale.

I have had a good life. I had very good parents who took care of me and protected me. They have both passed away now and I still miss them very much, but I have wonderful sisters that look after us and support us today. And then I met Ebba and my life changed. In the next session we are going to tell about our life together.

The story of Ebba and Jonni

EBBA

I met Jonni in the year 1990. At that time I lived by myself in a small flat in a basement of the group home. I first met him on a winter's day when I slipped on the ice and fell into his arms. I have been there ever since. I am sure we were meant to meet each other on that day and be together forever. That was our destiny. At that time I didn't feel very well. I had ended a relationship with a man who was not good to me; he was very abusive. Jonni and I fell in love and a few months later he moved into the flat with me and we got support from the staff at the group home.

After a while Jonni asked me out for dinner and few days later his mother invited me to their home. His father had passed away and I never met him. Even so I feel like I know him, I have heard so much about him. I was shy and afraid in the beginning but Jonni had a wonderful mother and I felt like I was so welcomed in the family. She always held our hands and after she died Jonni's older sisters have taken her place in supporting us. His family is wonderful and they have supported us from the beginning and still do.

We got engaged on Jonni's birthday in 1990 in our flat. Jonni bought the rings and afterwards we went to Jonni's mother and told her. After that we went to his sister's place and waved our hands so she could see our rings; we were so happy and proud. She invited us for champagne and after that we went out for dinner, just the two of us. It was so romantic.

My family also supported us but it took my father a time to accept this. In the beginning he doubted that we could manage our life together and he told us we should first move in together and see how that went. 'Don't get married until you are sure,' he said to us. I don't know why, I think he was protecting me. But after a while he became very fond of Jonni, as everyone else who gets to know him does, and he realised that we could manage well our life together.

After we first met I was anxious about telling Jonni about the sterilisation, but he thought it was all right. He knows we have no place for a child. Jonni supports me and loves me like I am. It doesn't matter to him that I had to undergo sterilisation. Jonni and I have never had enough money to raise a child. Also I couldn't bear to have a child who would be taken away from me like many women with intellectual disabilities have experienced. We do not want to be dependent on assistance from staff or our families and we could not raise a child without support. I want to be independent, I always have.

As I said earlier, we do not always agree. We do not have the same temperament. I get angry and I sometimes cry and scream. Jonni is much easier going, but it sometimes takes him a year to make one decision. That makes me mad sometimes because it doesn't take a long time for me to decide. I think this is like what many couples experience. Still we have a good marriage. I have learned that we have to accept each other like we are.

FIGURE 4.2 EBBA AND JONNI GOT ENGAGED SEPTEMBER 1990

We do everything together and although we do not always agree, that's all right, we are best friends. Since we got married I can be myself and I know that he accepts me as I am and understands me. That makes all the difference. His family helps us and now I have two families. We are happy together and we do things that people normally do: we travel a lot, we go to movies, to the theatre, to town and we meet our friends. We also go to meetings in the disabled people's movement and we take an active part there, fighting for a better life for disabled people. We have everything we want but sometimes we need more money. The benefits in Iceland are not good enough; sometimes we don't have any money by the end of the month but I am not complaining, we survive and many people have it much worse than we do. We are getting older now and I wish we could move to a little flat in a quiet neighbourhood where we can have more support than we have today. But we should be in control.

JONNI

I lived with my parents until I met Ebba. At that time I was 38 years old and she was 41. This was the first time I was in a serious relationship. I had all my life lived in my parental home and I was not used to standing on my own feet. Even so, I am used to being in control of my life. I sometimes say: 'I went from my mother's arms into Ebba's arms'. But it went well and we have been happy. And then it was the wedding. Our marriage was in April in 1993. It was a wonderful day, the weather was beautiful and the ceremony was in a church in our neighbourhood. And we had a big party afterwards. I think there were about 70 people invited, and we got lots of presents. It was a perfect day.

FIGURE 4.3 EBBA AND JONNI GOT MARRIED APRIL 1993

Some weeks later we went for a three-week honeymoon to the Canary Islands. That was the wedding gift from Ebba's father. We also celebrated my 40th birthday. He and his wife went with us. It was a very nice trip and we have travelled several times to the same place through the years.

After I first met Ebba I moved to her flat in the group home. The staff were nice and supportive and they were very happy about our marriage, but it was important for us to be on our own. The staff supported us but Ebba's father was not keen in the beginning. He worried about his daughter and that we would not have enough support in the new place. He thought it would be better for us to stay in the group home. The staff helped us to find the flat we live in today. I think we have managed our daily life well. We haven't had much support and we haven't asked for it. We can do most of the things by ourselves. Ebba does the cookery and I do the dishes. We go together to the supermarket and so on. I have the responsibility for our money and I go to the bank to pay some bills and things like that.

I am satisfied with our life today even though we sometimes need some more money and support. We often meet my sister and her grandchildren and I love to be around them. Sometimes I wonder if it would have been nice to have a child. I love children. Shortly after Ebba and I met she told me about the sterilisation. I think it is unfair that she was sterilised without knowing. The sterilisation has never had an influence on my feelings for Ebba and I am not sure that we could have managed to have a child. We haven't had enough money or support to have children and we want to be independent. Instead we have had the opportunity to travel and do other nice things. But even though I am pleased with our life, I sometimes wonder.

FIGURE 4.4 *'WE ARE BEST FRIENDS'*
EBBA AND JONNI IN CAMBRIDGE AFTER A
CONFERENCE AT THE OPEN UNIVERSITY IN 2008

Summary: What can other people learn from our stories?
EBBA AND JONNI

We have learned a lot by telling our stories and we hope that other people also learn from our stories. Our stories are different and we are different persons, and that is how it is. Everyone has a story to tell.

We think it is of great importance that people all over the world tell their stories and learn from each other. It is also important that the government and people without disabilities know that we are not different from them. We want to live a good life, have a partner, get married, have enough money, have the opportunity to travel, go to the theatre and do things on our own. We should be in control of our lives. People should understand that.

What people can also learn from our stories is that we are not victims. We have overcome barriers and challenges we have faced in our lives and managed to be independent together. If you believe in yourself you can do anything, but sometimes you have to fight for it.

About Iceland: the policy context to Ebba and Jonni's story
GUÐRÚN

In 1938, a law was passed in Iceland legalising sterilisation and abortion. The law was directed at people who were 'feeble minded'. This legislation reflected the influence of the broader eugenics on Iceland and remained in force until 1975. During the first decades of the legislation's enactment, the sterilisation of people with intellectual disabilities was uncommon, but between 1965 and 1975 it became progressively more widespread. Statistics were not published in Iceland after 1975, although findings from recent Icelandic research suggest that women with intellectual disabilities continued to be sterilised during the 1970s and 1980s. These findings highlight that sterilisations were usually carried out around times of transition: moving away from family to a group home, on the one hand, and from an institution to a group home on the other. Although involuntary sterilisation is no longer practised in Iceland, some recent research indicates that young women with intellectual disabilities are still being encouraged, by family members and carers, to undergo sterilisation as a form of contraception. The common justification for such practice is framed in terms of it being undertaken in the women's best interests. Current law (from 1975) on sterilisation in Iceland presupposes that: 'application shall include the declared consent of the individual in question, signed in their own hand, and she/he is aware of what the sterilisation entails, and that he/she by their own free volition requests the operation'. In the current law it is also presupposed that if the person could be categorised as contending with serious mental health issues or as having severe intellectual disabilities, then the law authorises sterilisation without given consent. In such cases parents or a legal advocate are authorised to provide consent on behalf of the person.

The law from 1975 should deal with safeguarding and risk but in practice it seems that the law has offered no protection. We have a special law for disabled people which should protect people in general and Iceland has also recognised the UN Convention on Human Rights (2006).

Iceland signed the UN Convention in 2007 but has not yet legalised it. It is commonly referred to as ' the Convention' and the disabled people's movement has put much pressure on the government to legalise it.

Although sex education is a requirement in the curriculum it is not very much practised and if it is, it focuses primarily on protection.

The population in Iceland is 321,000. At the time of writing we could not identify any statistics on the population of learning disabled people.

References

Hreinsdøttir, E.E. with Stefánsdøttir, G.V. (2010) *Lífssaga brautyðjandans Eygløar Ebbu Hreinsdóttur.* [The life-history of the pioneer Eygló Ebba Hreinsdøttir]. Reykjavík: Authors.

Hreinsdøttir, E.E. and Stefánsdøttir, G. (2010) 'Collaborative life history: different experiences of spending time in an institution in Iceland.' *British Journal of Learning Disabilities 38*, 2, 103–110.

Hreinsdøttir, E.E., Stefánsdøttir, G., Lewthwaite, A., Ledger, S. and Shufflebotham, L. (2006) 'Is my story so different from yours? Comparing life stories: Experience of institutionalization and self-advocacy in England and Iceland.' *British Journal of Learning Disabilities 34*, 3, 157–167.

Stefánsdøttir, G. and Hreinsdøttir, E.E. (2013) 'Sterilization, intellectual disability, and some ethical and methodological challenges: It shouldn't be a secret.' *Ethics and Social Welfare 7*, 3, 302–308.

CHAPTER 5

'I WOULD HAVE BROKEN THE LAW SEVERAL TIMES...'

Reflecting on the Criminal Law Sexual Offences Act (1993)
in the Republic of Ireland

Ger Minogue, Martin Corry, Marie Deeley, Patrick Kearney, Joe McGrath, Kathleen O'Leary and Pauline Skehan, Clare Inclusive Research Group (C.I.R.G.)[1]

Overview

- We worked with Kelley and Rob to talk about the law about sex and relationships in Ireland.

- At the moment, the law makes it difficult for us to have sexual lives.

- We decided to use our own names.

- People with intellectual disabilities don't know about the law and may have broken it.

- The law should be in plain language so people can understand it.

- We felt it was insulting to us, assuming that we would not need to understand.

- Some of us were in relationships.

- Some of us wanted to get married and have children.

- You have to be responsible for your actions if you have children.

- We worked on drama and campaigning to try to change the law.

---

1   C.I.R.G is supported by the Brothers of Charity Clare Services through co-ordinator Rob Hopkins and Kelley Johnson.

The writing process

We put this chapter together over a long time. We are a group of people with intellectual disabilities in the Republic of Ireland who do research about things that are important to us. We are angry about a law which makes it difficult for us to have good sexual lives. We have been working on trying to change this law. Kelley, who is a professor, told us about writing a chapter in a book that would tell others about what we thought of the law and how we wanted to change it. We thought about this and decided that we would like to write the chapter.

We met and talked about our experiences about what sexuality means to us and what the law means to us and why we think it should be changed. We decided that we did not want to write about our own lives and sexuality. They are private. We agreed not to talk about people's experiences outside the room. We talked together about the law with Kelley and she recorded what we said. Then she wrote a draft of the book chapter and came back to us with it. We then changed it and talked about it further. Kelley wrote some of the chapter which was about the law. We decided that we did not want our names on the book because then people would know what we had said.

However the group met later and we talked it through again and decided we hadn't said 'anything bad' and that, 'It's about us and what we think'. Others said, 'We want our names mentioned', 'There wouldn't be a book without us' and more poignantly, 'We don't want to be kept in the dark like before'.

When the chapter was written Kelley put the ideas that we all had in one kind of type and when an individual person gave their ideas she put it in another kind of type. We use the term 'intellectual disability' in Ireland.

Introduction

Currently, in Ireland there is a law called the Criminal Law Sexual Offences Act (1993). This law makes it illegal to have some kinds of sex with people with intellectual disabilities. It says that unless people are married it is not legal to have sexual intercourse or buggery with someone who is intellectually impaired, (that is if they have mental health problems or a intellectual disability) unless they are able to live independently in the community or are able to show that they are not likely to be exploited or abused. The law was passed at a time when there was a lot of concern about the sexual abuse of people with intellectual disabilities. But no one thought of (a) involving people themselves in the draft law or (b) that people with intellectual disabilities might want to have their own legitimate sexual relationships accepted and legitimised.

While no one has ever been prosecuted under this law it places people with intellectual disabilities, service providers and families in a difficult position. People with intellectual disabilities who want to have a sexual relationship outside marriage are legally prevented from doing so. Service providers have expressed concern that if they support two people who want to have a sexual relationship they may find themselves in the position of colluding with them to break the law. The law in the Republic of Ireland is currently in breach of the UN Convention on Rights of Persons with Disabilities (UN 2006) and is one of the reasons why Ireland has delayed its ratification of the Convention. There has been increasing recognition that the law as it stands needs to be changed to recognise the rights of people with intellectual disabilities to a sexual life (Law Reform Commission 2005; Redmond and Jennings 2006). We have put the actual wording of the law in the following box:

The Criminal Law Sexual Offences Act 1993

The Criminal Law Sexual Offences Act was passed in 1993. It states:

1. A person who –

    (a) has or attempts to have sexual intercourse, or

    (b) commits or attempts to commit an act of buggery, with a person who is mentally impaired (other than to a person to whom he is married or to whom he believes with reasonable cause he is married) shall be guilty of an offence and shall be liable on conviction on indictment to –

    (i) in the case of having sexual intercourse or committing an act of buggery, imprisonment for a term not exceeding 10 years, and

    (ii) in the case of an attempt to have sexual intercourse or an attempt to commit an act of buggery, imprisonment for a term not exceeding 3 years in the case of a first conviction and in the case of a second or any subsequent conviction imprisonment for a term not exceeding 5 years.

2. A male person who commits or attempts to commit an act of gross indecency with another male person who is mentally impaired shall be guilty of an offence and shall be liable on conviction on indictment to imprisonment for a term not exceeding 2 years.

---

3. In any proceedings undertaken in this section it shall be a defence for the accused to show that at the time of the alleged commission of the offence he did not know and had no reason to suspect that the person in respect of whom he is charged was mentally impaired.

4. Proceedings against a person charged with an offence under this section shall not be taken except by or with the consent of the Director of Public Prosecutions.

5. In this section *"mentally impaired"* means suffering from a disorder of the mind, whether through mental handicap or mental illness which is of such a nature or degree as to render a person incapable of living an independent life or of guarding against serious exploitation.

Our views about the law

We started our discussion by talking about the law. We think there are some real problems with it for people with intellectual disabilities. We all had very strong views that the law was wrong for the following reasons.

People with intellectual disabilities do not know about the law.

All of us now knew about the law but we all agreed that we had not known about it until we had joined the Clare Inclusive Research Group. For some of us this had been a shock. One person said:

When (it was) said to me, I was going along nice and comfortable. You know what I mean. He mentioned it to me over the phone. No one mentioned it to me that it was an offence, having sex; Rob explained it.

Another commented:

I did (know about it). It was discussed at some meeting how some people are not all incapacitated mentally and they could easily have a sexual relationship.

Although all of us are adults and use services for people with intellectual disabilities, no one in the service had told us about the law.

We all agreed that it was wrong that people with intellectual disabilities should not know about a law that affected them. One person commented:

I have possibly and probably broken the law since I joined the organisation.

Another person wondered if he hadn't been told because of his disability:

Is it because I'm Down syndrome no one's told me about this before?

People were angry about a law that they felt treated them as if they were not adults and could not make decisions. Some comments within the group included:

The law is making me very unhappy.

The law is like a military camp. It is very unfair.

Gives us no credit for common sense. No freedom.

It is unfair.

Understanding the law

The words in the law are difficult to understand and there is no plain language copy of it. When we talked about it, we realised that we did not always understand what it was saying. Some of us thought that it meant that people with intellectual disabilities couldn't get married and one person told a story about someone she knew:

I had a friend…who wanted to get married and she went to the priest and she found she couldn't get married. And she had a very dear friend and she wanted to get married.

We didn't know if this was because of the law but we thought it was wrong that people should not be able to have sex together or to get married if they wanted to. We thought that it was important that if there were laws about us then we needed to know what the words say and to understand them. Another researcher made the point that if having sex outside marriage was alright for 'normal' people then it should be alright for people with intellectual disabilities too.

Oh Jesus! Sex without marriage is normal; so called 'normal' people do it.

We had different views about having sex and marriage. We thought that being married meant that you were responsible but that meant that you had to know about sex.

All people need to know about sex…because if you get married you are taking responsibility for that person. If you sign the registry. That is important in getting married.

Some of us felt the law insulted us by implying that we had had no moral sense and some of us felt strongly that it was important to have sex in marriage in order to have children.

We should be able to decide for ourselves. We come from a moral place. What I want to say is that. I think that people should have sex with people because if I don't have sex I won't have a child and that is a bond between a man and a woman. You need to get married.

We thought that some people with intellectual disabilities might not understand about the responsibility of having sex and that they might need some protection.

You will have one group of people wanting to go in one direction. You have people who are able to make a decision, other people who need long-term support to get to where they are going. You have people like me, probably like...us round this table and we know all the complications and what they are getting into and know what they're responsible for.

Having relationships

We had different views about how we felt about relationships and what they meant to us. But we were in agreement that whatever we thought about this, people with intellectual disabilities should not be prevented by law from having relationships.

Some of us were involved in a relationship with someone else.

I had been in services (for a long time). I personally myself had gone out with one person in the service but she is no longer there. In 2008 I found out about the law and that is the first time I knew about it. I was involved. I came from a different place. I would have broken the law... several times.

Some of us wanted to have a relationship and a family.

I want to move out... I would prefer to have a family of my own.

One person commented about this:

But you would have to prove that you could live independently.

Some of us had not had relationships or did not want them.

I never had a relationship but I knew people who had and they said they were broken hearted. Wish to God they never had. Because the girl left them and left them stranded... I met this woman and she said, 'You have no money...so keep going.'

I don't want to get married because I am happy the way I am.

Some of us wanted to have children but we all saw this as a big responsibility.

All people need to know what they are getting into in that respect.

When you bring a child into the world if there is a health condition in the family you need to be aware of that.

You have to consider all the complications and all the things that might affect that child.

You have to be aware of that because otherwise... then you probably put the other person at risk.

Parents would have to know how to look after the child and teach the child what to do as well. That is very important. Very, very important; how to look after the child and send them to school.

When you bring someone into the world it is more expensive. You have to mind them... make sure they are looked after.

We didn't come to a conclusion about this but we thought it was really important to be responsible for our actions if we were to have children.

Knowing about sex

One of the problems with the law was that it suggested that if people did not know about sex it was because of their disability. But we thought that a lot of people did not know about sex because they had never had an opportunity to learn about it. We thought that it was really important that everybody knows about sex and has some education about it. If they don't have this information then they can't make decisions about it. When we talked about this we found out that people relied on their families for getting this knowledge and that none of us had had formal sex education.

I never heard about sex in school.

You could get information if your family was able to tell you... And if you had sisters and brothers and if they were getting married... Only by learning from your family.

Some people said they got no information from their families. But one person said:

I did get some information from my sister. And my brother had young kids growing up as well. A boy and a girl. And then they had another lovely baby as well.

We were angry and unhappy that service providers were expected to tell us about sex and the law, saying it was the responsibility of schools. Someone said:

We get training in the transport and we get training, and sex is life experience why should it be service providers, it should be at school. It should be that everybody finds the information that they don't know. And if you know people who have a disability... you need protection.

Someone else felt that service providers didn't know about the law or what to tell people anyway.

They won't explain anything. You ask them a question. They don't know... They don't know.

The effects of the law

We asked the question: why is the law there?

The law is there to protect people who are shy or afraid. I know it is there to protect people who are vulnerable. People who are vulnerable in our society.

We couldn't think of any other reasons for the law being there but we did think that it stopped people from having relationships. We talked about the services that we used and how it was important to trust each other and when we trusted each other relationships might happen. One person said:

At Christmas parties they invited us together to socialise together... And meet and get on with one another which we did do. We supported each other to do a day's work. So therefore relationships could form. We had to have a good work relationship and we had to know that people could be trusted to a certain degree.

But it seemed that sexual relationships were not part of this. One person said they were '*taboo*'. Someone else commented that:

It wasn't that easy because people didn't know and it was never suggested that if two people got along very well was that (a sexual relationship) a possibility?

One person said that it must be difficult for service providers to support people having a sexual relationship because of the law. They may be afraid of losing their jobs or being seen as helping people to break the law.

Changing the law

When we found out about the law we were angry and we decided that we wanted to let people with intellectual disabilities know about it. We wanted to find out why the law existed and we wanted to campaign for it to be repealed. 'Can we talk to people about it? And ask people why?' (see Hopkins 2009). That's where we began but we have done a lot of things since.

We used stories from people's experiences to write two plays. We talked to a group of people about relationships. One of the people in the group was involved with another person in a service for people with intellectual disabilities and they were caught kissing. Another service user caught them and told someone. And they had to report to the manager of the service.

So the first play was about that and the law and was called 'No Kissing'. It was the first one and we did it in Dublin and lots of other places. Later we performed a second play that was based on the experience of someone who wanted to leave home to live with his girlfriend.

His mother did not want him to do this and a social worker and the Garda (police) were called in. The man had to prove that he could live independently. This play was performed as a piece of Forum Theatre (Boal 1979). In this kind of play the actors give the performance and then people in the audience are asked to make comments or to come on stage and act out solutions to the problem. We did this play at national conferences in Ireland for people with intellectual disabilities and service providers. It did bring up a lot of issues for people. For example: how do you tell your mother or father you want a relationship? It's not easy unless you have a good relationship with them. And the person whose story the play was based on still hasn't managed to move out.

From plays to campaigning

Because of the plays we were asked to go on national radio and talk about them and about the law. This was as part of a panel about intellectual disabilities and sex education along with an advocate representative and the parent of a young woman with an intellectual disability.

Then the Law Reform Commission in Ireland began to do some work to review the law on sexuality. Because of the plays and the media, we were invited to consult with them. This was the first time researchers with an intellectual disability had presented to the Commission. We told them we thought the law was wrong and we said the language was too difficult and that people with intellectual disabilities needed to know what it said. People at the Commission said they would have to think about the language.

The Commission has since published (Law Reform Commission 2011) a Consultation Paper on Sexual Offences and Capacity to Consent which makes recommendations and asks for information from people with views about the law and the changing of it. We put our views into writing and sent them to the Law Reform Commission.

So far the law hasn't changed and we are still waiting. They are bringing in a law about people's capacity to make decisions and we are waiting for that to happen.

But there are other ways we can get heard too. We agreed that:

When we go to election we can tell people who make laws we don't like them. We have a vote in this country.

I think if you came to me and told me you wanted me to vote for you in the election, I might. But if you don't deliver on your promise then I won't vote for you again.

Summary

We don't think the Sexual Offences Act is a good law. Kelley told us that it goes against our rights in the UN Convention on Rights of Persons with Disabilities and we want to see the law changed. We know that some people need protection from being abused but we need to make sure that people have good sex education so that they know about sex and can have relationships. This chapter has been about what we think about the law and what we are doing to try and change it. It is taking a long time.

References

Boal, A. (1979) *The Theatre of the Oppressed*. New York: Urizen Books. (Republished by Routledge Press in New York/London in 1982.)

Hopkins, R. (2009) 'Making research live!' *British Journal of Intellectual Disabilities 37*, 4, 331.

Law Reform Commission (2005) *Consultation Paper on Vulnerable Adults and the Law: Capacity.* LRC CP 37-2005. Dublin: Government Printing Office.

Law Reform Commission (2011) *Consultation Paper on Sexual Offences and Capacity to Consent.* Dublin: Law Reform Commission.

Redmond, B. and Jennings, A. (2006) 'Social Work and Intellectual Disability' in N. Kearney and C. Skehill (eds) *Social work in Ireland,* 107-126. Dublin: Institute of Public Administration.

United Nations (2006) *UN Convention on Rights of Persons with Disabilities*. New York: United Nations.

CHAPTER 6

'ONCE IN SIX WEEKS? THAT'S NOT A RELATIONSHIP!'

Stories About Love, Relationships and Sex from Self-Advocates Living in Flanders

Our New Future Group with Toon Maillard

Overview

- The chapter brings several stories of love and intimacy in Flanders together in two tales.

- Fonske tells about his need for friendship, how humans are not meant to be alone:

  ◦ How he feels institutions are disabling, and love is not.

  ◦ How he feels love takes time – you need to invest in it if you want it to grow.

  ◦ How he feels a relationship is about the physical stuff, the romantic bits, but most of all, about those everyday life sort of things.

- Maurice and Peggy found each other through an online dating site.

  ◦ Maurice speaks of trust and conversation as the foundations for a relationship.

  ◦ Peggy talks about the mistrust she feels from Maurice's supporters.

  ◦ They are making plans to live (closer) together, but the system of care in Flanders does not make things easy.

The writing process

TOON

We set out on this chapter and had a few discussions about authorship and recognition, but about anonymity and privacy as well during the time we were writing. The project started as a personal project for some of the members, but now it's gone back to the entire group. There have been debates on ownership, but in the end, through shared ownership, it was suggested that the authorship should be carried as a group. The terminology used here is 'people (labelled with) learning difficulties'.

Introduction

OUR NEW FUTURE AND TOON

The authors all are part of Our New Future, a small non-profit organisation in the Flemish-speaking part of Belgium. Our New Future was founded back in 1997 as the first self-advocacy group in Flanders by and for people labelled with learning difficulties. Today it is still the one and only independent organisation for people with learning difficulties who want to speak up and fight for their rights. Their goals are expressed in the organisation's name:

> **Our:** 'We' people with learning difficulties are in charge in our movement. We lead by example. We decide as a collective what direction we are going in and what our priorities are. We get support from our advisors – for example, to type and translate this text – where and when we ask for it.

> **New:** We take on new challenges, and are not afraid of showing others our abilities. We're always open to new things and are eager to learn.

> **Future:** We want to work on a better future by raising awareness in society that we are people with our own rights. We want to get rid of the cliché that disabled people are incapable of doing things.

We want people to know their rights. Therefore we organise workshops on the United Nations Universal Declaration of Human Rights and the on the Rights of Persons with Disabilities (2006). We have translated both texts into two booklets in accessible Dutch and we have included an audio CD, for those who prefer listening. These rights are the basis for our actions. When it comes to relationships, to intimacy and managing our private lives, we often feel violated in our rights. The right to information, respect for privacy and respect for home and the family – articles 21 to 23 (United Nations 2006) – are still not guaranteed in the heavily institutionalised context of Flanders.

Official records are hard to come by and there are no definite numbers or registry of learning disabled people; most estimations are about 200,000 of the entire Belgian population of about 11,200,000 (European Commission 2013). Many people with learning difficulties spend their lives in institutionalised or segregated care, starting at an early age in special schools and living in group homes or with their parents depending on the support they need.

Special schools do not offer diploma courses, so most of the people with learning difficulties go on to sheltered or supported employment, or spend much of their adult lives in day-care centres. When parents are no longer able or willing to offer support, or people just want to stand on their own feet, there are numerous housing options ranging from group homes to independent living, depending on their label, support needs, personal network, and so on. Current legislation is promoting community support for people with learning difficulties who voluntarily decide to go and live together.

Due to the reality of many people living in larger institutions however, many of them experience a day-to-day power struggle with their care givers, especially in the area of relationships, intimacy and sexuality. In the mid-1990's some accounts of forced 'therapeutic' sterilisation surfaced in the media. Since then more attention has been given to the training and education of both disabled people and their supporters.

In mainstream education, sexual education is part of the curriculum in both primary and secondary education. In special education and day-care centres the curriculum contains RSV (relational and sexual education), following the European Framework and guidelines from the World Health Organisation in regards to Sexual Education. The curriculum only offers targets, so pedagogy and methods are open to the schools themselves. The aims are to support and guide relational and sexual development, to develop values and norms and to avoid risk and harmful sexual behaviours (Ministry of Education of the Flemish Community 2012). In a recently started European project on experience exchange, Flanders is considered amongst the leaders in the field of relational and sexual training for people with learning difficulties (IPPFEN 2013). However, in practice the focus remains mostly on protection and prevention of harm through sexual contact (e.g. in sex education and training offered through formal and non-formal education) and risk assessments in institutions (Lesseliers 2009). This often leads to over-protection and prevention of any sexual contact at all.

The United Nations Convention on the Rights of People with Disabilities and its optional protocol was signed and ratified by Belgium, its regions and communities in 2009. Since the ratification, all legislation should be interpreted in light of the Convention (D'Espallier 2011). This has had its effects on policies in education, independent living, employment, care and support and equal opportunities.

On a federal level the Anti-Discrimination Law of February 2003 was replaced by the law of 10 May 2007 explicitly prohibiting any form of direct or indirect discrimination in all life domains (participation in society, employment, social protection and social care, justice, goods and services, social security, etc.). In addition, the 2007 law also defines the obligation of any provider of services or goods, or employer to offer reasonable accommodations to guarantee equal participation in everyday life. This implies government services should offer necessary support to enjoy all rights on an equal basis with others.

In 2011 Belgium filed its first report to the Committee on the Rights of Persons with Disabilities. It only mentions services to support the development and enjoyment of sexuality by people with disabilities in relation to – limited – actions taken to prevent sexual abuse and a newly formed task force on the prevention of HIV. Only in the (small) German-speaking community is there an organisation that supports people with disabilities with relationships and sexuality (FGS Social Security 2011). In the shadow report made by an advocacy organisation for disabled people the focus lies on the lack of support through personal budgets that prohibits people from living independently and having 'fruitful' relationships (GRIP 2012).

In May 2010 Our New Future organised a conference called 'Love is all around'. We partnered up with a training organisation and the Department for Disability Studies and Inclusive Education at Ghent University. People with learning difficulties told their stories, their dreams and desires about fruitful relationships to other self-advocates, professionals, family members, policy makers and academics. This chapter brings an updated account of some of those stories. We wrote this together with the help of our coach. Some parts of the stories are very personal, but we think it is important that they get out there. So we asked Toon, our coach, to use aliases in the translation. We are Fonske, Peggy and Maurice.

Fonske's tale

We meet Fonske at the station. His bright fleece jacket stands out, even in the rush-hour crowd. He tells us we are taking the tram to his house, so we follow Fonske to the platform.

Fonske is a man in his early forties. He has been a member of Our New Future for about ten years now and has been working with the training centre on the topic of 'Love is all around'. He was recently contacted to participate in a new reality TV series, *The Undateables*, but he wants to start his story by showing us where he lives.

CASE STUDY: FONSKE ───────────────────────

I used to live in a group home. There I spent most of my youth, when I was not at school or at the football field. I lived there together with 15 other men. It was unthinkable to have women around. That is, until about ten years ago. Then a few women came to live in the group home. By that time I had already moved to a different house. I did not really mind. We do not get to choose who we live with. You do not automatically get along with everyone. Especially if there are six others, or even 15, but you get used to it.

A few years ago I decided to move closer to my work at the community centre nearby. Now I live here with two others. And there is room for one more, but I would prefer it to just have the three of us. I could have chosen supported living, just on my own, but I like to have people around. Every person has the right to choose who he lives with. Now we are three men with learning difficulties living together. We are living in a community amongst other people. But it would be better if others were living with us.

It really is a coincidence that we are living together with three guys, but I think it is for the best, so you don't have any arguments. Two guys and one girl; that is just looking for trouble. You know the problem with us men? We cannot really talk with women, you know? My care giver said the same.

Two men living with two women is no problem I think, but you just cannot find a perfect match just like that, for everybody. I would like that, and I do believe that others would want this too. Humans are not made to be alone, by themselves. If they would put us together, that could be the basis for a relationship. I have seen it before. People who got to know each other in a group home, and then went on to living together, just the two of them.

I also do a lot of volunteering work in the local community. Everybody knows me around here. I have a lot of friends. Friendship is very important to me. Maybe even more important than a relationship. For me, the most important part of friendship is getting to know each other. A friend is someone you feel comfortable with. Someone you can go out with. And a friend supports you when you need him.

Some of my supporters from the institution are my friends too. They come and have pancakes on my birthday. Not for long, because they have other houses to visit. But they do their work, and then they have a cup of coffee. It makes me feel at ease.

Friends can talk about relationships as well, because everyone has their own ideas about that. I cannot talk to everybody about relationships. It all depends on how I feel around people. I feel at ease at Our New Future, so I talk to the people over there. But some of them have had experiences of sexual abuse, and that is awful. It makes me angry. That is why they do not want to speak about it. And I respect that.

I have been in love. Five years ago. But it did not work out. It was going too fast, and I needed time. I just want to be friends with everyone. So I chose not to go through with it. It is not easy to let something like that grow. It needs time. You need to give a relationship a year or two to grow a decent basis. People need to get to know one another. If I get into a relationship, it has to be long term. That is my choice. Freedom of choice is my right!

I am not actively searching for a girlfriend right now, but it will happen when the time is right. I went to a meeting once for singles with learning difficulties. But only guys showed up. I don't know if any of them ever got together. You need to be patient in life. You need to come across the right person. It is different from person to person what you are looking for in a relationship. So you need to follow your heart. I am sure my dreams can still come true. I will just have to be patient.

It is not easy for someone with a disability to have a relationship with a girl. I think you should be able to have a relationship with people without a disability. I feel that is important, love is not disabling. It makes you stronger.

Everyone talks about inclusion. But if you are disabled, then you are disabled in relationships… Because of our lives in the institutions, others do not know us. They do not know who we are, or that we are just like any other person. We are strong people. Everyone should be open to one another regardless of labels. You can be friends with everyone. You can fall in love with anyone.

Now listen, for me, love is different from friendships. Love is physical. It is giving a hug, or a kiss. Being in love is something you do with the whole of your heart. The heart is a symbol. You have to open your heart like a rose that blooms. That's what being in love is. Love always brings something new. New feelings, new experiences.

A relationship is something you have to take your time for. It is something you have to realise. You need to invest in it if you want it to grow. Trust is important. Trust to talk about all things that are important to you. And knowing the other person will keep them to themself.

If you love somebody, you have to look after them, in your own ways, in your own capacities. If I am in love, if I have a girlfriend, I look after her by giving her all my attention. I do that by bringing her breakfast in bed, or by cooking her dinner. I will buy her a cake, or a rose. Just to get this romantic feeling.

My ideal partner is funny, likes to go out to bars, restaurants, festivals… She would also love to hike, that's the kind of girlfriend I am looking for. Someone who likes to cook, and help doing the dishes… Do not get me wrong, I do not want her to do it for me. I want to do it together. Being in a relationship is doing things together. Not just fun stuff, but also those everyday life things.

In any case she has to be sociable. Like me. At least, that's how I picture her to be. I have not met her yet, but she has to be the same type of person. My type of person. That makes sense does it not? If I were a parrot, I would go out and look for another parrot, wouldn't I? Blue, green, red, yellow, any kind of parrot I would like and get along with. But I wouldn't go out and find myself an elephant.

So I am still waiting, that is why I did not participate in that television show. I would love to have a girlfriend, but when you put that on television, it is easy to be ridiculed. At first I was very enthusiastic about it, they had me completely sold when they told me they would help me in my search... But after talking about it with some of my supporters and friends, I decided not to participate. It is just too personal to put out in the open.

But if it turns out they really want to bring honest and respectful portraits of people with learning difficulties looking for the love of their life, then I will be the first to call them and to apply for the next series. I wanted to get to know them first, get more information, but they just wanted to come by and start filming right away. You know, actually I really wanted to participate, but I won't. You have to be careful, because those media types... They are only interested in what works on screen, not in your personal well-being.

I write poetry as well, that is how they found me. I write poetry for a training centre, so they can use it to advertise their workshops on love and intimacy. There is always something about love or friendship in my poetry. That is a sign I find that important in life, so it shows in my hobbies as well.

I already know everything I need to know. I researched that myself. I look up everything on the internet. But not everyone has access to the internet, so it is good that there are places which offer training and information. That is why we organised the conference as well.

Not everyone got educated in school. They think we are not interested, or that we will not understand. Everybody was always laughing when we talked about love and sex in classes. They all made fun of the teacher and what she was saying. Especially when she talked about sex or pregnancy. I think most of them did not get it. I always asked questions, so I got laughed at as well, but I did not mind. I think it is important to ask questions about 'relationships', 'sex', 'having babies' and 'love'.

I also asked questions in the institution where I was living. Some told me about their own relationships, about what went well and what did not. Those were the most interesting conversations, where you can learn from other people. So, some of the care givers answered, but most of them did not. They were embarrassed or even got angry. It was a topic you did not openly discuss.

Even now, it is not easy. Sure, if someone in our house would say at breakfast, 'My friend is coming over for dinner tonight', that would not be a problem. People visit here all the time. If your girlfriend wants to stay over, not a problem either, at least if you are together for six months and if you ask for permission. The management of the institution needs to approve guests, so everything can be sorted with fire insurance, if something should happen... You ask for permission a week in advance. Our parents ask our care givers, they ask management and they approve or decline. The news is brought by our care givers, so you can imagine it takes some time. It is not just letting them know, like, we feel romantic tonight and want to be together... They are pretty easy going, but still, everything has to go through proper procedures.

I feel people with learning difficulties are still discriminated against. We do not have all our rights yet. Society has to move forward and people should have the freedom to choose for themselves if they want a relationship.

CASE STUDY: PEGGY AND MAURICE

Peggy and Maurice are both in their mid-forties. They met through a social networking and dating site for people with learning difficulties. Maurice had been looking on the website for quite a few years, but without any luck. Peggy had just come out of a relationship, and got a tip from a friend about the website. She got three responses. One was from Maurice.

Maurice came across as very well mannered and fitted the type she was looking for. After a few chat sessions, they met up in real life. They met at the station and told each other what they would wear. Maurice recognised Peggy immediately from the picture. He describes it as a moment where he knew that everything fitted together. They went for coffee and it gradually grew and grew.

Modern technology played a major part in Maurice and Peggy's story. They met through the online dating site and made contact through Skype and Facebook, which they use to keep in contact during the week. Without their own computers, they would not have met each other. At Maurice's place the shared-use computer has Facebook blocked so the care givers cannot access it during work hours. Peggy's former house did not even have a shared computer. The computer sat on a table in the middle of the room, with a sign 'do not touch, supporters only'.

Maurice thought it was a good idea that they got to know each other a bit before they met up. According to Maurice, trust is one of the most important foundations of a good relationship.

Maurice has had people looking over his shoulder his entire life. His parents, his big sister, his care givers...that is why he now makes it a point that his relationship is something he has to do himself, and no one should interfere or meddle: 'A relationship is between me and her. It is our responsibility to make it work.'

Their different ways of living and support do make a difference. Peggy lives in supported living, Maurice in a group home. Maurice feels they are reluctant to let him go. He asked Peggy to have her supporter send an email to his institution, to ask if he could stay over for the weekend:

> We needed to make some agreements, not just between us both, but also between our institutions. For example, the first time Maurice was staying over. None of my supporters minded, but Maurice's…oh boy, you'd think we're all grown ups. They sounded even more like embarrassed teenagers than we did.

The agreements were all sorted out by the supporters for Maurice and Peggy and after a lot of emailing back and forth, Maurice was allowed to stay over. They did not like it at first, they would only let Maurice stay over one night, but the people from Peggy's institution persuaded them.

> Just one night? That's not a relationship, is it? What can you talk about in just one day? What can you do in just one night? And just before I left, they asked me if we were going to sleep together… They asked me if she had an extra bedroom. So I gave it a spin. I told them that she has two rooms…which she does, the bedroom and the living room. She even has a bathroom! But they don't have to know she has three rooms, do they?

Maurice spends every weekend at Peggy's. He explains how the only reason he goes back home is because he has to work during the week. Maurice has three housemates. He does not get along with his housemates and his supporters are not too fond of the idea that Peggy would come over and visit or, even more unthinkable, stay over.

> They say there's already four of you, a fifth wouldn't be manageable. We don't have a key to our room and there's no lock on the bathroom, so they say Peggy wouldn't feel at ease. I told them I don't feel at ease there every single day… One Wednesday Maurice invited Peggy over because there was a music festival in town. Because of issues with public transport, she would have to stay over, so Maurice asked his supporters. One of them told him to ask his housemates. If they were okay with it, she would not mind either. When the other supporter heard about it, she came over personally to tell Maurice off: 'Privacy issues'.

> It went from 'sure', to 'however', to 'maybe another time'. I asked them why I couldn't have the key to my room for one night, if privacy was a concern, but I never got an answer… So we called it off. Next weekend there's a festival near Peggy's. We'll go there.

Maurice says that there is still a lot of control from the institution. It is better than it used to be, but still… He cannot invite his girlfriend over to his own home when he wants to, and when she is over, they'll just ignore her. At one time they were sitting in the living room and a supporter came in. 'She did not say anything; she just took place behind the computer right next to us; so she could overhear everything.'

> I am still better off than some of my friends at Our New Future. Peter for instance. I know his girlfriend; we work at the same sheltered workplace. They can only see each other once every six weeks. They're on the phone every evening! How hard can it be for the institutions and the supporters to arrange a meeting more often? She's in a wheelchair, but Peter can take the train. I think it's harder to work and build on your relationship if you don't see each other that often. And that's because of those institutions. Tony, another friend, has to make an appointment, not with his girlfriend, but with the institution. A week in advance. He can't even stay over for dinner. Just rules, rules, rules… And what for? So people with learning difficulties wouldn't need to worry? So we can live a happy life? Alone… Peggy is hopeful that one day all the arranging will be over and they can just live their lives together as a couple. She talks about the hassle they had to go through, just for the fact that Maurice told them he was at her place during the weekend and he needed money to eat. He figured that since he didn't eat at home, they didn't have to provide meals for him on Saturdays and Sundays. That way he could use the food money to pay for groceries at Peggy's. His supporters told him that was not possible. He had to pay even if he was not there and there was no way to give him a refund. So Maurice went to the only room in the house he could lock and called his lawyer. He called his lawyer from the loo. After he told them his lawyer would call them, there weren't any more financial problems. Maurice's supporter called Peggy to tell her she was his first girlfriend. Peggy explains:

> I told her how I did have some experience and Maurice would learn everything soon enough, if we got to know each other a bit better. She was impressed. When I met Maurice I told him not to worry.

At home they told Maurice it was his relationship, so he should figure it out for himself. Maurice explains how they took him aside and had 'the talk'.

> They told me I had to take these 'balloons' and use them, against viruses and diseases. They told me that the most important thing if I was feeling like having sex, was putting one of these on. I thought, the most important thing if I feel like having sex, is to talk to Peggy about it. Conversation is the basis of a good

relationship. If you don't talk to each other, you can't build a relationship. I tell her everything.

Maurice and Peggy had the talk as well.

When he came here, he told me they'd given him something. Maurice, he's very correct about those things. We talked about it and decided not to use them. I've been tested for work and I can't get pregnant. Maurice really respects me, sexually. He always says, if you don't feel like it, just say so. And I do the same. Because I am his first girlfriend, he was a bit nervous at first. But I told him that he shouldn't be embarrassed. His care givers asked him if he'd be able to… I told him he'd learn soon enough.

You know, for us, the most important thing in a relationship is communication. You don't know each other from day one. It's something that takes time. If you're prepared to give it time, I think you can make it work.

The issue of children came up as well. They would love to have a child, but they can't have any.

Peggy told me, yeah, I was disappointed. But I was glad she had trusted me enough to tell me about her operation a few years back. And I told her I was happy she had made it through. Otherwise I would never have met her. And that's the most important thing.

Maurice and Peggy just got engaged. They have bought each other rings. But it will stay at that. If they get married Peggy would lose her benefits. Maurice works in a sheltered workspace and she volunteers in a day-care centre for small children. If they married or moved in together Maurice would keep his wages, but Peggy would lose everything.

If it weren't for that, I think we'd be married already. Don't get me wrong, I think just being together is the most important. So maybe we'll find a way to go and live together. But hey, even if we never get married, we'll always be connected.

Maurice is planning on moving. He is looking for an apartment near Peggy's.

We figured that I would come here every weekend for now. But it just doesn't feel right going back each Sunday. We want to have a future together, not just two days in the week. I am really looking forward to that. Being together only one day in the week isn't a relationship!

Summary

In this chapter, stories from self-advocates – Fonske, Peggy and Maurice – provide valuable insight into the continuing impact of service procedures on people's lives and the quiet but routine regulation of people's activities, behaviours and experiences including their personal and sexual relationships. Although on the surface settings such as group homes and supported living may seem a far cry from the old institutions, these insider accounts bring home the impact of current service frameworks and everyday practice on people's lives and relationships.

These accounts clearly bring home the patience, resilience and optimism of people with learning difficulties committed to pursuing their dreams and plans for relationships whilst remaining reliant on staff and services for elements of their support. The stories provide practical examples of steps people have taken to overcome service barriers and, in Maurice and Peggy's case, to be together and build their relationship. We also learn how the internet is beginning to play a role in enabling people to access information about sex and to meet a partner.

References

D'Espallier, A. (2011) 'Draagkracht is geen toverwoord.' *Momenten 9*, 16–24.

European Commission (2013) *Eurostat. Population on 1 January by age and sex – Belgium.* Available at http://appsso.eurostat.ec.europa.eu/nui/show.do?dataset=demo_pjan&lang=en, accessed on 13 June 2014.

GRIP (Gelijke Rechten voor Ieder Persoon vzw) (2012) *Mensenrechten en handicap. Schaduwrapport Vlaanderen (België) 2011 voor het VN-Comité voor de Rechten van Personen met een Handicap.* Brussels: Gelijke Rechten voor Ieder Persoon vzw.

FGS (Federal Government Services Social Security) (2011) *Report on the Implementation of the UN Convention of 13 December 2006 on the Rights of Persons with Disabilities.* First Report from Belgium. Brussels: Federale Overheidsdiensk Sociale Zeberheid.

IPPFEN (International Planned Parenthood Federation European Network) (2013) *KEEP ME SAFE Project: Empowering Young People with Learning Disabilities to Protect Themselves Against Sexual Abuse and Violence across Europe.* European Commission, Daphne 111 programmes. Brussels: IPPF EN Regional Office.

Lesseliers, J. (2009) *Persons with Disabilities: Their Experience of Relationships and Sexuality.* [Proefschrift ingediend tot het behalen van de academische graad van Doctor in de Pedagogische Wetenschappen.] Gent: Academia Press.

Ministry of Education of the Flemish Community (2012) *Sexual Education.* Brussels. Available at www.ond.vlaanderen.be, accessed on 13 June 2014. Ministry of Education of the Flemish Community.

United Nations (2006) *Universal Convention on the Rights of People with Disabilities.* New York: United Nations.

CHAPTER 7

THE PARADOX OF INTIMACY IN JAPAN
Shifting Objects of Affection

Eiji Tsuda and Takako Ueto with an introduction by Louise Townson

Overview

- Despite disability equality being enshrined in Japanese law, discrimination is still prevalent.

- There is a persistent public perception that adults with learning difficulties are asexual in Japanese society.

- There have been public issues about sex education in special schools in Japan.

- However, self-advocates are starting to speak more openly about relationships.

- In Japanese culture the idea of independence is weaker than in many western countries.

- It is not unusual for adults to live at home with their parents for many years in Japan.

- This makes it even more difficult for people with learning difficulties to shift their relationships and live with partners.

- Even where people with learning difficulties have partners, they may not extend this to living with partners or getting married.

The writing process

This chapter is written by two academics, Eiji and Takako from Japan. When the chapter was initially discussed it was explained by Eiji that it would be too difficult to co-write the chapter directly with people with intellectual disabilities because of the nature of the topic. Louise has therefore read the chapter and written her views as a foreword. The preferred terminology used in this chapter is 'people with learning difficulties', which relates back to the People First movement in Japan, which both Eiji and Takako support.

Introduction

LOUISE

Having read this chapter it becomes very apparent that there are many differences in cultural values in Japan compared to the UK.

Many people may read this and think that people with intellectual disabilities who live at home for longer in Japan is wrong, but this can also happen for people with intellectual disabilities living at home all their lives within the UK. There is nothing wrong with that; (if that is their choice) it's just what people are comfortable with.

Relationships are often difficult to talk about regardless of whether you have an intellectual disability or not; this is a topic that can be difficult to talk about anyway.

In families years ago (and perhaps some are still like that) there were certain things that you just didn't talk about and relationships and sexuality was one of them.

I do think relationships and sexuality can be at different stages. By this I mean the ability to talk about these issues can vary from culture to culture and family to family.

Introduction: Japan's socio-cultural and legal background

EIJI

According to a Japanese national survey in 2006, the population of people with learning difficulties in Japan is estimated to be about 547,000 out of approximately 120,000,000 of a national population. They are recognised by the government as consumers of the social welfare service which is identified only by application. Consequently, there must be a lot more people who are not labelled as having learning difficulties in spite of having needs for social welfare services.

In this chapter we are going to describe the socio-cultural oppression of the sexuality of people with learning difficulties in Japan. The formal system, including our legal system, cannot be said to represent the real situation with regards to the sexuality of people with learning difficulties. For example, you will see in this chapter that people with learning difficulties suffer from socio-cultural barriers to marriage, although the Japanese Constitution admits the rights of all people, including people with any disabilities, to marry if both partners wish it.

Just the same as in western countries, eugenics prevailed in Japanese society until the mid-twentieth century. Even after the Second World War, the Japanese government tried several times to strengthen their Eugenic Protection Act to allow abortion for the reason of the impairment of a foetus. Fortunately they failed, due to the work of social movements, and then finally changed the Act to the Maternal Protection Act in 1996.

Now, under the law, it is nominally prohibited to abort a foetus for the reason of disability, but actually we know that informally there are still many such cases.

Additionally, because of the development of technology for prenatal diagnoses, a new eugenics prevails. As an extra chromosome equates to Down's Syndrome in many cases, we can say that there is a strong connection between abortion and learning difficulties, although the law in Japan does not formally allow the connection. It would appear the prevention of the birth of babies with disabilities is based on socio-cultural imperatives rather than legal backgrounds.

Discourses of sexuality

In Japan there are several discourses concerning the sexuality of people with learning difficulties. In many cases the theme is discussed from a social adjustment perspective. Some argue that the sexual behaviour of people with learning difficulties often deviates from cultural norms, and that such deviations should be controlled.

Miyahara and Aikama in the conclusion to their 2001 study state: 'The parents who think that their child with learning difficulty has difficulty with learning and controlling his/her sexual behavior tend to have (a) negative understanding of his/her sexual development' (p.65). This suggests that some parents do not want their children to behave sexually (as this would be seen as deviating from the social norm), or conversely they consider their children to be asexual beings. 'Don't wake a sleeping baby' is a saying that parents and supporters of people with learning difficulties often use when they want to keep people away from sexual knowledge and behaviour.

In 2003, disciplinary measures were taken by the Board of Education in Tokyo against teachers at a special school for explicit teaching materials in their sex education classes with students with learning difficulties (Nakagawa 2009, pp.48–53). During disciplinary proceedings it was argued that materials such as dolls with sexual organs ignored the developmental age of the children.

On the other hand, alternative discourses that recognise the sexuality of people with learning difficulties as an essential part of life are now emerging in Japan. Clearly this highlights an issue of oppressed sexuality. People with learning difficulties themselves have started to speak out as part of this discourse. For example some of the narratives from a book by people with learning difficulties (Chuo-Houki 2002) include: 'We boys could not have close relationships with girls in the institution'; 'I really hated that the staff of the institution decided what I wore and they forced me not to make up; and 'I – a man – was very embarrassed of helping girls to bathe in the institution'.

The rights of people with learning difficulties to be educated and given guidance about ways of expressing their sexuality have started to be discussed. An experienced teacher who has taught sex education for students with learning difficulties for many years, explains as follows: 'Students with learning difficulties surely have emotions of love but are often poor in nurturing the emotional expression inside them… They should be taught the way of expressing their emotion of love' (Shuppan 1996, pp.128–129). These discourses tell us that sexuality is an essential factor of empowerment: that people with learning difficulties should be encouraged to love themselves and others and to develop self-esteem and the social self.

In the following section, we draw upon this perspective to share some examples of how, in our view, people with learning difficulties in Japan have experienced oppression of their sexuality.

Shifting objects of affection

In modern Japanese culture, the central object of affection for most people shifts from their parents to a new partner whom he/she chooses in adolescence (Erikson 1968, p.247; Smith 1969). During this process, people commonly experience loneliness and struggle in finding their new object of affection. In Japan, however, we can observe that there are barriers which frequently prevent people with learning difficulties experiencing such a transition. These barriers can be attributed to Japanese culture as well as social prejudice against disability.

The authors are advisors of a self-advocacy group in Kobe, Japan. The group, called 'Friend', was established by parents of people with learning difficulties in 1999. We are going to introduce two scenarios from self-advocates in this group to describe their oppressed sexuality and, in contrast, the empowerment of people with learning difficulties in Japan.

CASE STUDY: YASU ————————————————————————

Yasu, a man in his fifties, has been a core self-advocate in 'Friend' from the first days of the group. He has been working very hard for a company since he graduated from special school. Yasu is a decent gentleman and is relied on by the other members of 'Friend'. Yasu lives with his mother and often shows us his affection for her. We frequently see him refusing to talk about independent living or living in a group home. He also refuses to participate in cooking programmes and lodging training programmes which the parents of the self-advocates prepare. We realise that he really hates to think of living apart from his mother.

The self-advocates from 'Friend' edit and publish a newsletter a few times a year. They decide the topic of the newsletter and write articles, or ask others to write. Their favourite topic is work. They write positively about what they do in their job and how hard they work. However, when the topic was love and marriage, some self-advocates could not write their thoughts, hopes or experiences. While another self-advocate wrote up a list of names of women who he prefers, Yasu refused to write the article. We realised that he had never demonstrated his sexuality.

We guess that his strong affection for his mother is something to do with his sexually disempowered state. Yasu has not lived apart from his family even after he became an adult, because he prefers to live his rather peaceful life cared for by his mother and does not have any motivation to leave. He probably has never had a chance to shift the object of his affection, to find and establish his new family, because his mother has been his object until today.

We think there are two reasons that could cause the failure of shifting affection for Yasu. One reason is that people with learning difficulties are often misconceived as asexual beings. Another reason is that the motivation to live apart from parents after becoming adults is relatively weak in Japanese culture.

It is reported that people with learning difficulties are viewed as asexual in Western culture too (Hasler *et al.* 2005, p.8). Also in Japanese culture, there is a pressure that keeps people with learning difficulties away from sexual knowledge and behaviour. Yasu may have internalised this part of his culture resulting in losing his voice to tell his sexual story, in exchange for a peaceful life with his mother.

Another reason that Yasu seems to have abandoned having a sexual life may be linked to a concept of family in Japanese culture. In Japan, it is generally not unusual for men or women to live with their parents even when they become adults. Young adults are not always required to be independent, and therefore the motivation to find their intimate partner seems rather weak in Japanese culture (Tsuda 2006). This may be one of the reasons why Yasu can remain living his rather peaceful life without shifting the object of his affection up until his fifties. We often forget the oppression imposed on Yasu, because he never complains about it and he says that he is satisfied with the status quo.

In an interview, another self-advocate, however, tells us about the oppression of sexuality for people with learning difficulties in general from her own experience of having a 'boyfriend'.

CASE STUDY: RIE

Another self-advocate of 'Friend', Rie, is in her forties and lives with her family. She has many social skills and has been working at a range of sheltered workshops since her graduation from a vocational school. After work and at weekends she enjoys a variety of leisure activities such as going to a baseball game and karaoke. Her leadership is a valuable asset for 'Friend', although she sometimes complains that the other members should be more active in self-advocacy activities such as participating in People First forums.

Rie has been dating a man who was her co-worker at one of the sheltered workshops where she worked several years ago. When asked how she and her boyfriend started dating, she replies, 'We shared common interests such as baseball and music. So we began to spend time together after work, talking about the things we both were interested in'.

According to her, when they started dating, her parents were against their relationship and would often scold and nag her. She would talk back, telling them, 'Just leave me alone!' This conflict with her parents made her emotionally unstable, but she was able to manage somehow. She would tell her boyfriend about what was happening at home. He would listen to her, show her empathy and advise her not to worry too much. His support meant a lot to her. She was very thankful to him and says, 'He stands by me.'

Although the conflict with her parents lasted for some time, she and her parents were able to make a compromise. Now the parents do not interfere or complain as long as she comes home before it gets too late at night.

She sees her boyfriend as a very reliable man. When she got into trouble with someone concerning money, he mediated between the two and helped them come to a settlement. Now, taking his advice, she tries to be careful not to repeat the same mistake.

Another thing for which she is grateful to him is his instruction about money management. In the past, she was not careful enough about spending her money. She would often spend all the money she had at once, find her purse empty and have to borrow some money from her mother, which became another source of conflict between the two of them. He taught her how to spend money more wisely and now she is free from this problem.

When asked who she turns to when she is in trouble or wants to be listened to, she says that she sometimes turns to her boyfriend and at times to other friends. When asked if she ever turns to her parents, she replies that she does talk to her parents about many things. However, she says, 'I don't go into detail. And I avoid discussing serious matters, because I will become even more confused and stuck in my thoughts after talking to my parents.' Moreover, it seems that her boyfriend recognises her as doing her best at work and encourages her to accept herself as who she is. She appreciates such positive regard for her, because she feels, 'Some people have prejudice against me'.

The more time she spends with her boyfriend, the less time she has available for her parents at home. Now all she does with her parents is watch TV and have supper together. However, it does not mean that she is refusing her parents. Rather, she is very concerned about them. When asked about her future plans, she says that she would like to live alone near her parents, rather than getting married to or living with her boyfriend. She would like to become more independent and to help her parents when they are in need of help. This is the reason why she wants to live near her parents. She and her boyfriend share the same idea about their own future, as he also wants to leave his parents and live by himself near them. She and her boyfriend agree that they will not live together, but will continue their relationship.

Towards the end of the interview, I mention to her that many people with learning difficulties do not have a boyfriend or girlfriend, and ask her if she would recommend those people to have one. She says, 'Yes, I really do!' Although one of the male members of 'Friend' sometimes says to her that it is no good for her to go out with her boyfriend so often, she thinks that he is wrong. To her, it is wonderful to have someone with whom you can feel so much intimacy and trust.

Discussion about Rie's story

TAKAKO

What I learned from the interview with Rie is that she is just like many adults who strive for independence and search for an intimate relationship with someone other than their parents. The difference between her and many other adults is that she experienced severe conflict with and oppression from her parents as she tried to shift the object of her intimacy from her parents to her boyfriend.

As she mentioned, her experience is viewed as an exception rather than the norm for people with learning difficulties. Her behaviour is regarded as undesirable by her family and by some of her friends; it is possibly regarded as somewhat deviant by society as a whole.

If we compare the experiences of Yasu and Rie, it seems paradoxical that what seems normal for many adults is considered deviant for people with learning difficulties. When people with learning difficulties express themselves, including expressing intimacy and sexuality, they often face a negative reaction from others; if such expression does not fit the generalised image of people with learning difficulties, the reactions received can be very oppressive.

It is also very important to note that Rie has been empowered though her relationship with her boyfriend in many ways. She has acquired good money management skills and she has learned to deal with problems at work. Above all, she has a more positive self-image and higher self-esteem. What brought conflict with her parents was her relationship with her boyfriend, but what made reconciliation possible was also her relationship with him.

From Rie's story, we can conclude that people with learning difficulties have the desire to be independent and search for an intimate partner, while maintaining a good relationship with their parents. What is needed is to understand their desire as normal and to help the process of shifting the object of their affection. Society needs to show genuine concern, accept people as they are and encourage them to accept themselves as they are.

Summary

EIJI AND TAKAKO

The pressure to become independent from parents as people reach their adulthood is relatively weak within Japanese culture. Consequently, most people with learning difficulties obtain independence only by struggling with their parents. An activist with cerebral palsy active in the Japanese disability movement in the 1970s expressed the relationship between people with disabilities and their parents very well: 'It is our fate to have to reject the partiality of our parents even while crying and apologizing for being undutiful to them' (Yokotsuka 1975, p.27).

Struggle or conflict among family members may be seen as a sign of deviance, whereas a peaceful relationship between people with learning difficulties and their parents represents a family with plenty of love. In such circumstance, people with learning difficulties tend to choose a dependent way of life with their parents, rather than struggling with parents to obtain their independence.

There exists a certain structure of family system, value system and prejudice against disability in Japanese culture that currently oppresses the sexuality of people with learning difficulties. We have to deconstruct the structure piece by piece to liberate people's sexuality and to create the best possible circumstances to enable people to self-determine their own lives.

References

Chuo-Houki (2002) 'I won't go back to the institution anymore', in *The Executive to Establish Group Homes for 100 thousand people* (in Japanese). Chuo-Houki

Erikson, E. (1968) *Identity, Youth and Crisis*. London: Faber and Faber.

Hasler, K., Yates, R. and Anderson, J. (eds) (2005) 'Sexual Health and Relationships: A review of resources for people with learning disabilities', *NHS Health Scotland*.

Miyahara, H. and Aikawa, K. (2001) 'A survey on sexuality of family of adults and children with learning difficulties.' *Bulletin of the School of Allied Medical Sciences, Nagasaki University, 14*, 1 (in Japanese).

Nakagawa, S. (2009) 'The trial of the study on mind and body in Nanao Special School.' *Quarterly Education Law* 161, 48–53 (in Japanese).

Shuppan, K. (1996) 'Expose love and sex of people with learning difficulties to light.' *Society for Life and Sex of People with Disabilities* (in Japanese). Tokyo.

Smith, E. (1969) 'The Date.' In D. Rogers (ed.) *Issues in Adolescent Psychology*. New York: Meredith Corporation.

Tsuda, E. (2006) 'Japanese culture and the philosophy of self-advocacy: the importance of interdependence in community living.' *British Journal of Learning Disabilities, 34*, 3, 151–156.

Yokotsuka, H. (1975) *Hahayo! Mothers! Don't kill! Korosuna!*. Suzusawa Shoten (in Japanese). US.

THE MALTESE ODYSSEY

Issues of Sexuality and Parenting for People
with Intellectual Disability

Claire Azzopardi Lane with an introduction by Louise Townson

Overview ————————————————————————————

- Maltese society does not always see people with an intellectual disability as people who have the same sexual needs and desires as non-disabled people.

- People with an intellectual disability want to have the same opportunities as non-disabled people to fall in love, have relationships, get married and have children.

- The law in Malta is influenced by the Catholic church and does not help to support this.

- It would help if there was a disability movement in Malta.

- People with disability under international law have a right to choose to become parents.

- People with disability in Malta should have a right to support from the state to help them be good parents.

The writing process

Claire has been working with Corinne, a 34-year-old mother with intellectual disabilities and her family, whom she describes as 'supportive'. They became research participants for a project on 'Motherhood for Women with Intellectual Disabilities'.

This was to counteract negative media attention Corinne had received through the Maltese press. Claire uses the term 'intellectual disabilities' in her writing. Louise read Claire's chapter and then wrote an introduction as a comment from her own perspective.

Introduction
LOUISE

When we talk or think about parenting we think more about parents who don't have the label of intellectual disabilities. Why is this? Everyone has the right to be parents regardless of whether they have a label or not.

Too many times I've heard horror stories about abuse or neglect of children, but we need to remember it's not just parents with intellectual disabilities that happens to. All too often people who are labelled don't even get the chance to be parents because the assumption is made that they wouldn't manage. If the correct support was in place then there is absolutely no reason why not.

One of my relatives is a social worker and we have many discussions where I've said that children are getting removed or fostered and adopted far too quickly if you're a parent with an intellectual disability. To this she has said, 'They don't just whip the kids away, procedures have to be followed!' But I think people aren't always given the support to understand what is happening and are pressured to just go along with what they are told by professionals and their own families.

Yet, in contrast, people with intellectual disabilities always have to prove that they are good parents.

The Maltese context

Malta is a southern European country, an island in the Mediterranean Sea. It lies 80 km south of Sicily, 284 km east of Tunisia and 333 km north of Libya. Malta is one of the European Union's member states. In 2013 Malta had a total population of 411,277. The Maltese government is in the process of drawing up a comprehensive register of people with disability to gain a clearer picture of this population and their needs. The most recent statistics by the National Commission for Persons with Disability (2011), estimate that there are over 30,000 persons with disability, 1,545 of whom have an intellectual disability.

Parenting and disability

Parenting is supposedly based on a principle of equal citizenship rather than parental competence, yet in Malta people with disabilities tend not to have children due to social and attitudinal barriers rather than the limitations imposed by their own physical or intellectual impairment. Parenting is all too often perceived negatively by sceptical family members, friends, health practitioners and complete strangers. As a consequence people with intellectual disability often find themselves in a position where choices and decisions about parenting are made for them by other people.

In order to make an informed choice about becoming a parent, knowledge of one's fertility and control over sexual encounters are required. Parenting by people with intellectual disability is also overshadowed by interrelated problems often linked to intellectual disability, such as low income, the risk of more than average health problems, ineffective professional support and lack of social networks as well as general negative public responses.

Malta has recently seen the first local report on State media of a woman called Corinne who has intellectual disabilities and has become a mother. She is not the first and will not be the last woman with intellectual disability to become a parent. Yet, since people with intellectual disabilities are generally perceived as asexual in Maltese society, this story evoked media sensationalism.

Corinne is aware of this and during the research said to me: 'When I show the photo of my daughter to someone they tell me how sweet she is but what they say behind my back I don't know' (Corinne, aged 34, mother of Mariah, aged one year six months).

The sexuality of people with intellectual disability has been suppressed since the beginning of time. In contrast with other EU countries, Malta lacks active movements formed and led by people with disability; furthermore movements working for disability and sexuality issues are unheard of. Azzopardi (2009, p.8) affirms that: 'In the last decade, the disability community in Malta has made significant progress on the "services" dimension but has fallen short in policy.' He confirms that when it comes to disability politics, parents are the only political and organised lobby that exists in Malta. He asserts that the local context at present is service dominated and people with disability are clustered in impairment-based groups whose agenda is overrun by charity-based campaigns.

The absence of a disability coalition in Malta has a great impact. If people with disability were organised, so as to be able to dictate their own agenda and contribute to developing policy, they could ultimately experience political power and control. In fact, disability policy is now starting to be drafted.

Law connected to intellectual disability in Malta

Although the United Nations Standard Rules on the Equalisation of Opportunity of People with Disability, which deals with Family Life and Personal Integrity

(Rule 9.2), recognises the right of people with disability to sexual expression, current Maltese law regarding the Capacity to Act of a person with an intellectual disability is listed under the Maltese Civil Code's (Chapter 16) Interdiction and Incapacitation (189, 1).

This law has not been reviewed since 1889 and terms referring to persons with intellectual disability include: 'imbecility', 'mental infirmity' and 'prodigal'. This legislation states that persons who are considered 'incapacitated from doing certain acts' may be interdicted (forbidden) or incapacitated, therefore legally rendered incapable of making a legal decision.

In addition, Malta's Marriage Act (Chapter 255, 4) maintains that a 'marriage contracted between persons either of whom is incapable of contracting by reason of infirmity of mind, whether interdicted or not, shall be void'. The Maltese Civil Code Legislation (Chapter 16, 190) is deemed automatically applicable to people who are 'congenitally deaf-mute or blind' and in 'any such case no further proof shall be required that such person is incapable of managing his own affairs'.

This law has possibly never been contested due to the beliefs and attitudes of many non-disabled people, who genuinely consider people with intellectual disability as incapable of sexual expression or sexual pleasure (Azzopardi Lane 2011; Bonnie 2008; Hamilton 2009). Furthermore many Maltese non-disabled people have a mentality locked into the eugenics era, and therefore claim that people with learning disability do not have the right to be sexually active (Azzopardi Lane 2011). Since international laws are only effective if individual countries adopt them into domestic law, then national legislation and adequate policies underpinning the rights of people with disability are necessary. Moreover, national legislation and policies are only useful if people with intellectual disability are given the necessary support to exercise these rights. Sexuality policies require a proactive approach to support the person with intellectual disability.

Yet in many other developed countries the stigma of asexuality is being challenged and progress has been made in developing strategies that empower people with disability to live an equally fulfilling life, where they have the same opportunities as non-disabled individuals.

The influence of the Catholic Church

The Catholic Church in Malta, as in the rest of the world, has influenced the image of people with disability, particularly people with intellectual disability, by portraying them in angelic and asexual ways. These images are an eminent influence on Maltese society, particularly on parents of people with intellectual disability and those who provide services for them: persuading them that their sexuality is non-existent since they are 'pure' beings. In both the Maltese and Irish constitutions, sexual expression is only recognised within marriage, and the Church encourages sexual relations only if two of the 'opposite sex' are bound by the sacrament of marriage with an intention of procreation. This leaves people with intellectual disability with limited opportunities, and a narrow margin of choices associated with intimate relationships.

Malta has recently ratified the United Nations Convention on the Rights of People with Disabilities. Article 22 of the Convention refers to the Right for Home and Family. This Article underlines the right of people with disability to have children and found a family. Once it is established that people with intellectual disability have a human right to a sexual identity, to procreate and to have a family, then measures need to be set in place in order to protect and empower this minority group.

A substantial part of this framework is accessible and suggests ongoing sex education for people with intellectual disability. This has been a requirement stated in national sexuality policies in various countries as well as in policies within services providing for people with intellectual disability. Such education would in turn empower the person with disability to make informed choices on whether to engage in a sexual activity or not, as well as on the use of contraception and family planning. Corinne and her family explained that she had not had the knowledge to make the link between sex and pregnancy: 'As it happened Corinne met a boyfriend, they were in love and she became pregnant without even knowing it' (Taina, Corinne's sister-in-law). Corinne became a media sensation when she admitted she didn't know she would get pregnant by having intimate relations with her boyfriend. She found out she would be a mother eight months into the pregnancy. Corinne recalls: 'I was feeling the kicking in my tummy, I didn't know what it was as I had never gone through it before.'

Social support given to people with intellectual disability at different stages of their adult life includes social services which are not just of financial nature. Being a socially just country involves giving people with intellectual disability the opportunity to have more control. Such autonomy translates into supporting adults with disability to be part of our communities and truly be able to realise their rights. Yet, rather than shouldering these responsibilities, our country still tends to give the respective families this role. It is this lack of support in Malta that endorses institutionalisation. Assuming that families will give all the support required by people with intellectual disabilities is far from social justice. While there are those blessed with a supportive family, who are ready to assume responsibility for all the needs of the mother and her child without separating the two from each other, others are not. There are known cases where women with disability have been denied their right to motherhood and their child put into foster care, because they did not have social or family support and could not raise a child on their own.

Corinne happened to be lucky, as her family supported her and her daughter. Corinne acknowledges: 'I'm glad I have my brother and Taina (sister-in-law), I don't know what I would do without them. They would have taken my daughter away if I hadn't had them, God forbid they took her away because she is part of me.'

Guardianship

A step in the direction of emancipation for people with disabilities was the introduction in 2012 of an Act to amend the Maltese Code of Organisation and Civil Procedure and the Civil Code, previously cited, with the purpose of including a Guardianship Act (XXIV). The Act is aimed at people whose condition renders them incapable of taking care of their own affairs, thus including some persons with intellectual disability.

With the introduction of the Guardianship Act (2012), a guardian or joint guardians are appointed by the Guardianship Board to safeguard the personal and proprietary well-being of a person and act on their behalf. Being subjected to a guardianship order does not mean that a person is stopped from contributing to decision-making. Unlike interdiction and incapacitation, the person subject to guardianship needs to have their will respected as much as possible. Most importantly the guardianship order will not be a universal order but it will be tailored according to the person subjected to that order, as this must be tailored to suit that person's particular needs. In relation to sexuality and people with intellectual disability, a person might be in need of a guardian to address their financial matters yet be in a position to decide about their sexuality, relationships or parental status without needing support (or with partial support).

Other issues and developments

Empowerment of parents with disability also relies on employment, a key component in financial stability and independence. Yet such an opportunity needs to be backed up by other forms of social support such as personal care assistance and public childcare that also cater for the needs of children with disability. Corinne, who was seeking employment to support her daughter and contribute her financial share as part of the family, asserted, 'I'll do anything for my daughter... I wish to work. I can clean and sort out papers and put them in envelopes. I tried working before...but then they fired me.' Taina, Corinne's sister-in-law, added, 'Corinne has understood more than ever how important it is for her to be able to work to support her child.'

The Equal Opportunities Act, which was enacted in Malta in 2000, gave people with disability in Malta a legal stronghold. The Equal Opportunities Act (2000) tackles equality in various domains, including education, employment and accessibility. Yet the enforcement of legislation still has a long way to go in Malta. A lack of policy is soon evident when issues of sexuality, such as sexual health, sex education and sexual abuse are discussed. Furthermore, this dearth is apparent when sexuality is combined with the topic of people with intellectual disabilities. The lack of policy to address sexual vulnerability, access to sexual health services, sex education and a right to be sexually active is evident in services for people with intellectual disability across Malta.

This situation may be linked to the fact that, in contrast with other countries, Malta lacks active movements formed and led by people with disability, as mentioned at the start of the chapter. Only recently has Malta seen the emergence of a small yet strong movement of this kind: Breaking Limits. This non-governmental organisation is working for the rights of disability at a political level, dictating its own agenda and contributing to developing policy and ultimately political power.

Moreover, in October 2013, the Permanent Secretary for the Rights of Persons with Disability and Active Ageing commenced work on a National Disability Policy. A consultative draft policy launched for public debate in Spring 2014 (Times of Malta 2014). One of the numerous issues included in these guidelines is sexuality.

Barriers to development

Malta recently launched a National Sexual Health Policy (2011) that had been in the pipeline for 11 years. Yet the policy publicised after such a long wait was a watered-down version of previous unpublished drafts, as the final version was sent to the Church's Curia for its views and its feedback was taken on board (Massa 2011).

Controversy erupted when a few days after the Sexual Health Policy was officially released, the Bishop of Gozo, Malta's sister island, stated that the educational system could be abusing students if, 'instead of helping them control their sexual energy, it offers them information and methods, such as contraceptives, inducing them to give in to the culture of pleasure' (Times of Malta 2010a). The Bishop of Gozo later clarified his comments reaffirming that any teaching on sexuality should address the 'respect and love between spouses before tackling the physical aspect' (Times of Malta 2010b).

Such propaganda at a national level, as Montebello (2009) concludes, is evidence that there is no serious strategic plan for a change in the structure of the Catholic Church so that it meets the reality of modern times or the contemporary needs of Maltese society. The Sexual Health Policy document makes no particular reference to people with intellectual disabilities and a sexuality policy specifically addressing the needs of people with disability at this point in time seems far removed.

Nonetheless research (Tabone *et al.* 2003) has claimed that young people's attitudes in Malta towards sexual issues contrast starkly with the Church's teaching.

Abela (1998) claims that Maltese youth are increasingly seeing sexual decisions as a private matter, no longer influenced by the traditional teachings of the Church. Yet religious minorities such as the Catholic Students' University Movement opposed the installation of a contraceptive machine on University Campus (Times of Malta 2009), arguing that they would feel offended and supplementing their argument by stating that university was not a place for sex and that the distribution of condoms promoted a promiscuous lifestyle.

The Catholic ethos

The Council of Europe (2003), which reports on the relationship between sexual values and the sexual health patterns and policies in European countries, asserts that western European countries are generally more tolerant towards sexual issues then eastern European countries. Yet they claim that strong Catholic countries in both East and West Europe, including Malta, have less tolerant attitudes overall (Cassar 2009).

The traditional Roman Catholic ethos has been an influential factor on attitudes in countries such as Ireland, Poland and Malta (Azzopardi Lane 2011; Bonnie 2008; Drummond 2006; Fairbairn 2002). It can therefore be said that historically, the morality of these countries has been dictated and shaped by the teachings and beliefs of the Roman Catholic Church. In both Ireland and Malta (Azzopardi Lane 2011; Selina 2008) the close relationship between Church and State has had a number of implications for the countries' citizens. Malta's official religion, as declared in the Maltese Constitution, is Apostolic Roman Catholic. Even though local socio-anthropologist Montebello (2009, p.115) argues that 'in real terms it probably does not mean much', the authorities of the local Catholic Church still seem to think that they represent the whole Maltese population and that they hold the right to speak on behalf of the whole nation.

To prove this point, various government discussions and decisions are regulated by the Catholic code of morality, even though this particular morality is probably not embraced by the majority of the Maltese population any longer (Montebello 2009). This could be witnessed by the results of the recent referendum on the legalisation of divorce, which surprisingly enough found the majority voting for the introduction of divorce despite the Church's tenacious crusade against it (Malta Today 2011; World News 2011).

Summary

The prospect of people with intellectual disability being able to exercise their right to equality and inclusion in Maltese society requires the introduction and the overhaul of existing legislation and policies that concern this sphere. Furthermore, the opportunity to be valued as a person who has the right to an active sexual life depends on a socio-political shift in attitudes and mentality in Malta. Women with intellectual disability who want to have a child believe that this is possible with the appropriate social networks. The need for supportive networks for these mothers is underlined and failure to undertake parenthood lies in inadequate support rather than the disability itself being an indicator for failure. Belief in the capabilities of people with intellectual disabilities as parents together with the provision of professional constructive, flexible and coordinated assistance has proved to be the most successful of strategies.

References

Abela, A. (1998) *Secularized Sexuality: Youth Values in a City-Island*. Malta: Social Value Studies.

Azzopardi, A. (2009) *Understanding Disability Politics in Malta: New Directions Explored*. VDM: Verlag. Dr Muller, Germany.

Azzopardi Lane, C.L. (2011) 'Sexuality and learning disability in Malta: realities and potentials.' Unpublished thesis submitted for the degree of Doctor of Philosophy. Canterbury, UK: Tizard Centre. University of Kent.

Bonnie, S. (2008) *Facilitated Sexual Expression in the Independent Living Movement in Ireland*. Available at www.independentliving.org/docs6/bonnie200208.html, accessed on 12 June 2014.

Cassar, M. (2009) 'Youth Culture in the Maltese Islands.' In J. Cutajar. And G. Cassar (eds). *Social Transitions in Maltese Society*. Malta: Agenda Publications.

Chamber of Deputies Malta. 'Permanent Committee for Social Affairs, Education and Prevention, Responsibility and Fidelity': The Best National Strategy towards Sexual Health. Office of the Prime minister, Annual Reports of Government Departments, (2009) p542. Available at www.gov.mt/en/Government/Publications/Publications%20and%20Policies/Documents/Annual%20Report%20of%20Government%20Departments%20-%202009.pdf, accessed 11 August 2014

Civil Code. Malta. Of Interdiction and Incapacitation. Chpt. 16. www.justiceservices.gov.mt/DownloadDocument.aspx?app=lom&itemid=8580, accessed 11 August 2014

Council of Europe (2003) *The Reproductive Health of Young Europeans. Population Studies, No. 42.* Strasbourg: COE Publishing.

Drummond, E. (2006) 'Attitudes towards a pilot study in Ireland.' *Learning Disability Practice 4*, 4, 28–34.

Fairbairn, G. (2002) 'Sex Matters: Practice and Research.' Learning Disability Practice 5, 2, 20. Ipswich, MA: EBSCO Publishing.

Hamilton, C. (2009). 'Now I'd like to sleep with Rachael': Researching sexuality support in a service agency group home.' *Disability & Society 24*, 3, 303–315.

Malta Marriage Act. www.justiceservices.gov.mt/DownloadDocument.aspx?app=lom&itemid=8749&l=1, accessed on 11 August 2014.

Malta Today (2011) *After Bishops' '10pm apology', Iva asks for extended voting time*. Available at www.maltatoday.com.mt/news/bishops-to-tell-voters-of-sorrow-for-church-s-words-and-actions, accessed June 2011.

Massa, A. (2011) 'Watered down sexual health policy sent to Curia.' *The Sunday Times of Malta.* Available at www.timesofmalta.com/articles/view/20110102/local/sexual-health-policy-watered-down, accessed 12 June 2014.

Montebello, M. (2009) 'Religion in Contemporary Maltese Society.' In J. Cutajar and G. Cassar (eds) *Social Transitions in Maltese Society.* Malta: Agenda Publishing.

National Commission for Persons with Disability (2011) Statistics on Persons with Disability from the 2011 Census. www.knpd.org/Issues/research.html, accessed August 4th 2014.

National Commission for People with Disability, Malta. Equal Opportunities Act (2000). www.knpd.org/mainlegislation.shtml#eoapubs

Tabone, V. (1995) *A sexual education programme for adolescents with Down Syndrome.* A dissertation presented to the Faculty of Education, University of Malta.

Tabone, C.,Buhagiar, A., Zammit, E., Pace, P., Lauri, M., & Bartolo, J. (2003) Religious Beliefs and Attitudes of Maltese University Students, University Chaplaincy, University of Malta.

The Sunday Times of Malta (2010) Sexual teaching should address respect before physicality – bishops. Available at www.timesofmalta.com/articles/view/20101128/local/sexual-teaching-should-address-respect-before-physicality-bishops, accessed on 12 June 2014.

Times of Malta (2009) 'University students in heated debate on sexual health.' Available at www.timesofmalta.com/articles/view/20091014/local/university-students-in-heated-debate-on-sexual-health.277398, accessed on 12 June 2014.

Times of Malta (2010b) 'Gozo Bishop's contraception comments deemed "unproductive and hysterical".' Available at www.timesofmalta.com.mt/articles/view/20101103/local/gozo-bishop-s-contraception-comments-deemed-unproductive-and-hysterical, accessed November 2010.

World News (2011) 'Malta votes for divorce despite hard lobbying by church.' Available at http://article.wn.com/view/2011/05/30/Malta_votes_for_divorce_despite_hard_lobby_by_church, accessed on 12 June 2014.

FIGURE 8.1 THE GRECH FAMILY WITH LITTLE MARIAH,
AT THE CENTRE BEING HELD BY HER COUSIN

FIGURE 8.2 CORINNE, MARIAH AND TAINA;
MATRIARCHY AND SUPPORT

CHAPTER 9

'MOLLY IS JUST LIKE ME'

Peer Education and Life Stories in Sexuality Programmes in Australia

Patsie Frawley and Christine Bigby with Janice Slattery

Overview

- In Australia people with an intellectual disability have not had much to do with developing or running sexuality and relationship programmes.

- This chapter talks about two programmes that have tried to change this – they are called 'Living Safer Sexual Lives' and 'Living Safer Sexual Lives: Respectful Relationships'.

- Janice Slattery has been involved in both of these programmes. She says this has been important because she has had a say about what kinds of things people with an intellectual disability get to hear about sexuality and relationships.

- It has also been important that she and other people with an intellectual disability have been the educators – not just professionals.

- In the first programme, people with an intellectual disability were involved in telling their stories, deciding how the stories were written and how they would be used in training for staff, families and people with an intellectual disability.

- In the second programme, people with an intellectual disability were involved in developing the programme using the same stories as the first programme.

- They developed training for people to become educators – these are called peer educators – and run the peer educator training. They have also presented at conferences and are still working on the programme in different ways.

- People with an intellectual disability who have been involved in this work have said:

  ◦ It is important to hear real stories about sexuality and relationships from people with an intellectual disability.

  ◦ The stories are about things that people experience.

  ◦ It is good to be able to talk about your own experiences using the stories.

  ◦ People with an intellectual disability are really good as educators because they share some of the same experiences as people in the group – they are 'in their shoes'.

'Bursting bubbles' and learning from each other: introduction

JANICE SLATTERY, SELF-ADVOCATE MELBOURNE, AUSTRALIA

In the late 1990s I was asked to be involved in a reference group for a research project about sexuality and relationships for people with an intellectual disability. The programme was called Living Safer Sexual Lives (LSSL) (Johnson, Frawley, Hillier and Harrison 2002).

I got involved in the work because I wanted to learn more about sexual stuff and relationships. We used to call them 'sex meetings' and we had some funny times at them. The main job was to talk about getting information to people with an intellectual disability so they could tell their stories to the researchers. I remember working on who should be involved in telling their stories and how we tried to get people with different experiences, like people who were gay, people who were in relationships or married, and women and men. We also helped the researchers put the stories together so people could understand them and then we helped with some other things like how to use the stories in training. I am even on one of the DVDs and I read 'Hanna's story'.

Before the LSSL programme I had been a peer educator in health programmes for women with an intellectual disability. One was about getting pap smears (Farnan and Gray 1994) and one was about getting breast checks (O'Shea 1997). I really loved this work. We learned about how to be peer educators and about the health information and we travelled all over the place running groups with women with disabilities, giving them information and talking about our experiences.

It was a long time before I got another chance to do anything about women's health, sexuality and relationships. Although I was involved in a self-advocacy group, they had never done anything about it. Because I had been involved in the earlier programme, Patsie [first author] asked me if I wanted to work with her and some other people to develop the second programme that was also going to use the stories but would talk more about having equal and fair relationships. It was great. I worked in a small team with Patsie, Amie, Danielle and two other women with intellectual disabilities – Linda and Rachel. I learned things that I didn't know before about how people experience violence and abuse in relationships and what makes a good relationship. And I was able to tell everyone else about how the stories were developed. We worked together for two years on this programme, meeting every couple of weeks at the University. It was good getting to know and work with other people and then to train all of the peer educators in Victoria and Tasmania so they could run the programme themselves where they live. It's a lot better when you work in a team because we came up with ideas that other people don't think about and we brought great values to the table and our own experiences as people with an intellectual disability.

All the women in the project team brought different skills and experiences and had a different impact on the programme. I was a project worker, a peer educator trainer and a peer educator and was involved in the evaluation. In the evaluation we did arts-based workshops as a team to evaluate the whole programme. We thought about what we had done to make it as good as it could be and what some of the problems were. One workshop was about 'bursting bubbles'; that was about how we had changed the way people thought about people with an intellectual disability and how we could do this as peer educators.

It has been important to talk about the programme and for Patsie and Chris [second author] to write this chapter so other people can know about our work. We have talked about the programme at disability conferences in Australia, Iceland and Sweden. We presented at a conference about women with disabilities and the peer educators have talked at a self-advocacy conference and a sexuality conference. Now I have handed it over to all the people we have trained to be peer educators in Australia – they are running their own groups. They now are working with organisations in their local area to show that people with an intellectual disability can be involved in stopping violence in relationships.

It is important to involve people with intellectual disabilities in developing and running programmes because it is important for us to have our voice about what is important to us and for people to listen to us. They need to know that we do know about sexuality and relationships and that we can help each other by sharing our experiences. It is also important for people with intellectual disabilities to know what they are getting into when they get into a relationship and what to expect from a relationship.

I hope people who read this chapter learn more about peer education by people with intellectual disabilities in sexuality and relationship programmes and how we can help each other.

Introduction

The sexuality of people with an intellectual disability is often overlooked by families, services and policy. People have few opportunities to develop a range of social or intimate relationships and lack access to the information and support necessary to determine how to express their sexuality and manage their relationships. Often their decisions are not supported by families, carers and services, they are sheltered from opportunities to learn about or experience relationships (Parley 2011), or they have negative experiences due to a lack of support. Governments have based policy frameworks on risk and protection, responding to real or perceived sexual health and safety problems of people with an intellectual disability. Education or intervention programmes have focused on teaching rules about sexuality and relationships or managing behaviour, often with little reference to real-life contexts (Gill 2012).

This chapter discusses the Living Safer Sexual Lives initiatives: Living Safer Sexual Lives (LSSL) (Johnson, Hillier, Harrison and Frawley 2001) and Living Safer Sexual Lives: Respectful Relationships (LSSL:RR) (Frawley, Slattery, Stokoe, Houghton and O'Shea 2011), which have taken a different approach. These two collaborative projects grew from a research project that involved people with an intellectual disability in developing life stories that focused on their experiences of sexuality and relationships (Johnson *et al.* 2002). In these projects people with an intellectual disability advised about research, designed training, developed a peer education programme and peer educator training materials, trained peer educators and worked as peer educators. These roles injected the perspectives and experiences of people with an intellectual disability into these relationship and sexuality education programmes.

The two programmes described and discussed here represent collaborative work with people with an intellectual disability that spans more than ten years. Through this work people with an intellectual disability have been positioned in sexuality and relationship programmes in very new ways in Australia. There is still more to learn about the way people with an intellectual disability want to get information, education and support about sexuality and relationships; the work described in this chapter could form the foundation for this future work.

In this chapter the voices of people with an intellectual disability are heard through their stories, through reflections gathered in research with people who were peer educators and through the evaluative comments of the women who were project workers in the second initiative. These reflections were gathered in the collaborative evaluation workshops used as one component of the evaluation of the second initiative LSSL:RR (Frawley, Barrett and Dyson 2012).

Background

Since the mid-1990s in Australia there has been little attention paid to sexual health, women's health, and sexuality and relationships needs of people with intellectual disability. Organisations like Family Planning have been the main recipients of funding to provide sexuality and relationships education, and changes to policy have in the main been driven by exposure in the media about issues such as abuse and sterilisation. Generally the focus of such policy and education has been on protection, risk management, reporting procedures and management of sexual behaviour. Australia, like other western countries, has grappled with the competing paradigms of risk and protection versus rights and self-determination in thinking about the sexuality of people with intellectual disability (Brown 1994; Hollomotz 2008; McCarthy 1999 and Brown 1999). Research suggests that disability support staff are working within a risk averse framework in regards to sexuality and relationships and lack guidance for their practice (Gore *et al.* 2011). Where policy guides do exist, they have been formulated by professionals and bureaucrats and pay little attention to the aspirations, needs and views of people with a disability (Touching Base 2011).

Innovative sexual health programmes were developed in the 1990s in collaboration with women with intellectual disabilities: *Janet's Got her Period* (Gray and Jilich 1990); *Paps I should* (Farnan and Gray 1994) and *Breast for Me* (O'Shea 1997). A rights-based framework, first articulated by Ann Craft in the 1990s (Craft 1994) underpinned some education and practice in Australia (Horsley and Azzopardi 1990). However, as Wilson *et al.* (2011, p.276) note, 'boundaries, or the limitation of rights and hence individual autonomy, continue to be placed on the sexual expression of people with intellectual disability'. People with an intellectual disability have had few opportunities to be engaged in advocacy, research or programme development about sexuality and relationships, and where advocacy has taken place it has tended to leave out the voice and experiences of people with an intellectual disability (Dillon 2010;

Healy *et al.* 2008; Johnson *et al.* 1998; Women With Disabilities Australia (WWDA) 1999, 2007).

The Living Safer Sexual Lives initiatives

The LSSL initiatives were developed in response to this relative absence of people with intellectual disability in education, policy and research about their own sexuality and relationships (Frawley, Slattery and O'Shea 2011; Johnson *et al.* 2002). These initiatives attempted to shift the control over content, delivery of programmes, and to some extent advocacy, away from professional 'experts' to people with an intellectual disability through the use of their 'experiential knowledge'. The involvement of people with an intellectual disability as members of a reference group advising on the development of the stories and how they were to be used in the first programme (LSSL), and as project workers and peer educators in the second programme (LSSL:RR), prioritised their knowledge and skills by positioning them at the centre of the programme. Further, these roles aimed to change the attitudes of staff, family, community members and peers about the place of people with an intellectual disability in sexuality and relationship programmes and advocacy.

Life stories: from research to practice

Life story methodology has become more common in intellectual disability research since the mid-1990s. Academics have worked alongside people with an intellectual disability to develop and use life stories, particularly about the impact of institutionalisation on the lives of people with an intellectual disability. These stories have also reflected on the important role of people with an intellectual disability in developing self-advocacy and advocating for rights (Atkinson and Cooper 2000; Cooper 1997). However, life stories had not been used in sexuality and relationship research or in education programmes in Australia until LSSL. Most programmes had used fictional case studies and stories rather than real-life stories.

The first programme developed using life stories was LSSL, an independently-funded study to look at how life stories could be used in the development of sexuality and relationship information and education (Frawley *et al.* 2003; Johnson *et al.* 2001). It was a participatory action research programme that aimed to involve people with an intellectual disability in defining the key sexuality and relationships issues in their lives, use their expertise to shape policy and practice and work collaboratively with them in researching and delivering new programmes (Johnson *et al.* 2002). The study reference group included people with an intellectual disability who became actively involved in writing the stories by listening to them and advising on wording, reporting and the formulation of a training programme (Frawley *et al.* 2003).

Twenty-five people with an intellectual disability were supported to write about their own relationships and sexuality. The main themes that emerged from an analysis of these stories were the hidden nature of people's sexual lives, inadequate or inaccessible education and information, failure by families and services to recognise rights, and abuse and loneliness (Johnson *et al.* 2001). These themes provided an organising frame for the stories which formed the core of the training programme for staff, families and people with an intellectual disability (Frawley *et al.* 2003). The key themes were also used to develop policy and practice recommendations for the government department responsible for disability services (Johnson *et al.* 2001).

The centrality of the stories in the training programme meant 'real-life' issues were 'heard' by service providers and families. These excerpts from the stories illustrate their power in conveying these messages:

> Kevin: Before we shared our room, a staff member knocked on the door and found us together. She said 'Get into your own bed.' I didn't like her that much doin' that. Because we were two adults and she should have let us do it.

> David: I meet women through school and through activities and that. I've had a girlfriend. No sex, touching, yeah, but not sexual... I don't really think about having sex with someone, but when I do I know it will be good.

> Hannah: I had one other sexual experience before him but I got rid of him – he was using me up sexually. He wanted to have sex all the time and I didn't, so I left him in the end... Since then I have had a relationship with a taxi driver...he was coming to see one of the other girls there, and to take her to a friend of his. And he ended up coming to pick me up each Friday and take me back on Sunday and that was a relationship... I have been raped twice. They asked me to go for a walk with them, then they raped me. Sometimes it was because I did silly things like go to the hotel or get drunk and that... There was a time when I would have liked children, but I never had the chance.

The training programme was designed around reflection, and rather than analysing the stories, workshop participants were asked to consider: what they might say to the story writer if they met them; what rights-based issues the stories raised for them; and how the stories challenged practice and policy (Frawley *et al.* 2003). This non-didactic approach kept the focus on the story and the person in the story, leading to reflection rather than analysis and intervention.

The programme was a rare example of sexuality education developed in collaboration with people with an intellectual disability, which drew on their experiential knowledge. Its strength derived from the basis in 'real life' of the accounts of people with an intellectual disability and the provision of 'a space for people with intellectual disabilities to discuss aspects of their sexual identities' (Barger *et al.* 2009, p.257). Evaluation of the programme suggested too that the use of stories helped to shift staff attitudes and provided an alternative perspective on issues like privacy, reproductive rights and abuse (Strong and Symonds 2001). Reports from staff who have undertaken the training reflect this shift in attitudes:

> We need to meet together as staff…and talk about our views about sexuality and relationships. It's difficult to help [people with an intellectual disability] if we aren't clear ourselves… We need to think about why we do things… It's really important to deal with people sensitively. We could wreck this guy's [person in one of the stories] life if we did the wrong thing. (Johnson *et al.* 2001, p.87)

> The course should be compulsory… Sexual issues are normally swept under the table. (Strong and Symonds 2001, p.9)

Collaborative project development and delivery

Living Safer Sexual Lives: Respectful Relationships (LSSL:RR) was funded as part of a national programme of violence and abuse prevention (Frawley *et al.* 2011). This programme uses four LSSL stories to focus discussions and activities on four themes: talking about relationships and sexuality; having rights and being safe; respectful relationships; and men and respectful relationships. The programme and the 'train the trainer' component were developed by a collaborative team that included three women with an intellectual disability. They brainstormed the 'key messages' from each LSSL story and developed additional activities about relationship rights, intimacy in relationships, gender and information on sexual assault. The team trained people with intellectual disability in five sites as peer educators to co-facilitate delivery of the programme with human service professionals from local agencies.

The team members with an intellectual disability were central to the success of the programme, having multiple roles as project workers developing the programme, trainers, peer educators and spokespeople for the programme at conferences and workshops. The programme evaluation, which used accessible arts-based workshops to elicit reflections from the project team (Frawley *et al.* 2012) found that for these women, these multiple roles enabled them to engage deeply with the programme and to become 'the experts' or as the women named themselves 'the A team'. Together the team reflected that these roles reinforced the following important ideas: that participation of people with an intellectual disability in the programme development and delivery,

> was important because they [people with an intellectual disability] have rights, thoughts, aspirations and insight; are adult learners, equal learners, and have the

capacity to learn and develop; can support each other; are experts; deserve this opportunity...[and] have guts, keenness and life experience. (Frawley *et al.* 2012 p.27)

Furthermore, these roles challenged and extended the women as women, as women with an intellectual disability and as educators. One evaluation workshop was called the 'award' workshop where the project team placed 'achievement stars' on the wall. The project workers with an intellectual disability gave themselves stars for the following: 'I answered a scary question", "I felt important at the conference", "People were asking me questions", "[I] opened up and shared my story so other people could feel comfortable sharing their stories", [I] was nominated for a [community] award' (Frawley *et al.* 2012, p.29). They also acted as role models, generating interest in becoming peer educators from others with an intellectual disability. Consistently participants reported peer education as the best thing about the programme, with comments such as 'I want to do what [Linda, Janice, Rachel] do'.

Peer education: experience and expertise

The first Living Safer Sexual Lives programme, LSSL, (Frawley *et al.* 2003) created a safe way for people to speak about themselves and their own experiences, demonstrating the importance of life stories as learning tools in a sexuality and relationship programme. As Barger *et al.* (2009) reported in their review of this programme, 'Participants got to share their sexual experiences which may serve to empower them and increase self-efficacy' (p.253). However, the programme was designed to be delivered by professionals. While there was an intention to develop it as a peer education programme this did not happen. The second initiative, LSSL:RR (Frawley *et al.* 2011), aimed to change this by embedding peer education into the model.

A review of the literature found very few examples where peer education by people with an intellectual disability has been used in relationship and sexuality programmes (Family Planning Northern Ireland 1999; Fitzsimons *et al.* 2000; WHGNE 2004). This is despite research that has found young people with an intellectual disability identified other people with a disability as 'top of the list' as potential sexuality and relationship educators (Shakespeare, Gillespie-Sells and Davies 1996). Although self-advocacy groups in the UK have played an important role in developing accessible resources and research (CHANGE 2010; Garbutt 2009), programmes have rarely been facilitated *by* people with an intellectual disability.

Sixteen of the twenty-three people trained as peer educators in the LSSL:RR pilot programme were involved in research about their experiences as peer educators. They consistently reported that the most significant aspect of their role as a peer educator was the opportunity to help others. Peer educators spoke about wanting to make sure other people did not have the sort of negative experiences they had had. They also talked about wanting to share their own positive experiences like being married, having a job, living independently or being a parent, in order to show that people with an intellectual disability can have good relationships and outcomes.

> *I guess if we can help, or if I can help people um in their situations um it's good for them. You know. Yes it brings…back bad memories but um…if you've gone through it and you know what it's like, you can help them.*

Peer educators felt they had developed skills to undertake the job from their prior experiences of self-advocacy and other representative and leadership roles. Importantly they felt that they were in a better position than professionals to talk to other people with an intellectual disability because they were 'in their shoes'.

> *Like, I go to [friend] as a person with a disability to a person with a disability…for help. Like, just between us, I have trouble dealing with [support worker] because she doesn't have a disability and I feel uncomfortable. I'd prefer to talk to [friend with a disability] because I know she's got a disability and I know she knows where I'm coming from. Well, some of my story could affect, like, go good with their stories as well sometimes.*

> *You, you get so much out of it. It's so worth it. Especially people with disabilities. There's no better way to get a message across from someone that you can relate to. And that's just putting it blunt. If you can relate to someone, you're gonna listen to them. There you go. Put it straight… [laughs]*

Furthermore, the stories from the original programme were revisited and used in a somewhat more focused way being delivered and discussed by peer educators in LSSL:RR. They provoked a sense of closeness from others with an intellectual disability who were being trained to be peer educators. They said, for example:

> *Molly is just like me.*

> *I think Hannah's was very sad. You know, very… Oh, about the brother, with the money. Like these are grown adults, consenting adults. They don't need to be treated like they're children. And yeah, that really got on my nerves. I had to go home and cool down after hearing that. Yeah, I was quite, 'Grrr'.*

> *Like, like certain bits in my story could help them. They might, they might think it – they're like what I've been through… Like if, like some, like if it's a woman it, they might think, like after they've had a kid or something, they might think how I feel, how they've, how I lost my daughter and I can only see her monthlies.*

> *Like talking, like when we show stories to 'em they think they're like, like Molly's story and that… And they talk about – when we talk about Molly's story they talk something about really about their own self and that.*

The peer education approach used in this programme enabled people to build on their existing skills, knowledge and experience and to work alongside professionals from the disability and community sector. In turn these professionals reported the approach and the use of the stories by peer educators strengthened the programme and put their role as co-facilitators into context (Frawley *et al.* 2012 p.30).

> *I think the power of the story is amazing and also the power of having their peers as facilitators. Reading the story, telling the story, I think it's really positive as well. The power is that it's a story from the person who has an intellectual disability; I think that is a strong connection... I think personal stories, they often...touch a chord, that's what these stories achieve. With the peer educators it's about when they can talk about stuff from a personal point of view. Again it's that true story...helping make connections for people...it makes it real in a way.*

Not everyone was supportive of the peer education role. The programme evaluation found that 'gatekeeping' by disability organisations was a significant barrier to participation in the programme by people with an intellectual disability (Frawley *et al.* 2012). This appeared to stem from an attitude that people with an intellectual disability were unable to be peer educators, particularly in a programme addressing sexuality, relationships and abuse (Frawley *et al.* 2012).

Some views put forward were that people with an intellectual disability might not have the experience needed to be peer educators where this experience was seen to be having a respectful relationship, or that a person with an intellectual disability would not be capable of supporting a peer if they disclosed abuse in the programme (Frawley *et al.* 2012). Such ideas have been found to be prevalent amongst disability support staff and are recognised barriers to the inclusion of people with an intellectual disability in decisions about their sexuality and relationships (Cuskelly and Bryde 2004; Evans *et al.* 2009; Gilmore and Chambers 2010; Gore *et al.* 2011; Hamilton 2009).

The LSSL:RR model sought to overcome these barriers by ensuring that people with an intellectual disability could nominate themselves to become a peer educator, rather than developing a set of criteria people had to meet for the role or a process that required them to be nominated. The only criterion was that the person was identified as a person with an intellectual disability and wanted to be trained as a peer educator. After the training some people chose not to continue as peer educators; there have been no examples where people have been deemed to be inappropriate for the role once trained.

Summary

People with an intellectual disability have a rightful place in planning and running sexuality and relationship programmes. The collaborative LSSL initiatives have demonstrated the importance of involving people with an intellectual disability in roles such as project workers, programme and research advisors and peer educators. These roles recognise and use their experiential knowledge about sexuality and relationships. As peer educators and project team members they can be in control of the information they get and give, and can use their own experiences to support key messages about positive, safe and happy relationships, as well as sharing how to deal with some of the negative experiences of relationships.

However, people with an intellectual disability in Australia are still seen as outsiders in the debate about sexuality and relationships. Whilst some progress has been made in recognising the rights of people with physical and other disabilities to determine their sexual expression, people with an intellectual disability are still in the main protected and restricted. Policy and practice that are informed and shaped by the experiential knowledge of people with an intellectual disability are an important step towards shifting the attitudes and values that underpin the predominant risk adverse environment that currently exists. Further collaborative research and programme development that build on this innovative work and that of organisations like CHANGE in the UK are needed to place people with an intellectual disability at the centre of education and support practices that determine their sexual expression, experiences and intimate relationships.

References

Atkinson, D. and Cooper, M. (2000) 'Parallel Stories.' In L. Brigham, D. Atkinson, M. Jackson, S. Rolph and J. Walmsley (eds) *Crossing Boundaries: Change and Continuity in the History of Learning Disability*. Kidderminster: BILD.

Barger, E., Wacker, J., Macy, R. and Parish, S. (2009) 'Sexual assault prevention for women with intellectual disabilities: A critical review of the evidence.' *Intellectual and Developmental disabilities 47*, 4, 249–62.

Brown, H. (1994) '"An ordinary sexual life?": A review of the normalisation principle as it applies to the sexual options of people with learning disabilities.' *Disability and Society 9*, 2, 123–144.

CHANGE (2010) *Talking about Sex and Relationships: The Views of Young People with Learning Disabilities*. Leeds: CHANGE.

Cooper, M. (1997) 'Mabel Cooper's Life Story.' In D. Atkinson, M. Jackson and J. Walmsley (eds) *Forgotten Lives: Exploring the History of Learning Disability*. Kidderminster: BILD Publications.

Craft, A. (ed.) (1994) *Practice Issues in Sexuality and Learning Disabilities*. London: Routledge.

Cuskelly, M. and Bryde, R. (2004) 'Attitudes towards the sexuality of adults with an intellectual disability: parents, support staff, and a community sample.' *Journal of Intellectual & Developmental Disability 29*, 255–264.

Dillon, J. (2010) *Violence Against People with Cognitive Impairments. Report from the Advocacy/Guardianship Program at the Office of the Public Advocate*. Melbourne: Office of the Public Advocate.

Evans, D.S., McGuire, B.E., Healy, E. and Carley, S.N. (2009) 'Sexuality and personal relationships for people with an intellectual disability. Part II: Staff and family carer perspectives.' *Journal of Intellectual Disability Research 53*, 913–921.

Family Planning Northern Ireland (1999) *Limelight: A Peer Education Project for People with a Disability.* Belfast: FPA NI.

Farnan, S. and Gray, J. (1994) *Paps I Should.* Melbourne: Women's Health in the West Centre for Development and Innovation in Health.

Fitzsimons, N.M. (2009) *Combating Violence and Abuse of People with Disabilities: A Call to Action.* Baltimore, MD: Paul H. Brookes Publishing Co.

Frawley, P., Barrett, C. and Dyson, S. (2012). *Real People, Core Business: A Report on the Living Safer Sexual Lives: Respectful Relationships Peer Education Program for People with Intellectual Disabilities.* Melbourne: Australian Research Centre in Sex, Health & Society.

Frawley, P., Johnson, K., Hillier, L. and Harrison, L. (2003) *Living Safer Sexual Lives: A Training and Resource Pack for People with an Intellectual Disability and Those who Support Them.* Brighton: Pavilion.

Frawley, P., Slattery, J. and O'Shea, A. (2011) 'Shifting the power in relationship education. Findings for a peer education model from Australia.' Paper presented at the Nordic Disability Research Conference, Reykjavik. Iceland, 27–28 May 2011.

Frawley, P., Slattery, J., Stokoe, L., Houghton, D. and O'Shea, A. (2011) *Living Safer Sexual Lives: Respectful Relationships. Peer Educator and Co-Facilitator Manual.* Melbourne: Australian Research Centre in Sex, Health and Society, La Trobe University.

Garbutt, R. (2009) 'Let's talk about sex: Using drama as a research tool to find out the views and experiences of young people with learning disabilities.' *Creative Approaches to Research 2*, 1, DOI: 10.3316/CAR0201008.

Gill, M. (2012) 'Sex can wait, masturbate: The politics of masturbation training.' *Sexualities, 15*, 3/4, 472–493.

Gilmore, L. and Chambers, B. (2010) 'Intellectual disability and sexuality: Attitudes of disability support staff and leisure industry employees.' *Journal of Intellectual & Developmental Disability 35*, 22–28.

Gore, V., Stancliffe, R., Broom. and Wilson, N. (2011) 'Barriers to sexual health provision for people with intellectual disabilities – a service provider and clinician perspective.' Presentation at the 46th ASID conference, Adelaide 9–11 November.

Gray, J. and Jilich, J. (1990) *Janet's Got her Period: A Resource Package.* Melbourne: Social Biology Resources Centre.

Hamilton, C. (2009) '"Now I'd like to sleep with Rachel": Researching sexuality support in a service agency group home.' *Disability and Society 24*, 3, 303–317.

Healey, L., Howe, K., Humphreys, C., Jennings, C. and Julian, F. (2008) *Building the Evidence: A Report on the Status of Policy and Practice in Responding to Violence against Women with Disabilities in Victoria.* Melbourne: Women's Health Victoria and Victorian Women with a Disability Network.

Hollomotz, A. (2008) '"May we please have sex tonight?": People with learning difficulties pursuing privacy in residential group settings.' *British Journal of Learning Disabilities 37*, 91–97.

Horsley, P. and Azzopardi, S. (1990) *Sexuality, Rights and Choices: Sexuality, Sexual Abuse and Appropriate Behaviour Education for People with Intellectual Disabilities.* Melbourne: Family Planning Victoria.

Johnson, K., Frawley, P., Hillier, L. and Harrison, L. (2002) 'Living safer sexual lives: Research to practice.' *Tizard Learning Disability Review 7*, 3, 4–9.

Johnson, K. (1998). Deinstitutionalising women: an ethnographic study of institutional closure. Cambridge, UK: Cambridge University Press.

Johnson, K., Hillier, L., Harrison, L. and Frawley, P. (2001) *People with Intellectual Disabilities Living Safer Sexual Lives.* Melbourne: Australian Research Centre in Sex, Health & Society.

McCarthy, M. (1999) *Sexuality and Women with Learning Disabilities.* London: Jessica Kingsley Publishers.

O'Shea, M. (1997) 'Breast for me: A developmental health education strategy for women with a disability.' *Australian Journal of Primary Health 3*, 1, 66–71.

Parley, F. (2011). 'What does vulnerability mean?' British Journal of Learning Disabilities, 39, 266-26

Shakespeare, T., Gillespie-Sells, K. and Davies, D. (1996) *The Sexual Politics of Disability: Untold Desires.* London: Cassell.

Strong, S. and Symonds, H. (2001) *Evaluation of 'Human Relations – an Introduction' and 'Living Safer Sexual Lives' courses.* Melbourne: Geoff Beeson & Associates.

Touching Base (2011) *Policy and Procedural Guide for Disability Service Providers Supporting Clients to Access Sex Workers.* Newtown: Australia.

Wilson, N., Parmenter, T., Stancliffe, R. and Shuttleworth, R. (2011) 'Conditionally sexual: Men and teenage boys with moderate to profound intellectual disability.' *Sexuality & Disability 29*, 275–289, DOI 10.1007/s11195-011-9203-y.

WHGNE (Women's Health Goulburn North East) (2004*) Empowerment. Women's Sexual Health Through Education: A Peer Leadership Model.* Wangaratta: WHGNE.

Women with Disabilities Australia (WWDA):Submission to the review of the National womens non government organisations funding program 1999, has a website wwda.org.au/issues/systemic/systemic1995/oswrev/

Women With Disabilities Australia (2007) WWDA Policy & Position Paper: 'The Development of Legislation to Authorise Procedures for the Sterilisation of Children with Intellectual Disabilities' (June). Available at www.wwda.org.au/subs2006.htm, accessed on 12 June 2014.

CHAPTER 10

EMERGING THEMES FROM PART I

Sue Ledger, Rohhss Chapman and Louise Townson

Overview

- This chapter explains how we identified four key themes from the chapters in Part 1.

- Part 1 highlights relationships as of central importance to people with intellectual disabilities.

- People have been able to support each other in a way that increases their independence.

- People with intellectual disabilities are often on the receiving end of rules and regulations. It is important that services support people in expressing their sexuality and to develop relationships.

- There is a lack of information about sex, relationships and the law.

- We talk about how a historical approach can enable people to understand how the past affects experiences today.

Introduction

SUE, ROHHSS AND LOUISE

This international part of the book opened with an overview of the historical context of relationships and sexuality during the twentieth and early twenty-first centuries. Across many countries, this period of history ostensibly witnessed a major shift in policy away from managing sexuality through the incarceration and sterilisation of thousands of people with intellectual disabilities to a far more enlightened stance that supports the right of people to form relationships, express their sexuality, marry and become parents.

The narratives in Part 1 bring to the fore issues that people with intellectual disabilities identify as important, in terms of relationships and sexuality. In doing so this collection of personal testimonies often presents a sharp contrast to the 'official' picture as conveyed through national and international legal and policy frameworks. Across these varied personal accounts a sense of pride, achievement, determination and optimism are frequently interwoven with continued experiences of personal struggle, confusion and frustration as people have taken steps towards developing relationships.

Before starting this chapter we re-read all of the Part 1 chapters in their final draft. In reading them as a whole we identified fresh insights, noticed new aspects of the stories and made new connections. The overwhelming impression, however, was that despite the richness and diversity of experience the same themes and messages continued to recur across individual lives, across cultures, across generations and across a range of service settings. This chapter brings Part 1 to a close by discussing these overarching themes and considering what they might mean for people with intellectual disabilities.

The themes that emerged in Part 1 are:

1. the value of relationships

2. rules and regulations

3. lack of information

4. the legacy of the past.

In Chapter 22 we make further connections between these themes and in Chapter 23 we answer the five research questions set out in Chapter 1.

The writing process
SUE

As we were close to completing the book Louise, Rohhss and I met up to draft this chapter together. Before the meeting we each identified what we considered to be the most important themes emerging from each chapter, using the five research questions in Chapter 1 to guide our thinking.

We also asked each of the five peer reviewers who worked on Part 1 chapters to identify three key themes for each chapter. We wrote these out on a grid to compare with our thinking and also as an attempt to introduce a kind of 'check and balance' to ensure that our ideas and values as an editorial team were not over-influencing how we interpreted the stories.

We had a large artboard and Rohhss and Louise called out their ideas whilst I wrote them up and then added in my own list. Once we had done that we compared our ideas to the feedback from each of our five peer reviewers, discussing each in turn. There was much agreement between us and our team of critical reviewers about the overarching messages to emerge from Part 1.

We grouped these into four clusters which we initially labelled as follows:

- together we are stronger

- regulated lives

- lack of access to sex education and information

- how the past still affects the present.

We then returned to the text to refine the headings to most accurately reflect all the material in the cluster. This is how they appear in the chapter. We chose Daniel Docherty's words from the opening of Chapter 2 to name our third theme and Lee-Ann Monk's phrase 'the legacy of the past' for our fourth theme.

Emerging themes

1. The value of relationships – 'together we are stronger'

In Chapter 4 Ebba Hreinsdøttir says, 'The best thing in my life that happened was that I met Jonni and we got married. That changed everything.' Similarly, her husband Jonni, joking about the journey from his mother's arms to Ebba's, emphasises 'but it went well and we have been happy'.

This couple's words, told through their respective yet intertwined life stories, provide powerful testimony to the fact that relationships are of central importance to people's happiness and well-being. This sense of happiness in being together is also very apparent in accounts from Peggy and Maurice who said 'we want to have a future together' (Chapter 6) and Rie's story (Chapter 7) 'it is wonderful to have someone with whom you can feel so much intimacy and trust'. As discussed in Chapter 1, for many people relationships make a huge difference to their life – the difference between a life lived with vitality and enjoyment and one of relative loneliness. The narratives highlight that this capacity of relationships to bring life-changing happiness must never be overlooked by services as they strive to fulfil their duty of care and to protect people from harm.

Yet the narratives not only reveal the importance of trusted, intimate relationships for happiness; they also reveal how, within relationships, people have been able to complement and support each other in a way that increases their independence. For example, in Japan Rie's boyfriend helps her with her money management and to deal with problems at work in a better way; in Iceland Ebba does the cooking whilst Jonni has the responsibility for going to the bank and paying bills. Interestingly, a number of the accounts reveal how interdependence between people in relationships and a determination to work together to solve problems strengthen their independence as a unit in relation to the rest of the world.

STANDING UP FOR RELATIONSHIPS

Through the stories we hear very clearly that people with intellectual disabilities recognise the importance of relationships in their lives and are taking action to stand up for what they want. In Chapter 4 Jonni and Ebba emphasise that from their life stories people can learn 'that we are not victims…we have overcome barriers and challenges we have faced in our lives and managed to be independent together. If you believe in yourself you can do anything but sometimes you have to fight for it.'

The Clare Inclusive Research Group put on a play (No Kissing), developed a piece of forum theatre and spoke out on national radio about the need for changes in the law about sex. Maurice in Chapter 6 phoned his lawyer in order to resolve a problem so he could be with Peggy. In Chapter 7 Rie continued to see her boyfriend and was eventually able to reach a compromise with her parents, and Chapter 9 tells how people with intellectual disabilities successfully assumed multiple roles as programme developers, peer educators and trainers to provide sex education, information and support based on life story material.

The narratives also evidence how people with intellectual disabilities are capable of making their own decisions if given the chance. The accounts provide examples of very practical thinking and decision-making about whether or not to have children. Life story accounts highlight that people are very aware of their disabilities. The stories enable improved understanding of how financial concerns (Chapters 4, 5 and 6), the fear of having a child removed (Chapter 4) and the desire to remain as independent as possible influence decisions about parenting, rather than the 'ability to parent', which tends to be the focus of service-based decision-making. In relation to decisions about having children people are aware of their limitations, responsibilities and the potential pitfalls of becoming parents. If given the necessary information and support many people with intellectual disabilities are capable in their own right of making informed decisions. As the narratives indicate, the decision may well be not to become a parent.

Making the transition from relying on family to relying on a partner for emotional support can be hard for some people (and their parents) to negotiate. Yet through the stories we see that relationships can bring opportunities for people to form new bonds and networks. In this way, supporting people to form relationships can play a part in reducing the sense of overwhelming desolation described by so many people with intellectual disabilities at the death of a parent whom they lived with and depended on all their lives. Ebba, whose own mother had died, says, 'Jonni had a wonderful mother... I felt like I was so welcomed in his family'; this is an example of how relationships facilitate acceptance and support in a way that cannot be replicated through services.

In their book *Towards a Good Life?* Johnson and Walmsley (2010, p.176) conclude that relationships 'are fundamental to the achievement of a good life' for people with intellectual disabilities. As discussed in Chapter 1, sexuality and relationships are a vital part of human existence; for all of us a feeling of belonging (hooks 2009; Ledger 2012), of being loved and not being lonely (Pitonyak 2003) are of key importance. The narratives in Part 1 of the book emphasise the happiness that good relationships can bring to a life and how being in a partnership that works can enable people to be more independent as a couple and to widen their social and support networks. In doing so the narratives highlight that this life-changing aspect of relationships must never be lost sight of by services as they strive to fulfil their duty of care and protect people from harm.

2. Rules and regulations

Being on the receiving end of a range of rules and regulations was a recurrent theme across chapters. Chapter 3 highlighted how increased recognition of the vulnerability of people with an intellectual disability to abuse has resulted in greater attention to safeguarding within services and legislation to ensure that people are better protected from a range of sexual offences. The stories in Part 1 suggest that services are often very averse to risk regarding relationships and sexuality.

The Clare Inclusive Research Group highlight that whilst they understand the law 'is there to protect people who are shy or afraid...people who are vulnerable' the group resent the underlying implication that they had little ability to make decisions and that for people with intellectual disabilities sexual relationships were a bad thing which should be stopped. The group also express feelings of anger that these laws could have been applied to them without their agreement or awareness: 'Can we talk to people about it? And ask them why?'

Stories highlight the impact of a range of service procedures on people's lives and emphasise the quiet yet routine regulation of people's relationships, behaviours and experiences. At times we learn how service systems can be potentially undermining of relationships, presenting obstacles for people to overcome rather than support. Despite apparent innovation in Flanders, practice still veers heavily towards protection and prevention of harm. Narratives from Fonske, Peggy and Maurice highlight the degree of scrutiny given to people's relationships before they are permitted to spend time together and show how service systems such as transport, finance and staff rotas can work against people being given the time and opportunity to develop relationships.

The story of Peggy and Maurice highlighted the positive part technology had played in enabling them to meet and build a relationship – they kept in touch through Facebook and Skype – yet even this was not immune to regulation in a way that prevented their access. In this way the stories raise questions about the extent to which relationships are seen as a priority in services: a point also picked up in the UK in a survey of the effectiveness of person-centred planning (Robertson *et al.* 2006).

The accounts also highlight the need for improved staff training in supporting people with sex and relationship issues. It may be that service systems have become so entrenched that staff and managers are not recognising their impact on the lives of people with intellectual disabilities.

From external to self-regulation?

In Chapter 2 Louise drew attention to the fact that people with intellectual disabilities are often 'shushed' or censored by staff if they speak about relationships or express their sexuality. Some members of the Clare Inclusive Research Group wanted to have a family but concerns were raised by other members about having to 'prove you could live independently'. Remarks such as these shed light on how people with intellectual disabilities are very aware that their lives are the subject of scrutiny and that their 'competence' in relationships and parenting is likely to be subject to assessment and professional decision-making.

Drawing upon the material in Part 1, we ask if people with intellectual disabilities are responding to this, consciously or subconsciously, by exercising 'self-censorship' or 'self-regulation'. In Chapter 4 Ebba Hreinsdøttir eloquently describes how as a person with an intellectual disability her 'default' position was to blame herself for the fact she had been sterilised without her knowledge: 'In the beginning I wasn't going to talk about the bad things that happened to me… I was ashamed… I thought it was my fault because I was so stupid.' In this way insider accounts support understanding of how people within institutional regimes can all too easily self-blame as opposed to questioning and challenging, as Ebba began to do once she had left the hospital.

Are people limiting their hopes, dreams and aspirations by not having relationships? (Fonske, Chapter 6; Yasu, Chapter 7); not aspiring to live with a partner? (Rie, Chapter 7); deciding not have children? (Chapter 4, Chapter 5, Chapter 6); not marrying or entering civil partnerships? (Chapter 5, Chapter 6). In Chapter 6, Maurice and Peggy have got engaged 'but it will stay at that'. Although very happy with her boyfriend in Japan, when asked about her future plans Rie says she would like to live alone near her parents rather than getting married or living with her boyfriend.

Of course it could also be that people are making their own decisions based on individual circumstances, but the recurrence of this theme raises the question as to whether people are making these decisions to appease, to steer a course of least resistance, to follow professional advice or simply to survive, as they fear, for example, the financial implications of living together. Such responses would be an understandable way of attempting to regain control in environments where people frequently witness relationships being counselled against.

It may be that limiting your dreams also avoids the pain of disappointment. If this is the case it would indicate that people may be internalising a view of themselves as someone 'unsuitable for relationships or parenting'. Such patterns raise serious concerns about people's future emotional well-being and lend strong support to the need for urgent sharing of stories of successful relationships and parenting by people with intellectual disabilities. Preferably, as advocated in Chapter 9, these would be delivered by people with intellectual disabilities themselves.

3. 'There is a big lack of information'

The difficulty experienced in accessing information about sex, relationships and the law was a recurrent theme across all cultures. The gaps in information were significant. In Belgium the focus of sex education is mostly on protection and prevention of harm. In Ireland people highlight that they have never received information about sex or the law about sexual relationships. In Japan the delivery of sex education to children in special schools remains very contentious. In Malta the Catholic Church continues to exert influence on policy in relation to sex education and sexuality across the population as a whole. There are no sexuality policies that address the rights of people with intellectual disabilities. Corinne and her family explain she had not had the education to enable her to link sex and pregnancy.

In Chapter 5 the Clare Inclusive Research Group highlight that it is often assumed that people don't know about sex because of their disability, whereas in their view, people don't know a lot about sex because they have never been given the opportunity to learn about it. This group draw attention to the failure of schools and adult services to provide information about sex and the law, a sentiment echoed by the experiences of self-advocates in Belgium and Corinne in Malta.

The stories also give some insight into how people with intellectual disabilities have obtained information about sex and relationships. Fonske explained how he looked up information on the internet and tried to talk to staff, although not all would be willing to enter into this conversation. Maurice was given some practical advice about condoms by his carers but in the end worked out a way forward with Peggy instead. The Clare Inclusive Research Group mention information from siblings and friends whilst the Living Safer Sexual Lives project emphasises the value of information being delivered by people with intellectual disabilities who have trained as peer tutors.

LOUISE

Sex education (or rather the lack of it) featured very heavily throughout. In the case of Chapter 5, from Ireland, people didn't know about the law. I think this is probably the case for most people with intellectual disabilities. If they do find out it is through their advocacy or People First groups. This isn't good because not everyone goes to one, so they will be the people who miss out. People do need to know about what the different laws are because it may affect their lives.

SUE

Access to information about sex, relationships and the law is crucial if people are to take an active role in determining their sexual lives whilst minimising the risk of abuse and exploitation. In this way the stories show how historically it has not been sufficient to assert people's rights to relationships (evident in normalisation policy since the 1970s) but that policy commitment needs to be operationalised with opportunities for people with intellectual disabilities and staff to learn about the law, relationships, sex, contraception and fertility. This information is crucial if people are to make their own decisions and adequately protect themselves from abuse.

4. Living with the legacy of the past

In Part I an international timeline and historical overview (Chapters 2 and 3) followed by life story narratives, enable links between past and present to be easily made. The continuing impact of past policy on the lives of people with intellectual disabilities is made painfully clear in Chapter 4 as Ebba Hreinsdøttir reflects on the fact that she was sterilised without her knowledge whilst she was a patient in a long-stay institution.

In the past people with intellectual disabilities were regarded as both a sexual menace prone to reckless sexual behaviour and as child-like and innocent (Baxter 1989). Both stereotypes provided rationales to prevent people from having sex and conceiving. The narratives in Part 1 show that many of the same anxieties about the sexuality of people with intellectual disabilities abound today – across different cultures – as in the past. In particular there has been ongoing social anxiety about women having sex and becoming pregnant, driven by a complex desire to both protect and control. In the past we hear how this was reflected in higher rates of admission to institutional care amongst young women. In the present it raises concerns about the higher usage of Depo-Provera as a contraceptive amongst younger women with intellectual disabilities, the continued practice of sterilisation and higher rates of childcare proceedings amongst mothers with intellectual disabilities. An example of this ongoing anxiety regarding conception is reflected in negative media coverage experienced by Corinne and her family in Malta after the birth of her daughter.

LOUISE

In Part 1 of this book there are many different themes. I thought that 'lack of education', 'sterilisation' and the difficulties of 'forming and sustaining relationships' were key ideas coming from the stories.

Lee-Anne Monk's Chapter 3 sets the scene for Part 1 very well. It made me think about how it brings the history of the past (about sterilisation) into the present (it is still happening). I found Eiji's Chapter 7 very informative because I didn't realise that people in Japan stayed living with their parents for a lot longer regardless of whether they had an intellectual disability or not; it's part of their cultural values.

Rohhss, Sue and myself and the critical readers did agree on many of the themes.

Summary

ROHHSS

The discussion of the themes emerging from Part 1 of the book is enlightening, if worrying. The commonalities across the different countries are sharp and I am looking forward to discussions with the authors when they have read each other's narratives. This sharing of stories and understanding the links into the public nature of these personal issues will be revealing. We have purposefully steered away from in-depth discussion about parenting in this book because it is the topic of a forthcoming Jessica Kingsley Publishers publication. Even so the tensions around parenting issues are straining through the text, particularly in Chapter 8, and should be noted.

One of the more worrying issues raised is about self-regulation and the impact of this on self-esteem. Sue suggests that compliance may be part of an armoury of self-defence. This aspect is built upon and discussed further in Chapters 11 and 22, as it is a recurring theme evidenced throughout the book, demonstrating the power and control of others in people's lives. Supporters and staff have a pivotal role in building confidence and enabling change; they stand alongside people with intellectual disabilities in their quest for equality, so this embedded opportunity needs to be used effectively.

The meta-narrative rooted in many of the chapters, especially from an historical/ policy perspective regarding people with intellectual disabilities as 'sexual menace prone to reckless sexual behaviour' and in contrast to 'child-like and innocent' (Baxter 1989), is also developed further through Part 2.

In Part 2 we consider a further set of stories, this time focusing on the experiences of people from the UK. At the end of Part 2 we identify emergent themes from these accounts before addressing our five research questions.

References

Baxter, C. (1989) 'Parallels Between the Social Role Perception of People with Learning Difficulties and Black and Minority Ethnic People.' In A. Brechin and J. Walmsley (eds.) *Making Connections: Reflecting on the Lives and Experiences of People With Learning Difficulties.* Sevenoaks: Hodder and Stoughton.

hooks, b. (2009) *Belonging.* New York: Routledge.

Johnson, K. and Walmsley, J. (2010) *People with Intellectual Disabilities: Towards a Good Life?* Bristol: Policy Press.

Ledger, S. (2012) 'Staying local: support for people with learning difficulties from inner London 1971–2007.' Unpublished PhD Thesis, Milton Keynes, Open University.

North, J. (2011) 'Making it happen' paper given at *Housing Options and Challenging* Behaviour Foundation Conference: 'Keeping it Local', Birmingham, 4th November 2011.

Pitonyak, D. (2003) *Toolbox for Change: Reclaiming Purpose, Joy and Commitment in the Helping Professions.* Available at www.dimagine.com, accessed on 4 June 2004.

Robertson, J., Emerson, E., Hatton C. and Elliot, C. *et al.* (2006) 'Longitudinal analysis of the impact and cost of person centred planning for people with intellectual disabilities in England.' *American Journal of Mental Retardation 111,* 6, 400–416.

PART 2

A UK EXPERIENCE

LAW, POLICY AND DIVERSITY

Exploring the Gap between Rhetoric and Real Life

Sue Ledger, Rohhss Chapman and Louise Townson

Overview ——————————————————————————

- This chapter sets the scene for Part 2 of the book.

- Part 2 is about law, policy and diversity in the UK.

- We set out a table summarising key laws and policy relating to sexuality and relationships in the UK.

- This should help people to become more informed.

- Diversity is about differences in the types of relationships people want or are involved in.

- We talk about how some people find it hard to accept diversity and difference.

- Sometimes services do not follow law and policy in the way they should.

- At the end, the individual chapters in Part 2 are introduced.

The writing process

This chapter was written by Sue, Rohhss and Louise. Much of the discussion about the chapter took place through exchanges of phone calls and emails. We use the term 'intellectual disabilities' in our discussion.

Introduction

SUE

In Part 2 of the book we shift our focus to the experiences of people with intellectual disabilities living in the UK.[1] This chapter sets the scene for a 'national' focus by outlining the legal and policy framework: the 'official version' of how sexuality and relationships should be addressed. We consider some of the potential barriers encountered by people as this translates into practice.

In the UK there are many Acts of Parliament and policies of relevance to the sexuality and relationships of people with intellectual disabilities (see Fanstone and Andrews 2009, p.124, for a recent summary). In order to be concise, we have focused on key legal and policy documents, each of which has a major function in promoting rights, protection and equality of treatment for adults with intellectual disabilities in the UK. We then move to a discussion about diversity.

Policies and guidelines are designed to help people with intellectual disabilities, families and staff know where they stand with regards to what are often sensitive and sometimes controversial situations and decisions. Within services, policies range from national guidance (such as *Valuing People*), to local government and NHS policy documents, such as local authority safeguarding procedures, organisational policies (for example, those held by charities or private sector companies) to individual 'policies' and 'house rules' for specific services such as group homes, employment services and day centres (Fanstone and Andrews 2009).

Implementation of polices

ROHHSS

There are frequent public and academic discussions over whether 'for profit' or 'not-for-profit' services provide better quality of care for recipients. Smaller organisations may have more room to manoeuvre in relation to innovative practice and quality care (according to the Institute of Public Care 2012). However, in the current economic climate of austerity, increasing numbers of charitable organisations are forced by commissioners to drive down costs (Community Care 2014). Effective funding of health and social care services is a key factor in consideration of the quality of everyday life experiences for intellectually disabled people, but other factors also need to be taken into account.

---

1   The four countries that make up the United Kingdom – Northern Ireland, Scotland, Wales and England – are governed by varying legislation and policy. Most contributors are writing about their experiences in England and accordingly the 'national' focus of legislation, policy and practice relates to that country. Reference is made to alternative UK legislation and guidance as appropriate.

As important as funding is, 'compassion' has been identified as crucial in the training of health and social care staff, according to 'The Independent Cavendish Review' (2013). This directive has come quickly on the heels of the Francis Report (2013), a public inquiry into the Mid-Staffordshire NHS Foundations Trust, where revelations of abuse and neglect of patients caused a national outcry.[2] Moreover, appalling abuse had been exposed in 2011 at Winterbourne View hospital (an admission and treatment unit for intellectually disabled people).[3] These scandals attack the very core values of much of the law and policy set up to protect and enable people to have satisfying lives, and show how far there is to go in the training and valuing of staff in their pivotal roles. Rather than the policy goals set out in Table 11.1, such as personalisation, person-centred approaches, localism and multi-agency working, we are frequently confronted with the actual reality of badly run services and institutions, isolation from families and failure of regulatory bodies.

More generally, the gaps between what a company or service policy sets out and real-life experience are often caused by a lack of resources or staff absence and other operational factors (Durham County Council 2004, p.24). Either way there is clearly a recognised gap between the rhetoric of policy and the reality of everyday life of people with intellectual disabilities.

As the 'Dignity in Care' guide from the Social Care Institute of Excellence pointed out, 'People in residential care and their relatives often complain of lack of stimulation, opportunities for social interaction, including sexual relationships and community participation' (SCIE 2010, p.12). It is clear then that services may not live up to the expectations of the people who receive them or pay for them. This becomes a crucial issue when it is combined with what we already know from research about the lives of people with intellectual disabilities (see Gravell 2012 and Chapter 1): that people are often lonely, have few friends and face many barriers in forming and sustaining relationships. These are the very issues that services need to be actively supporting (see Chapter 9).

Current law and policy

SUE

Table 11.1 summarises key national legislation and policy in relation to sexuality since the passing of the Human Rights Act in 1998. We hope that this will provide a useful guide for people with intellectual disabilities and their advocates, students and practitioners.

---

2   For more information see www.independent.co.uk/news/uk/home-news/jeremy-hunt-mid-staffordshire-nhs-trust-will-be-dissolved-9154787.html.

3   See www.bbc.co.uk/news/uk-england-bristol-20078999 for a timeline of the Winterbourne View Abuse Scandal.

TABLE 11.1 KEY MESSAGES FROM LAW AND POLICY (ENGLAND AND UK)

Law or policy	Key messages
The Human Rights Act 1998	• Act reinforces a 'rights culture' and a duty to ensure that everyone receives the benefit of the law • Key articles: **Article 2** The right to access education; **Article 3** No torture, inhuman or degrading treatment; **Article 7** No punishment without law; **Article 8** The right to privacy and family life (includes sexual relations); **Article 10** Freedom of expression; **Article 12** The right to marry and have a family; **Article 14** Freedom from discrimination; **Article 17** No one has the right to destroy or abuse rights

No Secrets (DH/Home Office 2000)	• Policy guidance which encourages all responsible agencies to work together to ensure a coherent policy for the protection of vulnerable adults at risk of abuse
	• Abuse is defined as a violation of a person's human and civil rights by another person or persons
	• Provides the following further definitions of abuse:
	  ◦ *sexual abuse*: including rape and sexual assault or sexual acts to which the adult at risk has not consented, or could not consent or was pressured into consenting
	  ◦ *physical abuse*: including hitting, slapping, pushing, kicking, misuse of medication, restraint or inappropriate sanctions
	  ◦ *psychological abuse*: including emotional abuse, threats of harm or abandonment, deprivation of contact, humiliation, blaming, controlling, intimidation, coercion, harassment, verbal abuse, isolation or withdrawal from services or supportive networks
	  ◦ *financial or material abuse*: including theft, fraud, exploitation, pressure in connection with wills, property or inheritance or financial transactions
	  ◦ *neglect and acts of omission*: including ignoring medical or physical care needs; failure to provide access to appropriate health, social care or educational services; the withholding of the necessities of life such as medication, adequate nutrition and heating
	  ◦ *discriminatory abuse*: including racist, sexist, that based on a person's disability, and other forms of harassment, slurs or similar treatment

Valuing People (DH 2001)	• States that services are to be underpinned by four key principles of rights, independence, choice and inclusion with advocacy and person-centred planning as key tools for implementing change • People with intellectual disabilities were closely involved in the groundwork for this policy • Highlights that people with intellectual disabilities 'are often socially isolated' and states that 'Good services will help people develop opportunities to form relationships, including ones of a physical and sexual nature' • The policy also emphasises the need for accessible sex education and information about relationships and contraception

The Sexual Offences Act 2003	• Defines consent to sex as: 'A person consents if he agrees by choice and has the freedom and capacity to make that choice' • Defines rape, assault by penetration and sexual assault • 16 as the age of consent to sexual activity (Sexual Offences Amendment Act 2000) • Defines a series of 'sexual offences against people with a mental disorder impeding choice' that recognise the vulnerability of people with intellectual disabilities to sexual abuse and apply to all people with mental disorder • Defines as sexual offence, causing a person with a mental disorder to engage in or agree to engage in sexual activity by inducement, threat or deception • Defines what is meant by a care worker and makes sexual activity between a person with intellectual disabilities and a paid or unpaid care worker engaged in a caring role with that person illegal

The Mental Capacity Act 2005	• Applies to everyone over 16 years
	• Presumes every adult has the right to make decisions and the capacity to do so
	• The Act outlines the following test for capacity to consent:
	Whether the person can:
	  ◦ understand the information relevant to a decision
	  ◦ retain that information
	  ◦ use or weigh up that information
	  ◦ *communicate* that decision (verbal or non-verbal)
	• A person is not to be treated as unable to make a decision unless all practicable steps to help her do so have been undertaken without success, including accessible information as appropriate
	• Each decision will be assessed separately
	• A person is not to be treated as unable to make a decision merely because she makes an unwise one
	• Any act done or decision made on behalf of someone must be in their best interests and least restrictive of their basic rights
	• Some types of decisions can NEVER be made by another person on behalf of someone who lacks capacity because they are either very personal or other laws govern such decisions. *These include the decision to enter into a sexual relationship, marriage or a civil partnership or divorce*
	• NB People who are incapacitated continue to have protection under the European Convention on Human Rights and the Human Rights Act (1998)
	• Recent case law has emphasised the need to balance rights and personal happiness with risk

United Nations (2006) *UN Convention on the rights of persons with disabilities.* New York: United Nations	• Reaffirms disabled people's human rights – another step in disabled people becoming equal citizens. Ratified by UK Government in June 2009. Sets out that disabled people face many barriers but requires governments to take actions to remove these barriers and protect disabled people.
Putting People First (DH 2007)	• The transformation of social care and the personalisation agenda is set out in PPF alongside the importance of investing in prevention and well-being. • It highlights the importance of supporting carers, person-centred planning, personal budgets and risk management. • Followed by very useful social policy guidance from *Equality and Diversity Matters, Commission for Social Care Inspection, 2008, Issue 7* which deals with equality and diversity regarding lesbian, gay, bisexual and transgender people using services.
The Health and Social Care Act 2008 (Reg11)	• Requires registered providers to take 'reasonable steps to identify the possibility of abuse and prevent it before it occurs'. • Staff in care homes must respect cultural background, sex (gender), age, sexuality (whether you are a lesbian, gay, bisexual or heterosexual person), religion or belief, and disability of people in their care.
Safeguarding adults: Report on the consultation on the review of *No secrets* (DH 2009)	• Report places new emphasis on prevention of abuse and on the empowerment of individuals to maintain their own safety. • Consultation found that safeguarding can be experienced as *'safety at the expense of other qualities of life, such as self-determination and the right to family life'.* • Report highlights the importance of achieving a balance between safeguarding and the independence associated with personalisation in adult social care.
Valuing People Now (DH 2009)	• Emphasises that the right to marry or have a civil partnership is both a civil and human right and states that local systems should enable practice that supports individual choice with regard to forming and sustaining relationships. • Recognises that people with intellectual disabilities often have very few relationships, limited opportunities to form or sustain them and that people are often lonely. • States the right of people to have relationships, become parents and continue to be parents, and that they receive support to do so. • Highlights the role of registered care services in supporting people to develop and sustain relationships, including sexual relationships. (Further information: http://webarchive.nationalarchives.gov.uk/2013)

The Equalities Act 2010	• Simplifies the way people are protected with regard to discrimination.
	• A person with any kind of impairment, including intellectual disability, who can demonstrate the difficulties they encounter carrying out everyday activities is defined and protected under the Act.
	• An important function is that the Act protects people from 'indirect discrimination', where policy or practice is applied in a way that may place some people with intellectual disabilities at a disadvantage (for example, providing written information but with no easy-read versions or health appointments of very short duration that mean people have very little time to process information or ask questions). (Further information: www.equalities.gov.uk).
	• The Equality and Human Rights Commission was established in 2007 and brought together the Disability Rights Commission, the Commission for Racial Equality and the Equal Opportunities Commission.
	• For people with intellectual disabilities, their families, carers, advocates and staff the Commission can be accessed to prevent inequality and unfair treatment and experiences.

In the UK, the different countries sometimes have separate policies and laws, so each document needs to be understood within its own boundary. However, most of these policies and laws have very similar foundations. The laws and policies summarised in Table 11.1 are in place to ensure that as citizens we are entitled both to a sexual life of our own choice and to equal protection before the law if our rights or bodies are violated. These are not alternatives; they are vital to our personal fulfilment, happiness and safety (Brown 2010). In general, the legal and policy framework aims to ensure that people with intellectual disabilities are both:

- *enabled and supported* to exercise the same rights as other citizens when it comes to their sexuality and sexual choices[4]

- *protected* as citizens from sexual violence and exploitation.[5]

Yet, Brown (2010) raises concerns that this twofold emphasis is ineffective. Within services, empowerment and protection are sometimes talked about as if they were mutually exclusive and this can lead to compromise rather than a clear commitment to do both well. As Louise will tell us later, protection can take the direction of limiting people's activities and choices.

Similarly, as seen in Table 11.1, consultation with vulnerable adults and their supporters as part of the review of the No Secrets guidance found that in practice, safeguarding can be experienced as prioritising safety over self-determination and the right to a family life.

Section 30 of the Sexual Offences Act 2003 says that it is against the law to have sex with a person 'with a mental disorder impeding choice', including women with intellectual disabilities who lack the capacity to make a decision to consent to sex. This law is there for a clear purpose, to protect people with intellectual disabilities who remain particularly vulnerable to sexual abuse. The purpose of the law is not to interfere in the development of positive, mutually beneficial relationships but to ensure that vulnerable women are not being pressurised or coerced into having sex against their wishes (City of Westminster 2010).

If two people have sex together but neither has the capacity to consent to sexual activity they will not be prosecuted under the Sexual Offences Act 2003. The Minister of State gave assurances on this point during the Lords committee stage of the Bill (Fanstone and Andrews 2009).

The existence of the Sexual Offences Act and the Mental Capacity Act means that staff must receive adequate training in the field of supporting relationships and

---

4   Rights enshrined, for example, in The Human Rights Act 1998, *Valuing People* (DH 2001) and *Valuing People Now* (DH 2009).

5   The right to protection is clearly stated in the No Secrets policy and enshrined in the Sexual Offences Act 2003.

sexuality. In terms of the law employees need to be mindful of their duty of care in supporting same-sex relationships including the provision of information, counselling and careful documentation of decisions made and the reasoning behind them (see Chapter 15). If this work is not undertaken the individuals and the organisation they are working for will be vulnerable to questioning of the nature and legality of their professional and organisational conduct.

The dangers of current law and policy

LOUISE

When we think about law and policies we may think they are boring and useless documents; well, that's how I've thought of them before.

I say this because, in thinking about risk assessments as an example, they can be used in such a way that people with intellectual disabilities wouldn't get to do anything. I agree that some people need to be protected at times but in doing so, are those people being stopped from living their lives the way they choose? That means having the same opportunities as everyone else has.

Often if you are in a relationship and a person wants to meet their boyfriend/ girlfriend away from a day centre, then there always seems to be a big issue and excuses about it. These are some that I have heard, "Oh, they don't need to do that!" or, "There isn't time (or transport) to sort it out" or, "Well, they see each other every day, don't they?" So obstacles keep getting put in the way.

Of course I think policies should be there to protect people who need it, but it should be recognised that this can also impinge on people's lives. Sometimes if people do things of a sexual nature that are deemed to be wrong, then it may just be that the individual doesn't have the knowledge of appropriate behaviour; it's education that people need, not blame.

A few years ago, a man who was an advocacy group member touched me inappropriately. I had been in People First for quite some time, plus my Mum has always been open about sexuality so I knew that what he was doing was wrong. I felt I had the confidence to say firmly, but nicely, 'Colin,[6] would you please take your hand away from down my leg!' He did and the matter wasn't ever discussed again. At the time I did tell a couple of friends and my Mum – who said I did the right thing. I didn't tell my Dad because things could have turned nasty, but at the end of the day he would have been protecting his daughter.

Colin left the advocacy group for a while and has recently come back but I don't hold any grudges; it was a mistake. If other people had got involved it would probably have escalated into a huge situation.

---

6   This is not his real name.

Having said that, people with intellectual disabilities don't always know about the policies in their services or workplaces, so they may not know what to do when things go wrong. It's assumed people with intellectual disabilities don't need to know about them, rather than make sure the policies are accessible and discussed.

A few years ago, as part of my job as a women's worker I had some safeguarding training which was really useful. I was in a situation once where I could see a friend of mine had been taken advantage of and financially abused. I remember thinking, 'something isn't right'. It was just certain things the person said or didn't say and eventually he no longer came to the advocacy group. If I knew then what I know now, then I would have referred it to the safeguarding team. If I hadn't had the training, I wouldn't have known.

Lost opportunities

ROHHSS

It is interesting to compare the contradiction in terms that runs through history regarding people with intellectual disabilities identified in Part 1 of the book – that of a person with intellectual disability as *sexual predator* or, in contrast, as *eternal child* – with the two aims of the current UK policy framework: that of *choice/protection* and *rights*. These are a clear binary and may not be too helpful in thinking through the complexities of a more sensitive approach to both protection and rights. As discussed earlier, it seems that despite major efforts, it is still very hard for the aims of current law and policy to reach effectively into the service sphere, and thus into people's everyday experiences, let alone alter attitudes of the public, including the friends that Sue and I mentioned in Chapter 1. Person-centred approaches, called for in policy since the early 2000s (DH 2001) would suggest a far more personalised and individualised approach to safeguarding.

Louise pointed out that this policy knowledge rarely reaches people with intellectual disabilities who are using and most likely paying for the service. This also seems to be a lost opportunity as accessible documents and knowledge transfer are useful to everyone. It will be interesting to read in Part 2 how much of this work is undertaken by the companies and services providing care and whether it is used in conjunction with providing training for people using their services about their rights and what can be expected in terms of support.

An aspect in much of the previous research we have reviewed has been the lack of acknowledgement of advice and support of friends or peers from services and advocacy groups. People with intellectual disabilities report that very often they are 'not believed' or 'listened to' (Chapman 2006, p.242; Gravell 2012), when expressing opinions or reporting on events. Yet there have been some excellent projects, written about in the public domain, that are run by advocacy and theatre groups and clearly demonstrate the power of peer support and education.[7]

SUE

We know that intellectually disabled people often find it hard to access information about sexuality. In addition there is relatively little research about how people with intellectual disabilities conceptualise their sexuality, develop a sexual identity and form and sustain relationships of their choice (Fitzgerald and Withers, 2013).

Fitzgerald and Withers (2013 p.8) conducted ten in-depth interviews with women with intellectual disabilities to explore how these women felt about sexuality and their sexual identity. Most of the women interviewed communicated that other people prohibited any expression of their sexuality and said that they were not allowed to have sex with their boyfriends and feared the consequences of 'getting caught'. Here is an excerpt from one of the interviews:

C: *I haven't been in trouble yet but I would do.*

Interviewer: Who would you get in trouble with?

C: *The staff, at home.*

Interviewer: You'd get in trouble with the staff at home?

C: *Yeah. If they found out.*

Interviewer: What would they do?

C: *They'd tell their boss.*

Interviewer: And what would happen then?

C: *They'd stop me from going to see my friend.*

Interviewer: And how would you feel about that?

C: *I'd be upset.*

The authors point out that this woman was clearly frightened of losing a valued person in her life as 'punishment' for having a sexual relationship with her boyfriend. This research raises issues about how people with intellectual disabilities living within services become 'regulated beings' whose sexual behaviour is often patrolled

---

7   See, for example: The Lawnmowers Independent Theatre Company, which performs participatory theatre and comedy (www.thelawnmowers.co.uk); CHANGE (see Chapter 18, http://changepeople.info); and The Josephine Project where Josephine is a life-sized anatomically correct woman made of cloth (www.themwifies.org.uk).

and documented by staff. In these situations a lack of legal knowledge may leave people vulnerable to violation of their rights to develop relationships.

Reading this excerpt really made me feel sad; it brought home the terrible vulnerability of some people and how easy it is for sexual expression to be controlled by behaviour from staff that, however well meaning, is in itself clearly illegal and abusive. For example, an organisation threatening punishment of withholding contact with a friend would be guilty of 'psychological abuse' under No Secrets (2000) guidance; the practice also contravenes her right to 'Privacy and a Family Life' under the Human Rights Act 1998, and represents failure to comply with the terms of the Health and Social Care Act 2008, which requires providers to support people with relationships, plus the Equalities Act 2010, which prevents discrimination in relation to disability.

LOUISE

I feel that this kind of reaction, that people would get punished by staff, is typical of some services. Why is this kind of oppression still going on? Would someone without a label get punished for having a sexual relationship? No! So why is it so hard for people who have a label to be able to have a relationship? This is wrong and makes me very angry.

ROHHSS

We can question why staff wield such extraordinary power. One possible way to understand this example resonates with a Foucauldian understanding of *discipline* as the apparatus of *power* that *regulates* behaviour. The stories demonstrate significant regulation of people's behaviour, especially within their homes (see Chapter 6). People with intellectual disabilities are 'overseen' by their staff to the extent that over time they automatically conform to the norms expected by staff even when they are not being observed. This is because staff are central in people's lives. Staff are employed to support, but sometimes *support* can be authoritarian (Gravell 2012).

Foucault demonstrated the powerful impacts of being 'overseen' using the imagery of a panoptican: 'Hence the major effect of the Panoptican: to induce in the inmate a state of consciousness and permanent visibility that ensures the automatic functioning of power' (Foucault 1979, p.201). So, in the above example, C, in speculating about what would happen, believed she would be prevented from seeing her friend; her past experiences of staff behaviour had led her to assume this. Her narrative presented no hint of her own power or resistance. This is, unfortunately, very typical of the narratives of people with intellectual disabilities in regard of services, but could be challenged if people knew their rights and were effectively supported.

SUE

Relatively little research exists on the prevention of abuse of vulnerable adults (SCIE 2011) and, as Rohhss mentions above, what exists has shown that adults with intellectual disabilities have little understanding of the general law relating to sexuality (e.g. age of consent, incest, abuse) as well as the law relating to sexuality and intellectual disability. For example, people just do not know if they could have sexual relationships, if they could marry, and what protection they could expect from the law. In O'Callaghan and Murphy's (2007) study, strikingly only 20 out of 60 people with intellectual disabilities knew they had a legal right to marry; only 50 per cent of people with intellectual disabilities realised that the law concerning sexual assault and rape also applied to them; and only around 50 per cent knew that there were laws to protect them from sexual relationships or assault from staff.

Issues relating to diversity

ROHHSS

Diversity cannot be separated from law and policy as aspects around equality (e.g. Equalities Act 2010) and inclusion (to counteract discrimination) are of course incorporated in the law and policy presented earlier in the chapter. What was important for intellectually disabled people in England in relation to diversity was clearly set out in *Valuing People Now* (DH 2009).

Essentially, *Valuing People Now* was a review of the 2001 *Valuing People* White Paper (DH 2001). Wide consultations took place throughout England with all stakeholders (over 10,000, including people with intellectual disabilities, DH 2009, p.6) prior to the publication of the 2009 document.

This new momentum was based on evidence gained that some specific groups had fared badly so far, mainly people with more complex support needs, Black and Minority Ethnic groups, people with Aspergers and autistic spectrum conditions, and offenders with intellectual disabilities (DH 2009, p.17). It also set out a three year delivery plan.

Some good progress was also evidenced, but issues to do with 'harder to reach' (DH 2009, p.17) groups caused concern. The new plan was to link *Valuing People Now* to changes in healthcare based on an independent enquiry called *Healthcare for All* (DH 2008) which particularly focused on problems with access to healthcare for intellectually disabled people. It also linked with a Joint Committee on Human Rights support, *A Life Like Any Other?* (JCHR 2008). *Valuing People Now* went on to set out that people with intellectual disabilities were entitled to the same opportunities and achievements as any other citizen, and that vision was based upon a number of other additional policies around children and carers (see DH 2009, p.14)

On reflection, the issues around 'harder to reach' people mirror the English experience of closing the institutions and long-stay hospitals. The institutions had moved people into the community who were more independent first and those with high support needs had languished incarcerated for many more years. What becomes apparent is that this is a repeating pattern. Policy impacts take longer to achieve where more intensive support is required. Dealing with issues around diversity requires a depth of knowledge about people. Interestingly, a recent Independent Commission on Whole Person Care report (Labour Party 2014), sets out a 'new' vision to coordinate care so it better meets the holistic needs of individuals. When we hear the stories of people's experiences, such ideas may seem aspirational; the point is to work out how to put these aspirations into practice.

LOUISE

Over the years I have been involved in the National Forum[8] and the Government Task Force[9] which was set up from the *Valuing People* (DH 2001) White Paper. There was a wide range of people on the National Forum from different ethnic minority groups and people with different types of intellectual disabilities.

After I left I was told a tale that someone with high support needs was on the National Forum but did not get the correct support because of their multiple needs and so they had to come off it. To me, this is discrimination. The person had to have two supporters with them to be able to attend, but they were told by the Forum that there was not enough money to warrant this.

I think people with higher support needs don't get included because it's assumed that they don't understand. If they are assessed as needing two supporters, then so what?

I can also remember a guy from People First with high support needs; he used a touch talker to communicate and new professionals used to shout at him because they thought he was deaf. He calmly put in his touch talker, 'I'm not deaf'!

I do think it's very sad, because we talk about discrimination, but it even happens within our own advocacy groups. We can be very bad at including people with high support needs, and people with intellectual disabilities can themselves be prejudiced and may not even value their peers.

---

8   National Forum – 2 people with intellectual disabilities from 9 areas of England are elected to the National Forum to represent the views of people with intellectual disabilities in their area. See www.nationalforum.co.uk/all-about-the-forum.

9   Government Task Force – was set up under 'Valuing People' (DH, 2001) to take forward the implementation of national action. It was to act as a champion for change and advise the government on Learning Disability policy (see DH 2001, p.118)

By this I mean we used to have advocacy group members ringing the office to ask when the next meeting was. I would answer the phone and know the information, but people with intellectual disabilities didn't want to speak to me, they wanted to speak with a support worker. They were very reluctant to accept support from me, a worker with intellectual disabilities.

ROHHSS

Sadly many people have a problem with accepting diversity, as evidenced in current publications about hate-crime (Gravell 2012), and as Louise remarks, even within People First. This shows the importance of work around values and attitudes. One day at an advocacy group, a transgendered woman, Pauline, came to work with the group on a voluntary basis. Some members seemed not to notice any difference but some of the staff behaved appallingly towards her, snickering behind her back and avoiding working with her. If advocacy supporters cannot confront their prejudices then it's going to be hard to support others to do so. Eventually Pauline left, with what I imagine to have been a very poor opinion of a 'rights-based' group.

Summary

SUE

Part 1 of the book documented how legislation and policy concerning the sexuality of adults with intellectual disabilities have changed considerably during the last 100 years. It also identified and questioned two recurrent yet paradoxical themes:

- People with intellectual disabilities as sexually promiscuous and irresponsible – associated with concerns about pregnancy, parenting and the birth of further intellectually disabled children.

- In contrast, people with intellectual disabilities as innocent, child-like and asexual and in need of protection from sexual information, activity and exploitation.

In Part 2 of the book these themes recur as we hear how risk and rights are responded to in a range of UK settings. The stories in Part 2 raise new questions, one of which is how services respond to perceived 'differences' or diversity in sexual expression: people who identify as lesbian, gay or transgender. In the UK, whilst there is a need to empower adults with intellectual disabilities and to reinforce their right to consensual sexual expression, there is also a very genuine need to ensure protection from sexual abuse. Research has now established that there is a significantly higher rate of sexual abuse perpetrated against people with intellectual disabilities (particularly women) and there is evidence that people are at risk of being targeted for sexual exploitation (see Chapter 20). Given the high prevalence of abuse it is not surprising that families and staff trying to support people with their sexuality whilst ensuring their protection often become confused and worried. The danger – as we have seen in Part 1 – is that it can all too easily result in separating people or 'halting' relationships as a solution to managing perceived risk.

In *A Life Like Any Other?*, the Joint Committee on Human Rights (JCHR 2008) noted that adults with intellectual disabilities are particularly vulnerable to breaches of their human rights and that sadly for many of them this is seen as a normal part of their everyday lives.

In Chapter 10 the interpretation of law and policy in relation to sexuality at local level was a recurrent theme. In Part 2 of the book we hear more about how the legal and policy framework impacts on people's experiences in the UK context. In doing so we see how the balancing act of enabling rights whilst protecting people from abuse is played out on a day-to-day basis. The chapters in Part 1 make it possible for these accounts to be viewed in an international context.

Overview of Part 2

ROHHSS

Mirroring the structure of Part 1, we start with a contextual chapter by Rachel Fyson, providing a foundation for the chapters that follow. Chapter 12 explores connections between public and professional acceptance of the changing rights of intellectually disabled people alongside broader changes in societal attitudes to sex and sexuality in the UK. Rachel demonstrates how greater sexual freedom has been impacted by an increase in awareness and concerns about sexual abuse.

Chapter 13 by Jan Walmsley, Carol Hamilton, Nigel Ingham and Steve Mee with Sharon Harrison, explores the experiences of people with intellectual disabilities and staff living and working in the former long stay institutions. These authors question whether it was easier for people with intellectual disabilities to form sexual relationships whilst living in institutions than in contemporary community settings. It is often assumed that developments result in improvement, but this chapter highlights how people with intellectual disabilities may have had more opportunities to have sex in the institutions than happens now in smaller, more tightly observed, community settings.

Chapter 14, by Alice, recounts her experiences of growing up. She was born a boy but realised that she was not comfortable living as a male and wished to live as a woman. Alice is transgendered and lives in a rural area. She comments on the cruelty and discrimination displayed towards her and how she has attempted to resist it and move on in her life.

'Gay women might need a Rainbow Fairy Group', Chapter 15, is about lesbian women and the support they receive from their organisation. It is co-written by Clare Miller, Adam Koronka, Lindy Shufflebotham and Sue Ledger. The chapter raises many questions about how to meet people when being a lesbian is such a hidden issue within services. Lack of knowledge by staff regarding the law connected to lesbian relationships is addressed. The chapter provides useful and insightful information.

Chapter 16 is written by two gay men, Craig Blyth, an academic, and Daniel Docherty (co-editor), a man with intellectual disabilities who struggled with 'coming out'. It traces and questions the ongoing reactions of staff towards his sexuality. Daniel's section is based on a conference paper he presented for the Social History of Learning Disabilities Group at the Open University.

Developing further the issues of diversity, Chapter 17, by Jackie Downer with Linnette Farquarson, reflects on her experiences as a Black heterosexual woman. Jackie makes the point that quality of support is an essential part of feeling comfortable, where her cultural background is fully understood. She also discusses how she feels other people perceive her and who she feels is looking out for her interests.

Chapter 18 is about CHANGE and their research on sexuality. This is written by Ruth Garbutt with Lyndon Strickland, a man with intellectual disabilities. They talk about sex education in schools and the views of parents and young people. They identify innovative methods for sex education. CHANGE is an organisation which specialises in the rights of intellectually disabled people.

Chapter 19 is from 'The Men's Room' and is written by Bill, Peter and Alan with Niall McNulty. It captures conversations between men with intellectual disabilities around sexuality and relationships. This chapter sets out some of the stark realities of long-term feelings of rejection but also demonstrates the men's resilience and humour as well as identifying barriers to starting and maintaining relationships.

Chapter 20 is a preliminary overview of previous literature undertaken by Craig Blyth and Rohhss Chapman about people with intellectual disabilities selling or being sold for sex. Very little is known about this topic although it is mentioned in passing in a number of other studies. This chapter explains why it is such an important area to research despite the hidden nature of the topic. The authors raise the importance of ensuing health issues.

Chapter 21, written by Rohhss Chapman, Louise Townson and Sue Ledger, candidly reflects on the partnership approach taken throughout the book, both from an author and an editorial perspective. They discuss some of the advantages that arise out of writing together but also critique the approach and acknowledge some of the grittier problems that emerged along the way.

Chapter 22, again written by the editors, pulls together the main themes of the stories presented in the book in the same way as Chapter 10.

Chapter 23, the final chapter by the editors, discusses the findings in relation to the research questions set out in Chapter 1. We present some recommendations and ideas for supporting people with intellectual disabilities in their quest for a full and safe life in relation to sexuality.

References

Brown, H. (2010) 'The Process and Function of Serious Case Review', *Journal of Adult Protection 11*, Issue 1, 38–50.

Chapman, R. (2006) *The role of the self-advocacy support-worker in UK people first groups: Developing Inclusive Research*, Faculty of Health and Social Welfare, Open University, Milton Keynes, Unpublished PhD.

DH Department of Health (2000) *No Secrets: Guidance on Protecting vulnerable Adults in Care*, London, Department of Health.

DH (Department of Health) (2001) *Valuing People: A New Strategy for Learning Disability for the 21st Century* (Cm 5086). London: The Stationary Office.

DH (Department of Health) (2007) *Putting People First: A Shared Vision and Commitment to the Transformation of Adult Social Care*. London: Department of Health.

DH (Department of Health) (2008) *Healthcare for All*. Report of the independent inquiry into Access to Healthcare for People with Learning Disabilities, The Michael Report. Available at www.dh.gov.uk/prod_consum_dh/groups/dh_digitalassets/@dh/@en/documents/digitalasset/dh_106126.pdf, accessed on 12 June 2014.

DH (Department of Health) (2008) *Carers at the Heart of 21st-century Families and Communities*. London: Crown Copyright.

DH Department of Health (2009) *Safeguarding Adults: report on the consultation on the review of No Secrets*. London: Crown publications.

DH (Department of Health) (2009) *Valuing People Now: A New Three-year Strategy for People with Learning Disabilities*. London: The Stationery Office.

DH Department of Health (2013) *The Cavendish Review:an independent review into healthcare assistants and support workers in the NHS and Social Care settings*. London: Department of Health.

Durham County Council (2004) *Sickness Absence in the Social Care and Health Service*. Available at www.cfps.org.uk/domains/cfps.org.uk/local/media/library/626.pdf, accessed on 6 February 2014.

Fitzgerald, C. & Withers, P. (2013) *I don't know what a proper woman means: what women with intellectual disabilities think about sex, sexuality and themselves*. In British Journal of Learning Disabilities, Vol 41, Issue 1, 5–12.

Faulkner, A. and Sweeney, A (2011) *Prevention in Adult Safeguarding*, Social Care Institute for Excellence Adult Services Report 41, London. SCIE.

Fanstone, C. and Andrews, S. (2009) *Learning Disabilities, Sex and the Law: a practical guide*, London: Family Planning Association.

Foucault, M. (1979) *Discipline and Punish: The Birth of the Prison*. London: Penguin Books.

Gravell, C. (2012) *Loneliness and Cruelty: People with Learning Disabilities and their Experiences of Harassment, Abuse and Related Crime in the Community*. London: Lemos and Crane.

Institute of Public Care (2012) *Leading the Way: The Distinctive Contribution of the Not-for-Profit Sector in Social Care, Paper two: Innovation*. Oxford: IPC at Oxford Brookes University.

JCHR (Joint Committee on Human Rights) (2008) *A Life Like Any Other? Human Rights of Adults with Learning Disabilities* (HL Paper 40-1 HC 73-1). House of Lords, House of Commons, Joint Committee on Human Rights.

Labour Party (2014) *One Person, One Team, One System: Report of the Independent Commission on Whole Person Care for the Labour Party*. Chaired by Sir John Oldham. Available at www.yourbritain.org.uk/uploads/editor/files/One_Person_One_Team_One_System.pdf, accessed on 12 June 2014.

McNicoll, A., and Stothart, C., (2014) *Deeper cuts to Adult Social care packages planned as council budgets drop by 4%* in Community Care www.communitycare.co.uk/2014/04/09/deeper-cuts-adult-social-care-packages-planned-council-budgets-drop-4, accessed May 15 2014.

Social Care Institute for Excellence (2010) *Common Safeguarding Issues – Lack of Social Inclusion*, Guide 46 available at www.scie.org.uk/publications/guides/guide46/commonissues/lackofsocialinclusion.asp, accessed September 2014.

CHAPTER 12

PROMOTING SEXUALITIES AND PROTECTING FROM ABUSE

Rachel Fyson with an introduction by Louise Townson

Overview

- Louise introduces the chapter with her own views about sexuality and protection. She feels that intellectually disabled people do not get a good enough education around relationships and sexuality.

- Rachel writes about equal sexual rights for people with learning disabilities. She says that the battle is far from over.

- The chapter raises the issue of what people want for themselves and what society does to protect people seen as 'vulnerable'.

- In the past people have believed that intellectually disabled people have huge sexual appetites and are a danger to society.

- It has also been believed in contrast that they are adult 'children' and do not have an interest in sex at all.

- These opposite views do not make any sense.

- Attitudes towards sexuality and people with intellectual disability began to be challenged by the rise of the disability movement.

- At the same time the public became more aware of sexual abuse and the dangers of HIV/AIDS.

- In England *Valuing People* policy (DH 2001) stressed the importance of independence and choice but this has been hard to uphold in a lot of services.

- Service providers are very wary of risk in relation to sex and sexuality.

- This leads to a constant tension between people's rights and desires and protection from abuse.

The writing process

Rachel wrote the chapter. Louise then read it and made comments about it from her own perspective and to include the voice of a person with intellectual disabilities. Rachel uses the term 'people with learning disabilities' in her writing, which is used in UK policy-making and by the Department of Health.

Introduction

LOUISE

This chapter looks at the topic of abuse and policies and the impact they have on the lives of people with intellectual disabilities. We generally think that over time policies have changed dramatically, but this chapter questions that view.

My concern is that of course people with intellectual disabilities need to be protected against harm and abuse, but the methods of going about this in services may get in the way of people living their lives how they want to. Part of that is being able to have a sexual relationship.

The question I ask is that when this right is taken away from people by their supporters, parents or carers, then is it being done because law and policy demand it or because law and policy are being interpreted in a way that forces their own values and beliefs on people?

It makes me angry when I hear of a relationship that is going well but other people are sticking their noses into it and looking for problems and issues when there aren't any. At the same time I have also known of when an individual has been abused and nothing happens because of having to have a court case approved by the Crown Prosecution Service (in England). I knew a woman who reported she was raped and it was reported to the police. Eventually it was decided that her account would not hold up in court and so nothing happened about it. This woman eventually took her own life.

Abuse can take many paths. It can be sexual, mental, financial or physical. During my work with People First we held women's conferences, the first of these was in 2004. We talked about relationships where many of the women talked about their own experiences with men and partners. Some of the women didn't realise that what they were experiencing was actually abuse; they had assumed it was a natural part of a relationship. A lot of this confusion seems to come from a lack of useful sex and relationship education. As the lives of women with intellectual disabilities can be very monitored and protected, these women were not experiencing the same life opportunities that other women benefit from.

When I was employed as a women's worker we held workshops on topics that women with intellectual disabilities wanted to learn about. These included assertiveness, relationships and health. In these workshops it became apparent that women knew very little about these subjects. For example, when we held a health workshop there was an exercise where we put a long piece of paper along one wall. Written on it was an age-line, 0 to 80+. We gave each woman laminated photos of a baby, a teenager, a pregnant woman and sanitary towels. Each person came up and put their photos in the age bracket they thought it went into. This demonstrated that many of the women didn't really know which event would occur at around which age. If women had more education about their health and relationships then they would have much higher expectations, know what their rights were and be empowered to make their own decisions, rather than have others mistreat them or dictate to them about their lives.

At another conference about sexuality and relationships in 2009, we had a talk by a county officer on 'safeguarding adults'. The feeling of the day was positive and the delegates were keen to focus on how to make and maintain relationships. However, the presentation focused on the negatives about relationships rather than the positives. It was about how to avoid risk rather than how to lead a full life, taking risk into account. The audience were disappointed and frustrated. Afterwards the Lawnmowers, a drama group run by people with intellectual disabilities, put on performances about issues that affect people's relationships and lives. It gave information through role play on how to deal with barriers to relationships and what could be said and done to allow more individual freedom: the type of information really valued by the delegates.

I'm of the firm belief that people who have profound intellectual disabilities and have very little or no verbal communication have their rights to relationships (and many other matters) ignored. This is due to the assumption being made that the person doesn't understand or have an opinion. They can; as a self-advocacy slogan sets out, *'just because I cannot speak does not mean I have nothing to say'*. It's just that time needs to be taken to understand that person's needs and to find alternative ways to communicate. One of my male friends is in a relationship with a woman who has profound and multiple needs but manages to get her voice heard very well with the aid of a touch talker that speaks for her and with a very supportive family.

Relationships can go wrong for anyone, regardless of whether you have an intellectual disability or not, but supporters, parents and carers appear to have a tendency to focus on the negatives of having a relationship rather than the positive effects. I think they are afraid and understandably want to protect people, but this actually treats adults like children. If you study these policies and procedures and interpret them negatively then people with intellectual disabilities would never end up doing anything they really wanted to.

Rachel's chapter traces the tension between rights and protection and how it impacts people's lives.

Promoting sexualities and protecting from abuse
RACHEL

> To be a human being is to be a sexual being. Although there may be a range of intensity, varying over time, we all have sexual needs, feelings and drives, from the most profoundly handicapped to the most able among us. Although we can shape (and mis-shape) sexual expression, sexuality is not an optional extra which we in our wisdom can choose to bestow or withhold according to whether or not some kind of intelligence test is passed. (Craft 1987, p.19)

This chapter explores how public and professional acceptance of the right of adults with learning disabilities to a sexual identity and to consenting sexual relationships has echoed, though within a lagging time frame, broader changes in societal attitudes to sex and sexuality in the UK. It will also consider how progress towards greater sexual freedoms has been affected by a simultaneous increase in awareness of sexual abuse.

Segregation

Although, as will be shown, the course of change for both people with learning disabilities and the wider population has been similar, public attitudes towards sex and people with disabilities in general – and learning disabilities in particular – have continued to be complicated by a fundamental contradiction (Priestly 2003). On the one hand, the (unfounded) belief that people with learning disabilities had 'monstrous sexual appetites' played a part in encouraging the development and continuance of large-scale institutional services in which people with learning disabilities were not only segregated from society but were also sexually segregated from one another through the use of same-sex wards. On the other hand, the (equally unfounded) belief persists that people with learning disabilities are childlike and asexual and therefore need to be protected from any knowledge of sex or sexuality (Craft and Craft 1978). Both of these arguments were used as rationales for segregating people with learning disabilities from the general population and denying their right to sexual expression, with the height of segregationist policies also linked to eugenicist beliefs (Roulstone and Prideaux 2012). Whilst more recent times have seen such attitudes and policies being challenged – not least by people with learning disabilities themselves – the battle for equal sexual rights for people with learning disabilities is far from over.

Sexual liberation?

In the UK, the modern era of sexual liberation is generally accepted to have started in the 1960s, with the post-war baby boomer generation creating pressure for social change. This changing social dynamic was enabled in part by technological developments such as the contraceptive pill, which for the first time gave women a safe and effective means of preventing unwanted pregnancy. It was secured by changes in the law, including the legalisation of abortion in 1967 and, in the same year, the legalisation of homosexuality. At this time, however, little changed for people with learning disabilities, the vast majority of whom lived either with their families with minimal support from the public purse, or in large-scale segregated institutions. In the 1970s, the 'sexual revolution' was further consolidated by legislation which made divorce easier to obtain. At the same time, active political campaigning saw significant advances in the legal rights and public acceptance of a range of disadvantaged and/or minority groups, including women, gay and lesbian people, people from ethnic minorities and people with disabilities. In 1972, Union of the Physically Impaired Against Segregation (UPIAS) was founded and began to both campaign against the segregation of people with physical impairments and develop a new theoretical model of disability – now widely known as the 'social model' – which challenged pre-existing understandings of disability and impairment (Shakespeare 2006).

Sex and marriage

Although the disability movement began to take off on the UK in the 1970s, it did not initially encompass people with learning disabilities; the right of people with learning disabilities to live in the community was only slowly beginning to be acknowledged at this time, and did not always include people with high support needs (HMSO 1971). In this context, the early UK writings in support of the right of people with learning disabilities to have intimate and sexual relationships were both echoing the wider context of increasing sexual and personal freedoms which characterised the era and the first steps in an ongoing struggle for equal sexual rights. The first authors to venture into this territory were Anne and Michael Craft; their book entitled *Sex and the Mentally Handicapped* was published in 1978, followed a year later by a research monograph *Handicapped Married Couples*. Whilst the language used in these book titles is now outdated, the content was revolutionary for its time. The first book opens by exploding the myths of sexual innocence and sexual depravity long associated with people with learning disabilities before moving on to set out the need for sex education and consider psycho-sexual development across the lifespan, including the importance of love and marriage. It also includes a chapter on contemporary law, which notes that 'the law in relation to sex for the handicapped in England and Wales has not changed greatly in recent years, in spite of our so-called permissive age' (Craft and Craft 1978, p.64) and goes on to record that, at the time, it remained 'an offence to have sexual intercourse with one who is severely subnormal' (p.65). The second book describes an empirical study of 45 marriages in which one or both partners had some degree of learning disability. It concludes that the research subjects' understandings of marriage were broadly the same as those of people within the general population; that most felt that 'marriage has brought them satisfaction which a single existence had not afforded' (Craft and Craft 1979, p.71). The book also highlights the largely positive outcomes achieved by children of these marriages and critiques the concept of 'problem families', a category to which many of these couples had been assigned by social services.

Sexual abuse

Throughout the 1980s and 1990s pressure from people with learning disabilities and their families (Rolph *et al.* 2005) began to achieve significant progress in the closure of long-stay segregated institutions and provision of services in the community. During this time, Ann Craft – and a small but increasing number of other activists and academics – continued to research on and campaign for the sexual rights of people with learning disabilities. In the wider world these decades were a period of time in which public consciousness of sexual abuse increased exponentially. This burgeoning awareness of the sexual abuse of children developed first in North America, and then crashed into the public sphere in the UK with the Cleveland 'scandal' in which 121 children were removed into care following suspicions of sexual abuse which were vigorously denied by their parents (Campbell 1988).

Recognition that not only children, but also people with learning disabilities, were at risk of sexual abuse followed – albeit with a slightly different international trajectory. The early 1990s saw professionals and academics working in North America (Sobsey and Doe 1991; Sobsey and Mansell 1990), Australia (Carmody 1991) and the UK (Brown and Turk 1992) all contributing to a sudden upsurge in research on the sexual abuse of adults with learning disabilities which appeared, at least temporarily, to eclipse the earlier focus on promoting a right to sexual expression. This period also witnessed the founding, in 1992, of the National Association for the Protection from Sexual Abuse of Adults and Children with Learning Disabilities (NAPSAC), which was later renamed the Ann Craft Trust.[1]

Academic research

By the mid-1990s, work in this field in the UK was dominated by academic researchers rather than people with learning disabilities themselves, and although the work was wide ranging it tended to focus on adults with learning disabilities as victims of sexual assault. This included studies of the sexual abuse of adults with learning disabilities (Brown and Turk 1994; Brown, Stein and Turk 1995); examinations of how different types of service provision including long-stay hospitals (McCarthy 1993) and community-based group homes (McCarthy and Thompson 1996) contributed to the sexual abuse of women with learning disabilities; explorations of sexual abuse perpetrated by men with learning disabilities (Thompson and Brown 1997); and practice guidance for front line services on how to identify and respond to abuse (Churchill, Craft and Holding 1993; Craft and Churchill 1997). Whilst some work with a focus on sex education continued to be published (McCarthy and Thompson 1993; 1997), including studies which recognised the sexual needs of people with profound and multiple learning disabilities (Downs and Craft 1996), at this time the research focus was predominantly on the sexual vulnerabilities of people with learning disabilities. In the UK, fear of sexual abuse was reinforced by media coverage of the Longcare Inquiry, where failure by local authorities to adequately monitor people placed in residential homes enabled ongoing sexual abuse of residents to continue undetected (Buckinghamshire County Council 1998; Pring 2003). Part of the reason for this apparently sudden association between sex and danger was, again, a reflection of changing social factors. Part of this can be linked to the rapidly growing public awareness of HIV/AIDS (see McCarthy and Thompson 1994, for an overview of a safer sex project for people with learning disabilities). But, more widely, this period saw the growth of what has been termed a 'culture of fear' in which abuse (and sexual abuse in particular) has been foregrounded, dangers of all kind are emphasised and the world is constantly presented as a risky and unfriendly environment (Furedi 1997).

Policy regarding good practice

For people with learning disabilities, the turn of the twenty-first century saw a breakthrough in the recognition by policy makers of the importance of the self-advocacy movement, with the *Valuing People* White Paper (DH 2001) being the

---

1   See www.anncrafttrust.org.

first national policy document to have actively involved service users in its design and implementation. The White Paper set out a blueprint for the 100 per cent closure of segregated institutions and the improvement of existing community-based services through a focus on the rights of people with learning disabilities to be independent, make choices and be socially included. The White Paper, moreover, explicitly recognised that 'good services will help people with learning disabilities develop opportunities to form relationships, including ones of a physical and sexual nature' (p.81). Since then, there does appear to be some evidence of an increasing acceptance by paid support workers of the right to sexual expression of adults with learning disabilities, though this was not found to be reflected in the attitudes expressed by family care givers (Evans *et al.* 2009); and the same research project also found evidence to suggest that people with learning disabilities were themselves increasingly aware of their sexual rights (Healy *et al.* 2009). However, a full translation of the *Valuing People* principles into practice remains problematic, and other studies have shown that when it comes to putting principles into practice some learning disability service providers remain highly risk averse in relation to sex and sexuality (Hollomotz 2011).

Changing views

It is undoubtedly the case that the last 50 years have been witness to a tremendous change in attitudes towards sex and sexuality and these changes are reflected in the lives of people with learning disabilities. Homosexuality, which half a century ago was outlawed, is no longer a matter of concern to the majority of the population (National Centre for Social Research 2010) and this more relaxed and open attitude towards sexuality is steadily but surely leading to a recognition that people with learning disabilities who are lesbian, gay or bisexual should be equally free to express their sexuality (Abbott and Howarth 2005). The Sexual Offences Act 2003 both removed some of the legal barriers to sex which previously existed for people with learning disabilities and sought to provide a degree of protection for the vulnerable by changing the definition of consent to include a requirement that anyone consenting to sexual activity must have the 'freedom and capacity to make that choice'.

Summary

Young people with learning disabilities growing up today can expect to receive sex and relationships education as a core element of their school curriculum. Adults with learning disabilities are increasingly likely to live in ordinary houses on ordinary streets and be freer to associate with whom they choose. With this greater sexual freedom, however, has also come a much greater awareness of the darker elements of human sexual behaviour and it is now understood that some adults with learning disabilities may be particularly vulnerable to sexual abuse. There is a pressing need to ensure that we succeed in promoting sexualities, providing opportunity for people to form, develop and continue consenting relationships, and providing protection from abuse.

References

Abbott, D. and Howarth, J. (2005) *Secret Loves, Hidden Lives? Exploring Issues for People with Learning Difficulties Who are Gay, Lesbian or Bisexual.* Bristol: Policy Press.

Brown, H., Hunt, N. and Stein, J. (1994) '"Alarming but very necessary": working with staff groups around the sexual abuse of adults with learning disabilities'. *Journal of Intellectual Disability Research 38,* 4, 393–412.

Brown, H., Stein, J. and Turk, V. (1995) 'The sexual abuse of adults with learning disabilities: Report of a second two-year incidence survey.' *Mental Handicap Research 8,* 1, 3–24.

Brown, H. and Turk, V. (1992) 'Defining sexual abuse as it affects adults with learning disabilities.' *Journal of the British Institute of Mental Handicap 20,* 2, 44–55.

Buckinghamshire County Council (1998) *Independent Longcare Inquiry.* Aylesbury: Buckinghamshire County Council.

Campbell, B. (1988) *Unofficial Secrets: Child Abuse – The Cleveland Case.* London: Virago Press.

Carmody, M. (1991) 'Invisible victims: Sexual assault of people with an intellectual disability.' *Journal of Intellectual & Developmental Disability 17,* 2, 229–236.

Churchill, J., Craft, A. and Holding, A. (1993) *It Could Never Happen Here.* Chesterfield/Nottingham: ARC/NAPSAC.

Craft, A. (1987) *Mental Handicap and Sexuality: Issues and Perspectives.* London: Costello.

Craft, A. and Churchill, J. (1997) *There are No Easy Answers.* Chesterfield/Nottingham: ARC/NAPSAC.

Craft, M. and Craft, A. (1978) *Sex and the Mentally Handicapped.* London: Routledge & Kegan Paul.

Craft, M. and Craft, A. (1979) *Handicapped Married Couples: A Welsh Study of Couples Handicapped from Birth by Mental, Physical or Personality Disorder.* London: Routledge & Kegan Paul.

DH (Department of Health) (2001) *Valuing People: A New Strategy for Learning Disability for the 21st Century.* London: Department of Health.

Downs, C. and Craft, A. (1996) 'Sexuality and profound and multiple impairment.' *Tizard Learning Disability Review 1,* 4, 17–22.

Evans, D., McGuire, B., Healy, E. and Carley, S. (2009) 'Sexuality and personal relationships for people with an intellectual disability. Part II: staff and family carer perspectives.' *Journal of Intellectual Disability Research 53,* 11, 913–921.

Furedi, F. (1997) *Culture of Fear: Risk-taking and the Morality of Low Expectation.* London: Continuum.

Healy, E., McGuire, B., Evans, D. and Carley, S. (2009) 'Sexuality and personal relationships for people with an intellectual disability. Part I: service-user perspectives.' *Journal of Intellectual Disability Research 53,* 11, 905–912.

HMSO (1971) 'Better Services for the Mentally Handicapped' (Cmnd 4683). London: HMSO.

Hollomotz, A. (2011) *Learning Difficulties and Sexual Vulnerability: A Social Approach*. London: Jessica Kingsley Publishers.

McCarthy, M. (1993) 'Sexual Experiences of women with learning difficulties in long-stay hospitals.' *Sexuality & Disability 11*, 4, 277–286.

McCarthy, M. and Thompson, D. (1993) *Sex and the 3 Rs. Rights, Responsibilities and Risks: A Sex Education Package for Working with People with Learning Disabilities*. Hove: Pavilion Publishing.

McCarthy, M. and Thompson, D. (1994) 'HIV/AIDS and Safer Sex Work with People with Learning Disabilities.' In A. Craft (ed.) *Practice Issues in Sexuality and Learning Disability*. London: Routledge.

McCarthy, M. and Thompson, D. (1996) 'Sexual abuse by design: An examination of the issues in learning disability services.' *Disability and Society 11*, 2, 205–218.

McCarthy, M. and Thompson, D. (1997) 'A prevalence study of sexual abuse of adults with intellectual disabilities referred for sex education.' *Journal of Applied Research in Intellectual Disabilities 10*, 2, 105–124.

National Centre for Social Research (2010) *British Social Attitudes 26th Report*. London: NatCen.

Priestley, M. (2003) *Disability: A Life Course Approach*. Cambridge: UK Polity Press.

Pring, J. (2003) *Silent Victims: The Longcare Scandal and Britain's Continuing Failure to Protect Society's Most Vulnerable*. London: Gibson Square Books.

Rolph, S., Atkinson, D., Nind, M., Welshman, J. *et al.* (eds) (2005) *Witnesses to Change: Families, Learning Difficulties and History*. Kidderminster: BILD.

Roulstone, A. and Prideaux, S. (2012) *Understanding Disability Policy*. Bristol: Policy Press.

Shakespeare, T. (2006) *Disability Rights and Wrongs*. London: Routledge.

Sobsey, D. and Doe, T. (1991) 'Patterns of sexual abuse and assault.' *Journal of Sexuality and Disability 9*, 3, 243–259.

Sobsey, D. and Mansell, S. (1990) 'The prevention of sexual abuse of people with developmental disabilities.' *Developmental Disabilities Bulletin 18*, 2, 51–66.

Thompson, D. and Brown, H. (1997) 'Men with intellectual disabilities who sexually abuse: A review of the literature.' *Journal of Applied Research in Intellectual Disability 10*, 2, 140–158.

CHAPTER 13

'FAR MORE PEOPLE WERE ABLE TO HAVE SEX LIVES'

Sexual Relationships and Reproductive Control
in Learning Disability Institutions

Jan Walmsley, Carol Hamilton, Nigel Ingham and Steve Mee with Sharon Harrison

Overview

- This chapter asks if it was easier for people with learning disabilities to enjoy sex in the old institutions than it is now, when people are living in the community.

- Sharon Harrison, a woman with learning disabilities who used to live in an institution, read the chapter and put forward her own views.

- Research today shows that people are still very concerned about women with disabilities becoming pregnant and having children.

- Lots of women with learning disabilities today are on long-term contraception, which is not good for their health.

- If they do have children, many are taken away.

- Oral histories show that people with learning disabilities did manage to have sex in the past in the institutions.

- Sometimes this was encouraged by staff because people were easier to manage.

- Different staff had different attitudes. Some would encourage people to have sex; others would try to stop it.

> - Even then, the main issue was to prevent women from having babies.
>
> - Due to this, contraception and sterilisation for women was often used.
>
> - Overall it may have been easier for people with learning disabilities to have sex in the past than it is now.

The writing process

This chapter was written by authors who are also academics. After the chapter was completed, Sharon Harrison was asked to read over it with her supporter, Tim Keilty. He recorded her comments.

Sharon's words, reflecting on her days of institutional living, form an introduction to the chapter. These views and past experiences corroborate much of the discussion in the rest of the chapter gained through the oral histories of staff working in the institutions. The term 'people with learning disabilities' is preferred by the authors. This follows the practice of policy makers in the UK.

Introduction

WITH SHARON HARRISON

We asked Sharon Harrison, former resident of Prudhoe Hospital, Northumberland, to comment on this chapter. Sharon agreed that it was not difficult to have sex and that it was not always a good thing. This is what she had to say:

- *'Mary and June used to have sex in the coal house – they used to come out black as the ace of spades.'*

- *'There was different people at it.'*

- *'If you were boyfriend and girlfriend it was easy.'*

- *'Ash Villa was girls only but we used to go to the lads' end (of the hospital) in the bushes and have it there.'*

- *'There was a woman in another hospital who I heard would do it for a Mars Bar.'*

- *'Some staff enticed people – encouraged them to do it.'*

- *'Sex wasn't always a good thing in the hospital – sometimes people were raped.'*

- *'Some people who had bad experiences – it put them off sex for good, even on the outside.'*

- *'Like me, never again – put me off.'*

Thanks to Tim Keilty for recording Sharon's views.

Introduction

This chapter draws on unpublished documentary material and oral history data from now closed English institutions to discuss sex, sexual relationships and contraception in the era of institutional care. It poses the question – was it easier for people with learning disabilities to enjoy sex in institutions than it is now, when most people live 'in the community'?

It is widely known that learning disability institutions were set up, in part, to inhibit people with learning disabilities from becoming parents. Things are different now – aren't they? On paper it seems that they are. The update to the English *Valuing People* White Paper (DH 2001), *Valuing People Now* (2009), promised that: 'People with learning disabilities have the choice to have relationships, become parents and continue to be parents, and are supported to do so' (DH 2009, p.92).

The 2005 Mental Capacity Act (England and Wales) introduced a legal framework in which capacity is presumed, with assistance provided to ensure, as far as is reasonably possible, that people make decisions for themselves (Mandelstam 2009). Things should certainly be improving. However, we know that sexual relationships, setting up families and having children remain problematic in the lives of people with learning disabilities. We believe that the motive of deterring people from having children remains central when managing sexual relationships and contraception.

First, take for instance, the use of contraception by women. A small qualitative survey with women with learning disabilities conducted by Michelle McCarthy (2009) indicated that the women she spoke to typically had 'just in case' contraception; even if they were not in a relationship they started contraceptive use earlier and continued it later than other women, and they had little agency in the decision to use contraception in the first place, which type to use, and for how long.

Second, a web-based survey undertaken by the Open University in 2012 which elicited 90 responses lent some support to McCarthy's findings. Contraception was seen to be necessary in just under one-third of cases because the woman was sexually active. Other reasons cited by more than 15 per cent of respondents were an expectation that the woman would become sexually active; fear of pregnancy; and the management of menstruation. In only 15 per cent of cases did women initiate the discussion about taking contraception. More commonly it was a parent, a worker or a GP (Earle *et al.* 2012).

These two research studies indicate that although *Valuing People Now* (DH 2009) says people should be able to enjoy relationships and to have children, actually this is discouraged, and that in fact women are taking contraception to prevent this, 'just in case' they have sex.

We also know that although more women may have children, many will lose those children to the care system (Tarleton, Ward and Howarth 2006).

The third issue is that of sexual abuse. Brown and Turk put this on the agenda in the early 1990s. Hollomotz's more recent research (2011) shows that it remains an issue for women with learning disabilities (and some men). Scandals such as that in the Longcare homes in Buckinghamshire (Pring 2005) remind us what can happen behind closed doors.

These are just three of the issues faced by people with learning disabilities today when seeking to exercise the right promised in *Valuing People Now* (DH 2009) that they have the choice to become parents, and be supported to do so.

We now go on to discuss the possibility that, although policy may seem far more enlightened today regarding people with learning disabilities having sexual relationships (DH 2009), in practice, some people were able to have sex in institutions as long as this did not result in pregnancy. It draws on unpublished material, both documentary and oral history, to shed light on the management of sexual relationships and reproduction in the institutional era.

The historical context

It is almost a truism that learning disability institutional care was set up to deter people then known as 'mental defectives' from having children. The Mental Deficiency Act 1913 charged local authorities with setting up colonies where men and women would be segregated from one another. An explicit motive was to deter them from having babies which, it was believed, would mean that those of low intelligence would eventually outnumber more intelligent members of the population (Jackson 2000). Cox (1996) and Walmsley (2000) have argued that young women were disproportionately targeted for institutional care in the early years of the Act's operation, and that even those who remained outside institutions had their sexual behaviour policed through close supervision of the families with whom they lived (Walmsley 1997; Walmsley and Rolph 2002), or places where they worked (Rolph 2000).

The regime associated with the 1913 Act remained substantially in force throughout much of the twentieth century. Institutional populations peaked in 1969 (Walmsley 2005) by which time the prohibitions on mixing the sexes had been relaxed and mixed wards were fairly common.

Sex in institutions: the literature

Until 1983 very few formal studies examining the role of the support worker in relation to issues of sexuality and intellectually disabled people were undertaken.

Such findings as were published document fostering of sexual ignorance (Lutzer 1983). An absence of privacy, work overload experienced by staff, care systems based on discipline and authority, over-protection of residents and extremely restrictive social practices influenced residents' experiences (Trudel and Desjardins 1992).

Research studies hint that sexual activity was a feature of the lives of those who lived in institutions. In general, sexualised behaviours acted out in private were deemed more acceptable than those exhibited in public. Unacceptable behaviours could include 'public masturbation, public long kissing and public homosexual behaviours' (Kempton and Kahn 1991, pp.96–97). The consequences of private sexualised behaviour being discovered were inconsistent, sometimes resulting in very unpleasant outcomes for those concerned. In some mixed institutions heterosexual behaviour was punished, at times through the use of solitary confinement and shaven heads (McCarthy 1999).

In some single-gender institutions workers were found to focus on repressing and punishing homosexual behaviour until female residents were included 'whereupon it switched to repressing any expression of heterosexuality' (Gordon 1979, cited in Szollos and McCabe 1995, p.251).

Reports vary greatly in respect of how sexualised behaviours were addressed by managers and administrators. However, it was workers who were instrumental in how these behaviours were dealt with in practice (Saunders 1979). One study reported that 91 per cent of the discoveries were made by workers, who often reacted either in anger or in denial of what they had found (Trudel and Desjardins 1992). This study also revealed that the attitudes held by workers to sexualised behaviours were largely negative. Yet within this generalised discomfort a wide range of attitudes could be found. Some workers denied that learning disabled people had a sexual life, others adopted an attitude that sexual behaviour of any kind was inappropriate, while others were tolerant of limited expression of sexuality such as holding hands and kissing (Murray and Minnes 1994).

Other research studies undertaken reveal that the sexuality support aspect of their work was not discomforting to all workers. Some observations of worker/ resident interactions show that some hospital settings were highly permissive, with workers neither encouraging nor discouraging any form of sexualised behaviour to any great extent (Felce 1998). In addition, some workers reported being conscious of the residents' sexual needs (Trudel and Desjardins 1992). Other workers reported counselling those they supported about sexuality issues and expressed significant interest in assisting them with their sexual well-being (Saunders 1979). Yet other reports suggest that workers were fired for not adhering to the traditions of conservatism in this area they were supposed to maintain (Gordon, cited in Sweyn-Harvey 1984).

In addition to this information gleaned from academic studies, we know from the reminiscences of former residents that people managed to have sexual relationships (Potts and Fido 1991, Chapter 8), and we also know that despite precautions a few had babies (Potts and Fido 1991, p.113).

A source of information that has to date been little tapped in regard to sexual relationships in institutions is former staff. The chapter's authors have accessed oral history testimony from former psychiatrists, a psychologist and nurses who worked in three different institutions from the late 1960s, and use these to shed light on the way sex was managed. All names have been changed.

'Less sex went on after we'd given guidelines than before…'

One theme that emerged in the testimonies of former institutional staff was that staff had considerable freedom to allow sexual relationships until guidelines began to be issued by hospital management in the 1980s. Most staff apparently turned a blind eye, regarding what went on in dormitories as the residents' business, but one or two recognised people's sexual needs, and took steps to make sure they were met. This story was related by Colin, a former nurse in a north of England hospital.

> Now the sister on B1, looking back she was well out of time, she was nearing retirement, 'It's just a bunch of kids we've got. We treat them like a bunch of kids.' They were 18, 19 at the time. One of the young women, D, had no speech, but somehow she found E (the guy) and she used to go and grab him and they'd go off into one of the bedrooms, and sister was very strict about it. She'd say 'Leave them alone. Nobody must go in.' We were happy that there was no abuse because if she didn't like him she would have bit him until her teeth met. And he used to headbutt so if he didn't like it he would have headbutted. Sister said, 'There's no question of anybody exploiting anybody. They're both up for this.'

> D was usually the motivator, she would go and grab him. And we never did know what went on except some shouts would come from the room! And they found each other. And E used to headbutt through partition walls and smash things. When he got his sex life sorted he used to sit around and watch TV and have a smile on his face; he was happy, the happiest I ever saw him.

Sadly D died aged 20, and E died not long after, after headbutting a wall.

Reflecting upon this, Colin commented that a greater awareness of rights had, paradoxically, resulted in more control rather than less:

> When we really started to get to grips with law we realised that that sex was illegal, because D's level of ld [learning disability], she couldn't give consent to sex. Now as far as we were concerned, she could. But consent by the modern and airy fairy

controlling guidelines are that you have to understand the implications of your actions. So to consent to sex you have to understand normal, as we would classify them, sexual relationships, and that to understand what exploitation is. Technically E would have been guilty of rape.

D and E now wouldn't stand an earthly in community services of having a sex life.

Similar freedom enabled staff in the same hospital to help men who wanted to masturbate but did not know how. The same sister on Ward B1 was responsible for this incident:

And of the guys F used to get very frustrated trying to masturbate. Sister said, 'He's going up to Telford Upper this weekend. Will you take him up for his tea?' I said, 'Oh, he's moving?' She said, 'No. He's spending a weekend among the wankers; he'll come back sorted.' And when he came back he had learnt to masturbate. And so it was a deliberate policy – he can't masturbate, he can't climax so he'll go and learn, somebody's going to masturbate him on there at some point. And it worked, he came back and it was like he'd found this gift.

It is hard to imagine such a solution being advocated in present day services. Whether it was abusive behaviour or, as Colin put it, a 'gift', is a troubling point.

Staff informants indicate that despite its illegality pre-1966, homosexual activity was apparently tacitly condoned in institutions more readily than heterosexual activity (Potts and Fido 1991, p.114). Colin again:

There was a lot of homosexual sex went on – a lot, a hell of a lot. I got very close to another client Peter and I know he had a very active sexual life, quite often he needed help from us because he had a sore anus – I don't know what he did, he wasn't able to tell us but he used to get lacerations on his penis. I don't know what that was and he had bandage and cream and he'd pick at it… But he obviously had a very active life.

Initially, when staff began to draw up sexuality guidelines, these envisaged offering more opportunities for sexual expression. However, when it went to the Board for approval, the tone was changed. Colin recalled:

When we set the sexuality policy up they said, 'You don't allow this sort of thing to go on, do you? Sex is about marriage.' So we ended up limiting people in effect. That was a consequence. And I wish we'd never started doing it, because less sex went on after we'd given guidelines than before.

It is a paradox that within the confines of closed institutions, staff appeared to be able to exercise judgement about facilitating sexual relationships, far more so than staff working in modern services, despite apparent increases in respect for rights. This had both positive and negative implications.

Child-bearing and contraception

Whilst permitting sex, or turning a blind eye to it, staff also had to be mindful of the possibility of pregnancy. If having sex was OK (in the eyes of some staff) child-bearing was to be avoided at all costs. Said one informant, Mike, former nurse in another institution from the 1960s onwards: 'There was always this fear of sexual relationships and what would happen if someone was pregnant. Well what would happen is that there would have been a termination.' The reason why pregnancy was regarded as such a disaster is illustrated by a case taken from the records of a colony in the south Midlands. Nellie F was resident in the hospital when in 1945, aged 24, she fell pregnant. The father, Victor, it transpired, had entered the ward from the subway connecting to the boiler house. Nellie had previously gone to the woods with him, and he had absconded from the hospital while she was on leave at home, and visited her there, indicating that this was not a one-off encounter.

Nellie's parents were indignant. Her father wrote:

> I am more than amazed that my daughter has got into trouble while in the care of the colony. The only thing to do in this case is to let them marry and I give my consent to this, as the young man in question is capable of earning his own living. (letter dated 7/8/1945)

Unfortunately for Victor, the Hospital Board disagreed. He was to be sent to Rampton 'for the honour of our colony'. The Medical Superintendent, in making this recommendation to his Board, wrote: 'It is a great pity as he is a very useful man at the colony, but his morals have always been very bad. In my opinion the girl is just as bad.' The outcome may have been better for Nellie, despite her morals. Thanks to the indignation of her family, who threatened to involve their MP, the Board decided that she should be allowed out on licence to work if suitable employment could be found for her. The child was taken in by Nellie's parents. Unfortunately the record ends at this point – whether Nellie did leave is not known.

The case is enough to illustrate the seriousness with which institutions took pregnancy, as opposed to sexual relationships. Before there was reliable contraception, people were kept apart as far as possible. But the advent of the contraceptive pill in the 1960s may have enabled things to be more relaxed.

Management of contraception

It may be that surveillance relaxed in the later twentieth century as the possibilities offered by chemical contraception extended protection. Certainly the staff whose testimony informs this paper actively managed contraception.

Colin told this story:

> There were two men on Henry Ward who had girlfriends and one [of the couples] was a pair on the ward and one was a woman from outside. And I know that TH had a conversation with the sister on that area, to ensure that both the women had contraception. They weren't giving consent to taking this medication. And when the girlfriends used to come and visit them on Henry [ward], he would say they shouldn't be disturbed, they should be left alone.

It was explained that many women were on the pill, and that, like the women Colin mentioned, had not given fully informed consent: 'A lot of the "at risk" ladies were on the pill and probably didn't realise that they were.'

Mike also described more drastic measures to prevent childbirth in the institution where he spent his career:

> A lot of people, if they were considered or deemed to be at risk of pregnancy, there were two options, often one of them was quite severe, and that was fallopian tube ligation, so they would be sent to hospital to have their fallopian tubes tied, or oral contraception.

Mike's frankness is surprising. At no point was it legally sanctioned to conduct what amounted to sterilisation without consent in England. Yet he discusses it as if it is unremarkable, and the hospital was complicit.

Mike also admitted that if babies did materialise, they would be aborted: 'I do remember pregnancies and every one that I remember ended with a termination. That was in the 1960s and 70s.'

As previous literature indicates, not all staff were in favour of liberal attitudes to sexual activity. A social worker from Colin's hospital recalled how the medical consultant rather clumsily advocated abstention:

> We knew some of them had a normal sex life; we needed contraception in the hospital. And they need to be on the pill. And we had meetings (about one client)… and we said, 'She loves nothing more than a jam bread in one hand and having it off in the bushes with one of the men, She's quite willing and she loves it. There's nothing wrong with it.' But then the consultant told her, 'You must not show men your knickers'. That was the extent he thought about prevention. And the next thing is she goes in her room and takes her knickers off, and she goes without knickers.

This corroborates the literature which indicates inconsistency in attitudes to sexual activity at different levels in the workforce. The oral evidence suggests that workers managed these difficult issues, and that managers and or medical staff had less immediate impact.

Managing menstruation

There is some evidence that contraceptives were used to help manage menstruation in long-stay hospitals. A psychiatrist who had worked in hospitals in south west England recalled:

> The consultant who had worked there – who I don't think I ever met – his reputation was that he was kindly but he had this feeling I think that they shouldn't ever be allowed to grow up so all the women who came had been put on long-term progesterone to stop them menstruating. It wasn't in the context of expecting they might get pregnant, it was really partly because they thought they were doing them a service because they wouldn't have to bother with periods, but it was almost as if they didn't want to face what was almost a hidden thing that these were adults. That would be up until the late 1960s, early seventies. By no means did everyone do this, but this particular doctor did.

Similar attitudes persist today. Michelle McCarthy found that, in the early 2000s, 6 of the 23 women she interviewed were taking contraceptives to regulate their periods (2009); recent research in the Netherlands had a similar finding (van Schrojenstein Lantman-de Valk *et al.* 2011).

Consent, abuse and exploitation

The testimonies we have of sexual relationships and contraception in institutions do not offer much detail of the decision-making process, other than staff exercising judgement as to whether the relationship was voluntarily entered into, and the practicalities of preventing pregnancy.

Undoubtedly, there was also abuse and exploitation. Colin acknowledged this in relation to male/female relationships:

> But a lot of sex went on, a lot of it was exploitative, I realise that, and there wasn't proper protection and it was usually the women of course who almost in every case, M's crowd…a lot of them had women in tow but they would be less able women in every case, led round by the hand. That was one of the things for people; I don't suspect it was the good old days.

In common sex in institutions, abuse has also been little researched.

Summary

We have highlighted some of the barriers to people with learning disabilities enjoying the rights to relationships and children promised them in *Valuing People Now* (DH 2009) and other documents such as the UN Convention (2006). In practice, we have suggested that the priority is to prevent women having children, just as it was in the twentieth century, by widespread use of contraception, and by removal of babies or children born to women with learning disabilities.

We have used testimony from staff who worked in long-stay institutions to suggest that maybe people had as much freedom to enjoy sex as people now living in the community – as long as they did not have babies. We are not suggesting that all was rosy in institutions – undoubtedly, as Sharon points out, abuse was rife – but the evidence we have gathered reinforces the scant academic literature, which suggests that staff had the latitude to allow people to take risks around sex, if they so chose. The practices described here raise questions about what the role of staff could and should be in relation to facilitating and supporting people's sexual needs and relationships.

References

Atkinson, D. (1997) 'Learning from Local History: Evidence from Somerset.' In D. Atkinson, M. Jackson and J. Walmsley (eds) *Forgotten Lives: Exploring the History of Learning Disability.* Kidderminster: BILD.

Cox, P. (1996) 'Girls, Deficiency and Delinquency.' In D. Wright and A. Digby (eds) *From Idiocy to Mental Deficiency.* London: Routledge.

DH (Department of Health) (2001) *Valuing People: A New Strategy for Learning Disability for the 21st Century.* London: Department of Health.

DH (Department of Health) (2009) *Valuing People Now: A New Three-year Strategy for People with Learning Disabilities.* London: The Stationery Office.

Earle, S., Tilley, E. and Walmsley, J. (2012) 'Who makes crucial decisions on reproduction and contraception?' *Learning Disability Practice 15,* 8, 34–35.

Felce, D. (1998) 'The determinants of staff and resident activity in residential services for people with severe intellectual disability: moving beyond size, building design, location and number of staff.' *Journal of Intellectual & Developmental Disabilities 2,* 2, 103–119.

Hollomotz, A. (2011) *Learning Difficulties and Sexual Vulnerability: A Social Approach.* London: Jessica Kingsley Publishers.

Jackson, M. (2000) *The Borderland of Imbecility: Medicine, Society and the Fabrication of the Feeble Mind in late Victorian and Edwardian England.* Manchester: Manchester University Press.

Kempton, W. and Kahn, E. (1991) 'Sexuality and people with an intellectual disability: An historical perspective.' *Sexuality and Disability 9,* 2, 99–111.

Lutzer, V. (1983) 'Modification of inappropriate sexual behaviour in a mildly mentally retarded male.' *Sexuality and Disability 6,* 3, 176–182.

Mandelstam, M. 2009 *Safeguarding Vulnerable Adults and the Law.* London: Jessica Kingsley Publishers.

McCarthy, M. (1999) *Sexuality and Women with Learning Disabilities*. London: Jessica Kingsley Publishers.

McCarthy, M. (2009) '"I have the jab so I can't be blamed for getting pregnant": Contraception and women with learning disabilities.' *Women's Studies International Forum 32*, 198–208.

Murray, J. and Minnes, P. (1994) 'Staff attitudes towards the sexuality of persons with intellectual disability.' *Australian and New Zealand Journal of Developmental Disabilities 19*, 1, 45–52.

Potts, M. and Fido, R. (1991) *A Fit Person to be Removed*. Plymouth: Northcote House.

Pring, J. (2005) 'Why it took so long to expose the abusing regime at Longcare.' *The Journal of Adult Protection, Volume 7, Issue 2, 15–23*. Available at http://findarticles.com/p/articles/mi_qa4124/is_200506/ai_n14801693/pg_6/?tag=content;col1, accessed on 7 July 2011.

Rolph, S. (2000b) The History of Community Care for People with Learning Difficulties in Norfolk 1930-1980: The role of two hostels. Unpublished PhD thesis. Milton Keynes: Open University.

Saunders, E. (1979) 'Staff members' attitudes towards the sexual behaviour of mentally retarded residents.' *American Journal of Mental Deficiency 84*, 2, 206–208.

Sweyn-Harvey, R. (1984) 'Care staff attitudes to the sexuality of mentally handicapped hospital residents.' *Mental Handicap 12*, 3, 28–29.

Szollos, A. and McCabe, M. (1995) 'The sexuality of people with mild intellectual disability: Perceptions of clients and care givers.' *Australian and New Zealand Journal of Developmental Disabilities 20*, 3, 205–222.

Tarleton, B., Ward, L. and Howarth, J. (2006) *Finding the Right Support? A Review of Issues and Positive Practice to Support Parents with Learning Disabilities and their Children*. London: Baring Foundation.

Trudel, G. and Desjardins, G. (1992) 'Staff reactions towards the sexual behaviours of people living in institutional settings.' *Sexuality and Disability 10*, 3, 173–188.

United Nations Convention on the Rights of People with Disabilities 2006. Available at www.un.org/disabilities/default.asp?navid=15&pid=150, accessed on 3 August 2014.

United Nations (2006) Convention on the Rights of Persons with Disabilities. New York: United Nations.

van Schrojenstein Lantman-de Valk, H.M.J., Rooks, F. and Maaskant, M.A. (2011) 'The use of contraception by women with intellectual disabilities.' *Journal of Intellectual Disability Research 55*, 4, 434–440.

Walmsley, J. (1997) 'Uncovering Community Care: Evidence in a County Record Office.' In D. Atkinson, M. Jackson and J. Walmsley (eds) *Forgotten Lives: Exploring the History of Learning Disability*. Kidderminster: BILD.

Walmsley, J. (2000) 'Women and the Mental Deficiency Act of 1913.' *British Journal of Learning Disabilities 28*, 65–70.

Walmsley, J. (2005) Institutionalization: a Historical Perspective, in: K. Johnson and R. Traustadottir (Eds.) *Deinstitutionalization and People with Intellectual Disabilities*. London: Jessica Kingsley Publishers.

Walmsley J and Rolph S (2002) 'The Development of Community Care for People with Learning Difficulties 1913–1946.' *Critical Social Policy 21*, 1, 59–80.

CHAPTER 14

'THIS IS MY TIME, MY LIFE, THE WAY I AM'

Experiences of Being Transgendered in a Rural Setting

Alice

Overview

- This chapter tells the story of Andrew.

- As he grew up he realised he was not happy the way things were and wished to be a woman.

- He started to buy women's jewellery and clothes but it got him into trouble with his family.

- He was also bullied at school.

- He was abused in his community and went to live somewhere else.

- He changed his name to Alice and had to leave his past behind to become who s/he wanted to be.

- There have been many difficulties along the way.

- Alice likes to write and thinks she can raise awareness of the experience of being transgendered.

The writing process

Alice has written many stories and poems. Some of her articles have been worked together here to provide a life course presentation of her experiences. Some small amounts of editing have taken place but have been checked by her as a true representation.

Introduction

My name is Alice and I'm from a rural county in England. I consider myself female. I have what is called a 'gender identity disorder', a label I was given when I went to the gender clinic. I'm a male to female trans-woman.

I have been living as a woman since 2005, but have had some setbacks over the years. This is because I have had so much hassle for switching gender. It was totally draining on my mind, body and soul; I was ill and it took me a while to resume living as a woman again. However, in the process, I came across a skill that I have. I can write about what has happened to me and I hope it will bring awareness.

My interests are walking, socialising, being a pen-pal, going to charity shops for female clothes shopping, meeting my friends for coffee, going to the cinema and helping people if I can. I like perfume, make-up, shoes and handbags, anything that's feminine, as I consider myself female.

My younger days

I was born male but growing up was not so good. I had all the creature comforts at home; I wasn't short of food or clothes within reason. When I went to school I was bullied and when I went home I was being controlled and manipulated. One of my relatives was shaping me up for their view of who I should become. Any traits or direction that I was shaping myself into were being wiped out. I didn't know until later in life how much damage this caused, but I do believe that if my relative hadn't tried to mentally control me, then things may have turned out differently. It's no guarantee though that I would not have become transgendered or a cross-dresser.

I started to feel different – that I didn't fit into the male way of things. I didn't like football or rugby, I wasn't into sporty things; it just didn't click with me. I knew something wasn't right, but I was told all teenagers go through a phase of not feeling right with themselves.

When I was 16–17 years of age I was buying ladies' watches as gifts, but actually I was buying them for me. When I was told male watches were for males and female watches were for females, then I went and gave the watches away. But still I was being drawn to female items, rather than being drawn to male ones. By the age of 17 to 19, I was buying one female watch and one male watch, to make up for the other.

Cross-dressing

I found each trauma that I experienced drove me closer to liking feminine things. When I was between 19 and 21 years of age, I started to buy dresses, a few handbags, some black patent court shoes, some make-up. It wasn't too elaborate, but when I was told that it was wrong, I felt lost. I felt that I wasn't in the right body, I wasn't myself. In some ways I felt I was living my life for other people. It eventually became a tug of war: a battle that was going on within myself. I liked female things, but other people didn't like me liking female things, they wanted me liking male things. That didn't work for me, although at this stage I didn't realise fully the impact of me becoming a cross-dresser.

I have cross-dressed since my late teens. I felt more at ease wearing female clothes than male clothes. As I got older, and went out with friends or out for a meal with a group of people, I felt envious of women in their outfits, handbags and accessories. It was killing me inside that I was no longer content in living as a male in female clothes. The macho way of males – I didn't feel like I fitted in that world anymore!

I had to sort out what I wanted in contrast to what other people wanted.

I wore gold dressy watches in public, as it was the best way of wearing female attire. I bought elderly women's handbags as I could put my things in there with easy access and carry my handbag in a carrier bag. But when I was seen with a handbag, it was noticed more because it was too old a style of handbag for me.

With each following trauma I started to cross-dress more often. A relative found out by finding my first handbag that I bought. They had me see the psychologist before you could say 'handbag'! The relative didn't have any understanding of how I was thinking or feeling. They were far more concerned about what their friends thought about me and to be honest I didn't really care what they thought; it was me going through this experience not them.

When I was younger, this relative dictated a lot of what I wore. It lessened as I got older but once when I went on holiday they had picked out what I should wear without consulting me. It was about them doing what they wanted for me, so I didn't have a choice of what I wanted to wear and it felt to me that I was being controlled by them.

That played a part in me losing any happiness and liking of being male. When someone takes 90 per cent of what you have and changes or alters it to suit themselves, rather than you doing it yourself, it feels like your rights are being taken away.

I allowed my relative to do this because I was weak, but I didn't realise how much they had trampled over my thoughts and ideas. I had been tarnished by someone else controlling me. I felt degraded, unworthy: as if people had picked around with me and then when they were finished, I was left to find my feet. But I couldn't do this, because I was damaged.

As my feminine side started to increase and take over, then I saw more opportunities to choose the colours, handbags and outfits for me, so that they weren't altered, chosen or picked through by someone else. This was a battle. When my relative disapproved of my female side, they went and took my skirts and tights and disposed of them without my consent. They had forced their thoughts and demands on me and I felt violated (as I had done many times) by them.

Sadly the relationship I had with them was on its way out and in a way, it came at the right time, as I could establish myself as Alice for me. My old male name would be no more as I needed to find a new way for me. If this was going to be as a cross-dresser or a transvestite or living as a woman, then so be it.

I was now living in rented accommodation and my relative wanted me to tell the landlady that I was a cross-dresser. To me this was a way of trying to make me choose to either stop cross-dressing or be kicked out.

Unfortunately for my relative, it didn't work! I was accepted by the woman for my choice of dress, and it worked out well. But at this point I decided to ditch the relative because instead of being the support that they could have been, whatever direction I chose, they were not. So it ended up that I had to find a direction that worked for me rather than them.

The best years of my life

The best years of my life were when I switched from male to female gender. Life for me became so much better, even though it was very tough at the start of the first few years. I wouldn't say the male years of my life were good or exciting, or that I was happy within myself. Thinking back I was just going from day to day not being happy and just living life feeling unhappy within myself. So the best years started when I began living as a woman for what I thought would be two years. It was difficult and I experienced a lot of abuse and hassle. But I loved going out dressed as a woman, wearing make-up, lipstick and having a handbag and wearing jewellery without hiding it in case of people being disapproving.

My experiences of living as a woman

When I started to live as a female, I discovered that society didn't like anyone who was different. Although I was happy and content, it seemed that society didn't like the way *I* wished to be. I was subjected to a lot of mental and verbal abuse as well as being threatened.

I felt that I wasn't doing any harm living as a female but the intensity of living as a woman was severe. When I had a quiet time or place that I went to, there was always someone who would say nasty or cruel things to me. I felt that living as a female was just living how I wished to be, it was better than being dead. I had been so unhappy and miserable for many years in male mode.

When I was male, I didn't have many opportunities or things coming into my life, so I became isolated, but when I was in female clothes, then things picked up and looked brighter in my world!

In the space of nine months of living as a woman, I endured much abuse from the general public. I was stared at, a lot, by men. If I was sitting in peace at a cafe, people would come up to the window or where I was sitting to gloat, mock or comment. They would come over and knock the table I was sitting at. They would always do something to annoy or upset me, then eventually go off to where they were heading. People would also throw rubbish at me, like I was a piece of rubbish. I had people run me off the road. I also had death threats, threats to be burnt out of my home. Some people exposed themselves in front of me, not once but a few times over the years.

At the start, my quiet time for myself soon became very awkward. As the months went by, living as a woman in some areas of my life had become easier, but on the other hand it was affecting me emotionally inside. As the abuse carried on, it started to affect parts of my life and how I was feeling. I started to become anxious and stressed out from the level of continual hassle.

I was seen as a male in drag

I found no matter how much effort I put in to look like a woman, I was just being seen as a male in drag. I didn't get much time where I could actually put living as a female into practice, to learn the mannerisms of women, because most of my time was taken up being subjected to the comments of macho males, doing or saying something awful. Sadly, most of my time was taken up with sorting out issues of that nature. Men were more intimidating towards me, but women were insulting, ignorant and bitchy. Women saw me as an alien.

I felt confident of the way that I was dressed; I felt more comfortable and at ease wearing skirts, tights and high heels. I did my make-up quite well, wore a blouse and carried a handbag. At the start I wore white blouses where my bra could be seen and that seemed to open an opportunity for a lot of vulgar comments from men. It made me feel glad that I wasn't part of the male population if they treated women the way that they treated me. As time went on I got more confident and didn't worry about what people thought any more. But the more effort I tried to put in, the more hassle I got, so it didn't seem to work. I couldn't win either way. I felt it was like a constant battle to keep the public happy instead of myself.

Each day became a journey like climbing up Mount Everest. I put a lot into my appearance, I managed to build up a good friendship and support from a few women who showed me respect and appreciated how much courage I had to do what I was doing, even though it opened me up to a lot of intimidation and hassle.

The more effort I put into to making myself look beautiful, the more society had a go at me. I felt if I had time to be left in peace then perhaps I would have been very much more content in living the dream that I wanted. I was happy living as a woman and in some ways I am envious of women, because they have what I am wishing to have – a female-shaped body and to live as a woman.

There was some support

A lot of people who respected and knew me told me that it was about time I had made this change, because when I was previously a male, they could see that I didn't suit it. They could see it, so it showed me that some people couldn't deny it was part of me. I accept that people who don't know me don't understand, but surely there are a lot of worse things I could do!

There were some real positives from living as a female. I got a lot of support from females, probably a balance of fifty-fifty, so every time I was subjected to abuse from other people I would also have positive comments from female friends showing their support. I got some very nice compliments and comments about my outfits.

When I got compliments from women, it boosted my confidence and made me happy. It's OK for women to wear male-style clothing, nothing is said, because women can get away with it more than the opposite gender doing it in reverse, which I see as wrong. Nothing is said to women for wearing male clothes or not having a handbag. I just don't feel happy or content in male attire or with the male way of things.

Becoming a woman

I felt that I had partly achieved the dream that I wanted, and even though it was short of the two years I have no regrets about fully living as a woman. I didn't have a problem with it, only the people who didn't know me had a problem with it.

I had to live as a woman for two years before I was allowed to get hormone treatment. In 2009 I got a certificate in my new name of Alice, and then I started hormone treatment. I was on hormone treatment for a few years – I still am – which made me feel and look more feminine. I wore make-up and lipstick every day, I always had my handbag with me and I never left the house without my handbag, even to go to the post box!

At this time I also moved away from the town where I was unhappy and started a new life, miles away. This was seen as a negative action by some people, but for me, it was something positive and improving for my life. By 2009 I had written 12 articles that were published in the USA and parts of the UK. With being happy and being my true self, I wrote articles that would help awareness of people who experience gender identity disorder.

Improvements

Each year things were improving and getting better, far from the days when I used to leave my home and carry a carrier bag with my handbag inside, to disguise being seen as a transgendered person in order to avoid abuse. Now I could go out wearing a short-sleeved blouse, trousers, heels and my handbag off my shoulder or carrying my handbag in my hand.

One of the achievements I wanted to reach was to manage to swim in a swimming pool as a female wearing a bikini. I managed to achieve that, even though it was a bit problematic, due to my gender switching from male to female, but in time it will become a bit easier. In 2009 I also wanted to undertake sponsored breast cancer walks as a woman. I did two of these, one of which was over thirteen and a half miles – the 'Moonwalk' in Hyde Park, London.

It is just not easy – something happened

However, things didn't work out too well really. In autumn 2011, I experienced a traumatic situation and suffered a severe ordeal. The place and the situation that I was in wasn't allowing me to recover, that is, not until my recovery of positive action developed, which was many months after the trauma.

As the months went past I was still living in a state of shock. I had started to rebuild my social life and self-esteem, but I also started to suffer from depression. The health services were unable to help me, so I had to work hard to get over the depression which I eventually managed to recover from.

I started to attend a local church that was transgendered acceptant. This is in contrast to my previous visits to other churches where I experienced being 'bible bashed'. I met a friend at the new church, which was a stepping stone to helping me recover.

I met up with the friend a few times during the week; we went shopping and for coffee together, which was good. I then started to find out about places to go to during the evening, and set up counselling for myself and other things to do. During the year I went to watch the Special Olympics, but I didn't feel like taking part in the Olympic Flame procession.

I found an holistic counsellor who started to help me and I kept on with my self-healing. Before I found the counsellor, the self-healing was working slowly. Ten months on from the trauma my self-esteem and self-confidence were starting to bounce back.

The trauma affected my role of living as a female. I had scaled everything down from being hurt, and the pain and lack of self-confidence I felt. When my self-esteem and self-confidence improved, I started to regain my feminine sparkle. With the counselling in place, I then started a plan of action to get back to full power. I was starting to turn a corner but I had a bit of a way to go yet; I had to beat severe tiredness caused by the trauma. Instead of it getting worse, it was improving, but slowly. Once I came out of shock I was able to create a plan of recovery.

When I started exercising again, I started a Chakra morning and evening meditation. In September I went to a transgender conference, and although I was tired and fatigued, it felt really good. I have made good progress. With self-recovery in place I started a spiritual journey to pray for healing; I have filled my home with angel ornaments, as I get a form of comfort from them. With recovery I have started writing new poems, releasing my previous poems and sending them out again to the wider network.

Summary

Eventually I lost nearly a stone and I was back to the weight that I was before I experienced the trauma of 2011. I have started to put smiles on people's faces again and I am inspiring them, as I am back on form. My feminine sparkle is back and I have started to do retail therapy. I enjoy shopping again and have bought some patent shoes and a handbag from Marks and Spencer's. Even though it was a bit expensive I felt I deserved it, so I use it for church and for special occasions.

I recently went to a transgender ceremony, I read out some of my poems on transgendered issues. I feel that I have made good progress; I have managed to beat the fatigue and exercising is helping to improve it as well as eating and feeling better within myself. Angel card readings are helping me to find a positive direction.

'Positive Action'
Positive thinking in our thoughts,
Positive thoughts in changing our attitudes,
Positive action in helping people,
Positive action in putting smiles on people's faces
Love and Light

ALICE

CHAPTER 15

CLARE'S STORY

Gay Women Might Need a Rainbow Fairy Group

Clare Miller, Adam Koronka, Lindy Shufflebotham and Sue Ledger

Overview

- Lots of women with learning disabilities may be lesbian[1] or gay but very little has been written about their experiences.

- Before writing this chapter we talked to people with learning disabilities, families and staff about the experiences of women with learning disabilities who are gay.

- Many people said they did not understand local policy or the law about same-sex relationships.

- In this chapter Clare talks about her experiences as a lesbian woman with learning disabilities.

- Clare includes some art work and a poem to help people understand her feelings and ideas.

- Clare set up the 'Rainbow Fairy Group' so people who were gay or weren't yet sure could meet, talk and go out together.

---

1   The Care Services Commission for Social Care Inspection report *Putting People First: Equality and Diversity Matters* (CSCI 2008) defines 'lesbian' as a term used to 'describe a woman who has an emotional and/or sexual orientation to women. Some lesbian women also use the term 'gay' but some do not like this. In this chapter we use the words 'lesbian' and 'gay' interchangeably.

- Because so many people said they didn't understand the law and policy about same-sex relationships we end our chapter with a section about the law and good practice.

- We argue that better understanding of the experiences of gay women will improve support.

The writing process
CLARE

Work on this chapter started in 2011 after Sue had talked to Lindy about writing a chapter on the experiences of gay women with learning disabilities. Sue explained that she had been talking to people with learning disabilities, families and staff to understand more about the experiences of women who are gay and in receipt of services and support. Many people told Sue that they didn't know any gay women. People with learning disabilities, staff and managers said they didn't know for sure what the law said you could do, or what organisations could do to support gay women.

Lindy saw me in a show put together by people with learning disabilities for a theatre group called 'Moment by Moment'. Two of the performances were by gay women singing about their lives. One of them was me, performing a song I had written about the sort of girlfriend I would like to have. The other performer was singing about her girlfriend.

Adam coordinates these shows as a part of 'The Gate', an inclusive space where people can come to work on a range of arts, music and literature projects. It is run by 'Yarrow'.[2] Lindy asked Adam if I would be interested in talking about my experiences as a gay woman so that they could be included in a book alongside other stories from people with learning disabilities about relationships and sexuality. I told Adam I would like to do this.

Adam, Lindy and I met up to talk about the chapter. I asked Lindy to write it down – I did not want to do that. Lindy wrote down what the three of us said and then checked back with us to make sure that we agreed with what she had written. We changed some things and put other things in. When Lindy came to talk to me at The Gate, I showed her some of my poems on the wall. She asked if she could take a photograph and I agreed. My poem gives a good idea of how I feel to be a gay woman with a learning disability in a relationship that's going well and makes me happy.

---

2   A West London housing association that supports people with learning disabilities.

CLARE'S POEM FOR HER GIRLFRIEND

Your eyes are like the sea

Your hair shines like the star

You got a lovely smile

You got red lips like yum strawberries

When I kiss them make me smile

Your a princess like in a fairy tale

I love you and being your girlfriend

You make me smile and you rock my world

You got a kind heart and make me laugh

BY CLARE LOUISE MILLER

This is a poem that Clare wrote for her girlfriend

When we had written a first draft of the chapter we sent it to Sue. Sue added some writing about the law and good practice. She also helped us think about what we wanted in the summary.

We discussed whether I should use my real name or not. I do not see why I shouldn't use my name. I have nothing I want to hide. However, the names of contacts and friends in the story have all been changed.

We used the term 'learning disabilities' because that is the term we use in Yarrow.

Introduction

SUE AND LINDY

In this chapter Clare talks about her experiences as a gay woman with learning disabilities. To provide context the chapter begins with discussion of the estimated numbers of gay women in the general population and the prejudice encountered by many people in same-sex relationships. Clare then talks about her experiences with two of her supporters, Lindy and Adam. This is written up in a largely conversational format and covers: setting up a support group, school, coming out, feelings of isolation and finding a girlfriend. Clare also includes art work as a means of sharing her feelings about her sexual identity.

Lindy then talks about supporting gay relationships from an organisational perspective. Sue and Lindy highlight the invisibility of lesbian relationships and ask what personalisation might mean for future support to gay people who are reliant on services. Our pre-writing discussions identified gaps in knowledge about the law and local policy in relation to lesbian women with learning disabilities. Responding to this we conclude with a question-and-answer section about the law in England.

Some facts and figures

LINDY AND SUE

Relatively little is known about the experiences of gay women with learning disabilities (Noonan and Taylor Gomez 2011). Abbott and Howarth (2005) researched the experiences of people with learning disabilities who identified as lesbian, gay, bisexual or transgender (LGBT). Their findings suggested relationships between women remain more hidden than same-sex relationships between men. At the end of their study the authors noted: 'It was relatively easy to find men to interview but we struggled to find nine lesbian or bisexual women with learning difficulties to interview across the whole of the UK' (p.4).

Walmsley (1993) has noted that the lack of positive information, role models and sex education available to women with learning disabilities results in it being extremely difficult for them to develop lesbian identities although a few have done so publicly (Teuben and Davey 2000). Burns and Davies (2011) and Fitzgerald and Withers (2013) found that women with learning disabilities had very little knowledge of lesbianism and tended to express negative views towards same-sex relationships between women.

Stonewall, a charity for lesbians, gays and bisexuals, endorses the UK government estimate that 5–7 per cent of the population is gay. No national census has ever asked people to define their sexuality (Stonewall 2013) so prevalence is reliant on estimation.

The National Learning Disabilities Observatory (IHAL 2013) states that there are just over one million people (2 out of every 100) in England with a learning disability. This equates to approximately 908,000 adults. Applying the government 5 per cent estimate would give a potential population of over 45,000 gay people with learning disabilities – many of whom would be lesbians. This is a sizeable number.

The National Observatory has only recently been established to collect prevalence data on the incidence of learning disability and, as in the wider population, there is currently no national means of gathering data on the sexual identity of people with learning disabilities.

In England, the last decade has witnessed legislative and policy changes intended to ensure that people with learning disabilities are appropriately supported to build relationships (DH 2001; 2009), including sexual ones. Yet for many people, the opportunity to explore and express their sexual identity and to meet people and form relationships remains problematic. All too often when sexuality is acknowledged it is assumed that people are heterosexual (Ledger and Tilley 2010).

Whilst we have witnessed significant progress in terms of acceptance of the rights of people in same-sex relationships, rejection of lesbian and gay people as valued members of communities continues (Thompson 2010). For people with

learning disabilities, many of whom already lead marginalised lives, a sexual identity as gay could present a further barrier: a double discrimination (Docherty 2007). Gay people with learning disabilities may want a different approach to their support. Some may encounter particular barriers with sexuality and relationships, including prejudice and discrimination from staff, family and friends as well as from wider society (Abbott and Howarth 2005; Ledger and Tilley 2010). The attitudes of people providing support, both family carers and staff in services, can make a huge difference to opportunities for people to express their sexuality. Whilst some carers believe that their family member can benefit from the opportunity to form relationships, have sex and find a long-term partner, Thompson (2010) points out that this support rarely extends to the possibility of same-sex relationships. Good services will be alert to this risk of discrimination, openly acknowledge it and be ready to respond in a sensitive and positive manner.

Setting up the Rainbow Fairy Group to support gay and lesbian people

CLARE, ADAM AND LINDY

Clare created the poster My Dream Girl (figure 15.1) when she first began to think about whether she might be gay. Clare said that when she is interested in exploring something she uses art and poetry to bring out her thoughts and ideas. Adam saw the poster that Clare was working on about her ideal girlfriend. They began a discussion and the idea of creating a group for young people identifying as LGBT came to Clare.

Clare said that the name of the group just popped into her head as she was doing the drawing – the Rainbow Fairy Group was born. Clare's idea was that the Rainbow Fairy Group would provide a space for young people – men and women – to come together to discuss sexuality, and in particular a place for people who identified as LGBT or who were thinking about their sexuality and were beginning to think they might be gay: 'I decided to make a group for people who use The Gate who are lesbian or gay or who weren't yet sure of their sexuality.'

Adam supported Clare to facilitate the group. This involved drawing up a list of what people wanted to talk about. Agendas included socialising and finding gay places that members had heard of but not yet visited. Two other gay women with links to The Gate came to the group. These women were a long-established couple who lived separately in staffed flats. Each was dependent on staff support to attend. Adam noticed that on some occasions, due to staffing pressures, only one of these women came. For us this raised questions about how staff prioritised supporting this gay couple to see each other and socialise.

Adam explained that he and Clare talked about who might like to come to the group and remembered that Clare had wanted her best friend, David, and her close friends, Jessica and Millie, to join.

School and college
CLARE

We talked about what it was like at school for Clare and whether there had been any discussion of same-sex relationships in her sex education classes. Clare said that the teachers didn't really say much about it but that she had had a male teacher at college who she knew was gay.

She said on one occasion at college she told a teacher in an LGBT group that she was a bit confused about her sexuality. Clare said it was at college that she had come across different names for different types of gay women 'like butch, femme and dyke'.

Describing herself Clare said, 'I'm not a girly girl, I'm a Tom boy'.

Coming out
CLARE

I came out in my early 20s – I kissed a boy once and I thought 'I am not into boys. That's not for me'. Then I kissed a girl and I thought that is more for me 'cos I like boobs'. I was a bit scared about coming out to my parents. I came out in my early 20s – I am 23 now. My Mum was cool with it; she said some of her friends are gay. Some people are scared of coming out to their parents in case their parents don't want to know them. My mum introduced me to two of her gay friends, but they were old though, and they were guys.

Before the Rainbow Fairies: the problem of isolation
CLARE AND ADAM

Clare had attended sessions at The Gate run by Image in Action.[3] They told Clare about an umbrella group for young LGBT people with learning disabilities. This group met in Ealing, some distance from Clare's home. Clare attended the group and enjoyed it but explained that she was not able to keep going because it was difficult for her to travel there. Clare had really wanted something similar that was closer to home.

---

3   An organisation that supports the rights of people with special needs to be provided with accessible information about sexuality, sexual relationships and sexual health.

Rainbow Fairies go to Gay Pride
CLARE, ADAM AND LINDY

Clare recalled a trip that the Rainbow Fairy Group organised to Gay Pride in Brighton:

> I went to my first Gay Pride in Brighton. I wanted to go to the toilet and I saw a man in a dress! It was me and Millie saw two guys wearing dresses. It didn't bother me. I always wear boys' clothes. If someone put me in a dress I'd take it off and bin it!

Local gay places
CLARE, ADAM AND LINDY

Clare has a close friend, Robert, who is also gay and he knew some of the local gay venues that had friendly and approachable staff. 'There was a nice pub in Hammersmith, there was a nice woman working there: you could get books and leaflets there. There was a pool table and I used to play pool with Robert.'

Clare also talked about gay venues in the West End of London that she had visited: 'There is another bar called Candy Bar. I haven't been there but I've been to Madame Jo Jos to see a band.'

> I wanted to set up the group because I am into girls. It's nice to go to pubs and clubs together. The gay, lesbian, bisexual and transsexuals are a bit like family because I am a lesbian; I've got a best friend who is gay.

FIGURE 15.1 'MY DREAM GIRL'

Finding my girlfriend

CLARE AND ADAM

Clare and Adam spoke about the song Clare had written and performed with the Moment by Moment Theatre Group. Talking about the song, titled 'Where can I get a hot and sexy girlfriend?', Clare said that she had missed this year's London Gay Pride, but that she was not so bothered as she had found a girlfriend:

> I missed the London Pride this year. I was single when I went to the Brighton Pride – it doesn't matter that I missed this one. In my head I thought I won't meet someone…then I met someone wonderful. I asked her out and she said yes. We went to a Japanese place. I drew a picture of my dream girlfriend [see above] then I found one. On my poster I said I did not mind if they are an EMO or a Goth or Punk. I just want a cool chick. She is 19 and she is cool. I do not think age matters. I want to cook her a romantic dinner. I was an EMO, a Goth Vamp. I used to do drawings for them then I did a poster for being a lesbian.

Language, attitudes and discrimination

CLARE AND LINDY

I asked Clare if she had experienced any difficulties or discrimination as a gay woman. Clare said that she had not felt discriminated against but that sometimes people thought that her girlfriend was her sister and she hated that. Clare was adamant about people who express anti-gay sentiments: 'I hate homophobics. When people call you horrible names it's bullying. Sometimes I do not say that I am gay as I am not sure how people will react.' Clare gave an example of how the subtleties of language can present problems: 'I am confused by how we can call ourselves queer but other people can't.' The re-appropriation of words that were previously considered disparaging of a particular group is a complex concept and the gay community, like any other, has its own language. At present the extent to which people with learning disabilities are able to understand and access these vocabularies remains largely unknown. Clare explained how when she wants to bring her girlfriend back to the house she shares with four others, that she has to ask her flatmates if they are okay with this: 'They seem alright with it. Some people were a bit funny about me being gay. Me and some people; we don't talk to each other much any more.'

We discussed whether the rules and the law are different for gay people and Clare responded, 'I kiss my girlfriend outside and I've not had any trouble.'

> I heard in the news about gay marriage, you can't get married in a church[4] though. In some countries you get shot or put in prison if you are gay. I get upset and angry

---

4   Gay marriage is now legal in England.

about that. When I was staying in a hotel with my girlfriend there was a bible and that says that it's not good to be gay. Some churches don't mind though.

Advice for young people with learning disabilities who think they might be gay

CLARE

We discussed whether there was any advice that Clare felt she would like to give to other young people in her situation. Clare replied: 'Talk to someone really close to you. Don't be scared. If people don't like it, tell someone. Find a group for young people and go to it. Gay people should stick together because we are like a big family'. This advice is reflected in a poster that Clare made about being gay.

FIGURE 15.2 'I'M HAPPY THAT I'M A LESBIAN POSTER' BY CLARE

Reflections on Clare's story from Yarrow's perspective

LINDY

Yarrow's sexuality policy highlights the right of all people with learning disabilities to develop relationships and to explore and choose their sexual identity. There is very little literature concerning how women with intellectual disabilities conceptualise their sexuality or develop a sexual identity (Fitzgerald and Withers 2013).The opportunity to explore and name sexual feelings and talk about attraction is fundamental if people are to recognise themselves as lesbian, bisexual or gay.

The policy and accompanying easy-read version endorse the rights of individuals to same-sex relationships. This is not always explicitly included in sexuality policies for people with learning disabilities and I wondered if Yarrow's policy had influenced the way Clare had been supported. In fact Clare said she had never seen it, nor had it been mentioned to her by any of her support team. Nonetheless it seems that staff had worked positively with Clare to support her to explore her sexuality. Whilst this may be a good reflection of support, we must remember that Clare is still campaigning for greater opportunities for young LGBT individuals: 'I think there should be more groups for young people. The Rainbow Fairy Group has stopped now but I am thinking of starting it again.' In addition, for both Clare and another gay couple supported by Yarrow, practical obstacles of transport and staff support limited their ability to access LGBT support groups.

In my view, at the time of writing this chapter, the law and other obstacles don't seem to have stood in Clare's way. At the time this story was told she was in a relationship that she described as 'very happy'. However, more stories are needed – Clare said she found it hard to meet other women and so she set up her own group. Others may be more isolated, perhaps worrying about their feelings of attraction or lacking sympathetic support to enable contact with other gay women. This raises a further set of questions about women with learning disabilities who are relatively independent and have been assessed as requiring little or no support. How do these women get advice, information and help if needed?

Building on Clare's advice to others to come forward and meet up, it seems more research is needed to explore how more women can be enabled to seek support and new relationships. However, as highlighted in the report *Putting People First: Equality and Diversity Matters* (CSCI 2008), individuals will make different choices based on their preferences; some may consider contact with organised gay scene groups as essential for their well-being whilst for others this may be seen as less important or even an intrusion (p.9).

Invisibility of lesbian relationships
SUE AND LINDY

The invisibility of lesbian relationships within support services also merits more research attention. In preparation for writing this chapter we talked informally to a range of people (over 35 in total) about their experiences of gay women with learning disabilities. This included detailed conversations with people with learning disabilities, family members, advocates, front line staff, social workers and managers. Across these conversations only three lesbian women with learning disabilities (Clare and the other two members of the Rainbow Fairy Group) were identified as currently supported.

Abbott and Howarth (2005) suggest that within services expressions of intimacy and touch between women may more easily be characterised as platonic and essentially unproblematic. Lesbian relationships do not run the risk of pregnancy and so may generate less concern within services.

From our own pre-writing conversations it appears that within services in England relationships between women remain largely unacknowledged. It seems that more stories need to be told if we are to gain greater understanding of the experiences of lesbian women with learning disabilities and how people who are gay would like to be treated and supported. However, we acknowledge that for gay women in receipt of support there may be substantial benefits to their relationships being largely overlooked within services for one this situation may afford more privacy.

The introduction of increasingly personalised services in England (HM Government 2007; 2010, Thompson and Westwood 2008) should offer improved opportunity for individually tailored support for women who may be gay or wanting to explore their sexuality. Yet Robertson *et al.* (2006) found that sexuality was rarely addressed in person-centred planning, an essential tool (DH 2001; Thompson and Westwood 2008) for delivering individualised support in England. It also has to be acknowledged that the introduction of personalised services, with greater dependence on family members or smaller numbers of staff, raises questions about how those providing support through individualised budgets receive training and support on sexuality and relationship issues (McCarthy and Thompson 2010). In the UK, many local authorities are having to make very significant savings in their social care budgets. As a result services are increasingly targeted at those in need of the highest level of support. Further exploration of the experiences of gay women with mild disabilities, often not in receipt of services, may also be of benefit.

Lesbian women with learning disabilities: the law and good practice
SUE AND LINDY

In preparation for writing this chapter Sue spoke to a wide range of people about lesbian women with learning disabilities. Many staff said they were unsure what they or their organisation would do if it came up as an issue and were not clear if their organisation had a policy that covered same-sex relationships. A particular area of concern was work with women with high support needs. In this context queries were repeatedly raised about what was legally permissible and who made decisions about sex under the 2005 Mental Capacity Act. All the people with learning disabilities said they did not know what the law said.

We were taken aback that so many people (including senior managers) said they did not understand the law and were unable to explain the approach of their organisation to supporting gay relationships. Many front line staff and families were sympathetic to providing support but said they did not know about where they would find information. Lots of people said the issue had never arisen.

Such significant gaps both in experience of lesbian women with learning disabilities and in knowledge of the legal and policy context are clearly of importance to future support. Mindful that supporting same-sex relationships can give rise to particular legal, cultural and sometimes religious concerns we decided to end our chapter with a section that provides responses to some of the key issues that arose through our pre-writing conversations. The question-and-answer format and content of this section draw substantially upon a book by Fanstone and Andrews (2009) entitled *Learning Disabilities, Sex and the Law* and upon material provided at a Family Planning Association course entitled Learning Disabilities, Sex, Law and Policy held in November 2013 (FPA 2013). Reference was also made to a range of legal documents and good practice guidance (City of Westminster with FPA and Image in Action 2010; Department for Constitutional Affairs 2007).

Useful information

This summary provides an overview of some of the main legal parameters that affect the sexual expression of women with learning disabilities who identify as lesbian. As in Chapter 11, this is not intended as a definitive summary of the law. Application of the law to individual circumstances is a complex area with new case law emerging and law being reviewed and updated. Expert legal advice may be needed to address individual circumstances and levels of support.

The section is intended to promote open discussion and provide basic information about the legal/policy context for people with learning disabilities who may be gay. Used alongside Clare's story, we hope it will be helpful to frame discussion with people with learning disabilities (gay and straight), families, advocates and staff and for organisations seeking to review their sexuality policy and practice to embed improved support for gay women.

Q 1 Is the law about sex education and sex different for gay women?
In England the law used to be very different for lesbian, gay and bisexual people but most of the differences have now been removed. For example, in 2000 the Sexual Offences (Amendment Act) equalised the age of consent making it the same for gay and straight people. Another example is 'Section 28', which was the term often used to talk about Section 2a of the Local Government Act 1986. This prohibited local authorities in England and Wales from promoting homosexuality, including giving information about sex and parenting by people who identify as gay. It was repealed on 10 July 2003 in the House of Lords. Even so, the legacy of Section 28 still confuses staff in services who believe it may still be illegal to support people with learning disabilities in exploring gay relationships.

Q 2 Is the law different for gay women with learning disabilities?

It is now legal for anyone aged 16 or over to engage in consensual sexual activity with partners of the same sex. Gay or lesbian couples can declare a civil partnership and legislation to allow same-sex marriage in England and Wales was passed by the Parliament of the United Kingdom in July 2013 and came into force in March 2014. This applies to anyone with a learning disability, providing the person has the capacity to consent to sexual activity, civil partnership and marriage.

Q 3 Can people with learning disabilities have civil partnerships?

Since 2005, in the UK, it has been possible for two women or two men to enter into a civil partnership providing they both have capacity to consent to the partnership. Entering a civil partnership is, therefore, an option available to gay women with learning disabilities.

Q 4 What does the law and associated good practice guidance
say about consent to a lesbian sexual relationship?

The law is the same for women consenting to sex with a person of the same or different gender. Good practice guidance (Family Planning Association 2013; Fanstone and Andrews 2009) recommends, when working with people with learning disabilities, the use of the Sexual Offences Act 2003 definition when considering issues of capacity to consent.

As discussed in Chapter 11, the definition of consent within the law in England is 'a person consents if s/he agrees by choice and has the freedom to make that choice' (Sexual Offences Act 2003).

The 2005 Mental Capacity Act encourages those supporting decision-making to do everything possible to support a person with learning disabilities to make their own decisions and to ensure they are fully involved in this process. In the case of women with higher support the Mental Capacity Act principles outlined in Chapter 11 apply.

Q 5 Can someone consent to a lesbian relationship on behalf of someone else?

The Mental Capacity Act (2005) makes it clear that no one else like a parent, advocate or member of staff can make a decision about consent to a sexual relationship, civil partnership or marriage on behalf of someone else.

Q 6 So what happens with women with high support needs?

See Chapter 11. In relation to people with high support needs in same-sex relationships, the purpose of the law is to not interfere in the development of positive, mutually beneficial relationships but to try to protect and ensure that vulnerable women are not being pressurised or coerced into having sex against their wishes (City of Westminster 2010). The same guidance in relation to staff providing skilled support and documenting decision-making apply.

Legal framework: supporting the rights of gay women

As discussed in Chapter 11, it is now illegal to directly or indirectly discriminate against or insult someone at work on the grounds of their sexual orientation. All health and social care employers should have a policy that prevents such discrimination. The public sector equality duty came into force in April 2011 underpinned by the 2010 Equalities Act. It ensures that public bodies consider the needs of all individuals in their day-to-day work: in shaping policy, in delivering services and in relation to their own employees. The new equality duty describes sexual orientation as a protected characteristic; its intention is to foster good relationships and to provide a clear framework for addressing discrimination on the grounds of sexual orientation if it occurs.

The following are examples of legislation and practice guidance that give broad support to the rights of women with learning disabilities to express their sexuality, develop sexual relationships and to receive appropriate support and guidance to enable this to happen with due regard to privacy, confidentiality and safety of themselves and others:

- The Human Rights Act (1998)

- The UN Declaration on the Rights of Persons with Disabilities (United Nations 2006)

- *Valuing People* (DH 2001)

- *Valuing People Now* (DH 2009).

What good practice guidance has to say

If a person with learning disabilities is lesbian then an issue may initially be in realising and accepting that for themselves (Fanstone and Andrews 2009). If a person with learning disabilities thinks they may be lesbian, gay or bisexual they should be offered full support by workers to help them explore this. It might involve contacting agencies to meet other lesbian, gay or bisexual people, or to access specific support or counselling.

Thompson (2010) emphasises that care must be taken in separating a person's sexual interests from their sexual identity. This means, for example, not labelling a person as lesbian just because she expresses an interest in sex with women. Thompson emphasises that in terms of sexual identity what is important is that people with learning disabilities should know:

- that some people who want relationships with people of the same sex call themselves lesbian, gay or bisexual

- that these are not bad names

- that they may choose whether or not to identify with these terms.

Finding acceptance from others, such as parents, family and staff, and avoiding discrimination may also be very important to the person and so should be fundamental in the delivery of support. Moving away from the assumption that all clients are heterosexual is a necessary process for organisations (Beckett 2004; Noonan and Taylor Gomez 2011).

Promoting the involvement of people with learning disabilities in policy development and review

Policies and guidelines help everyone know where they stand when working in highly sensitive and often controversial areas such as supporting same-sex relationships. Policies and guidelines to support gay women with learning disabilities could range from national guidance on the law and good practice (as discussed in Chapter 11), local authority policy documents, to 'house rules' for individual homes and meeting places (Fanstone and Andrews 2009). Sex and relationships is an area in which there are often strongly held personal, cultural and religious views as well as great potential for both harm and scandal. It is also an area where there remains much confusion about the law and issues of capacity and consent. Many staff still feel that keeping people apart can be an easier way of managing complexity than working through and addressing sexuality issues. Clear guidelines, developed with people with learning disabilities themselves and circulated in accessible formats, should protect people with learning disabilities and promote their rights. It would at the same time support families and carers in their roles and help to prevent agencies making avoidable mistakes. Policies should provide clarity regarding the law and enable a clear, supportive and flexible approach.

The following are examples of policy documents that make specific reference to supporting gay relationships:

- *Adults with Learning Disabilities Personal and Sexual Relationships.* A policy for providers in Westminster, (2010) City of Westminster/NHS Westminster with Image in Action and the FPA

- *Let's Talk About Sex: Your Sexuality Rights and How Yarrow Can Help You.* A booklet about sexuality for people that Yarrow supports. (Sterling *et al.* 2002).

Summary

Clare, Adam, Sue and Lindy have worked together on this chapter, attempting to shed light on the experiences of women with learning disabilities who identify as gay and how staff in organisations can support these women. We have endeavoured to provide some basic information on the law and good practice so that supporters can be confident in the information and advice that they provide to women. Clare has shared her experiences and feelings about her lesbian identity. It is an uplifting and largely positive account that affords insight into what can be achieved and what could be better supported. Clare has told her story for this book in the hope that it will inspire other women with learning disabilities who are – or who think they might be – gay not to struggle in isolation but instead to come forward, meet up with others and follow their heart: in Clare's words to 'take the step to be part of a bigger family'.

References

Abbott, D. and Howarth, J. (2005) *Secret Loves, Hidden Lives? Exploring Issues for People with Learning Difficulties who are Gay, Lesbian or Bisexual.* Bristol: Norah Fry Research Centre, University of Bristol. Available at www.bristol.ac.uk/norahfry/research/completed-projects/secretlovessummary.pdf, accessed on 21 September 2013.

Beckett, C. (2004) *Crossing the Border – locating heterosexuality as a boundary for lesbian women and disabled women* in Journal of International Women's Studies, Vol 5, Issue 3 pp 44–52; available at www.bridgeew.edu/SoAS/jiws/May04/Beckett.pdf, accessed on

Burns, J. and Davies, D. (2011) *same-sex relationships and women with intellectual disabilities in Journal of Applied Research in Intellectual Disabilities,* 24, Issue 4, 351–360.

City of Westminster and Westminster NHS in association with Image in Action and FPA (2010) *Adults with Learning Disabilities Personal and Sexual Relationships.* A Policy for Providers. London: Westminster City Council with Image in Action and FPADH.

Care Services Commission for Social Care Inspection (2008) *Putting People First: equality and diversity matters, 1 - Providing appropriate services for lesbian, gay and bisexual and transgender people,* in Social Care Policy and Practice, Issue 7, March 2008. London: Department of Health.

Department for Constitutional Affairs (2007) *Mental Capacity Act Code of Practice.* London: The Stationery Office.

DH (Department of Health) (2001) *Valuing People: A New Strategy for Learning Disability for the 21st Century.* London: Department of Health.

DH (Department of Health) (2009) *Valuing People Now: A New Three-year Strategy for People with Learning Disabilities*. London: The Stationery Office.

Docherty, D. (2007) 'Good as You 2.' Paper given at Social History of Learning Disability Conference, Learning Disability, Relationships and Sexuality: Past and Present. Open University Milton Keynes, 5 July.

FPA (Family Planning Association) (2013) Training course materials. *Learning Disabilities, Sex, Law and Policy*. Course date 12 November.

Fanstone, C. and Andrews, S. (2009) *Learning Disabilities, Sex and the Law: A Practical Guide*. London: Family Planning Association.

Fitzgerald, C. and Withers, P. (2013) '"I don't know what a proper woman means": what women with intellectual disabilities think about sex, sexuality and themselves', *British Journal Of Learning Disabilities*, 41, 1, 5–12, Education Research Complete, EBSCOhost, viewed 26 August 2014.

HM Government (2007) *Putting People First: A Shared Vision and Commitment to the Transformation of Adult Social Care*. London: The Stationery Office. Available at http://webarchive.nationalarchives.gov.uk/20130107105354, accessed on 27 January 2014.

HM Government (2010) *Think Local, Act Personal: Next Steps for Transforming Adult Social Care*. Available at www.thinklocalactpersonal.org.uk, accessed on 2 December 2010.

The Improving Health and Lives Observatory (IHAL) (2013) People with Learning Disabilities in England 2012. Available at www.improvinghealthandlives.org.uk/about/faqs#q2, accessed on 1 July 2013.

Ledger, S. and Tilley, L. (2010) 'Reminiscence, identity and developing a living archive of learning disability history.' Paper given at LGBT Seminar, LM Archives, December.

McCarthy, M. and Thompson, D. (2010) 'Introduction.' In M. McCarthy and D. Thompson (eds) *Sexuality and Learning Disabilities*. Brighton: Pavillion.

Noonan, A. and Taylor Gomez, M. (2011) 'Who's missing? Awareness of lesbian, gay, bisexual and transgender people with intellectual disability.' *Sexuality and Disability 29*, 175–180. Available at http://dx.doi.org/10.1007/s11195-010-9175-3, accessed on 4 June 2013.

Robertson, J., Emmerson, E., Hatton, C. *et al.* (2006) 'Longitudinal analysis of the impact and cost of person centred planning for people with intellectual disabilities in England.' *American Journal on Mental Retardation 111*, 6, 400–416.

Sterling, J., Anderson, C., Bevan, M., Cover, M. *et al.* (2002) *Let's Talk About Sex: Your Sexuality Rights and How Yarrow Can Help You*. London: Yarrow Housing.

Stonewall (2013) *How many lesbian, gay and bisexual people are there?* www.stonewall.org.uk/@_home/sexual_orientation_faqs) 2694.asp, accessed on 4 November 2013.

Teuben, S. and Davey, M. (2000) 'Gina's Story' inTraustadottir R. and Johnson K. (eds) *Women with Intellectual Disabilities: finding a place in the world,* 162-171. London, Jessica Kingsley Publishers.

Thompson, D. (2010) 'Sexual Interests, Opportunities and Choices.' In M. McCarthy and D. Thompson (eds) *Sexuality and Learning Disabilities*. Brighton: Pavilion.

Thompson, J. and Westwood, L. (2008) 'Person centred approaches to educating the learning disability workforce.' In Thompson J., KilbaneJ. and Sanderson H. (eds) *Person Centred Practice for Professionals*. Maidenhead: McGraw-Hill/Open University Press.

Walmsley, J., (1993) 'Women First: Lessons in Participation.' Critical Social Policy, Issue 38, 86–99.

CHAPTER 16

GOOD AS YOU 2 (GAY2)

A Peer Support Group for Intellectually Disabled LGBT People

Craig Blyth with Daniel Docherty

Overview

- Craig talks about some of the issues of writing in partnership.

- He explains the process of writing the chapter.

- He explains it is difficult to be gay and disabled in the UK.

- Daniel talks about some issues around being a disabled gay man.

- He looks at the attitudes of other people and how he has experienced a 'double discrimination'.

- As a response to these barriers a group was set up in Manchester called 'Good As You 2' (GAY2).

- GAY2 was for lesbian, gay and bisexual people with learning disabilities.

- Finding the right support for the group was crucial.

- Daniel points out some of the things that have changed since the group came about.

- He also looks at some issues still to be solved.

- Craig talks about some of his experiences.

The writing process

Writing this chapter 'together' was difficult as we both lead very different lives. As a lecturer and an academic, I spend lots of my time writing and undertaking research and, importantly, get paid to do that. Daniel, on the other hand, is not paid by the university and although he has done a lot of teaching and writing at the university, it is not his job. Consequently, getting together to write this chapter was challenging because when I had time to work on it, Daniel had other commitments – and vice versa.

In talking it over, we decided to use a previous conference paper that Daniel had written for the SHLD conference in 2007 (see Chapter 1).[1]

This approach to writing is explored more in the next section of the chapter. Everything that is written here has been approved by Daniel as an 'authentic' representation of his views. The terminology used is 'learning disability' and 'learning disabled people'. The latter is based on a social model of disability understanding and is the term preferred by a group of learning disabled people who are involved in doing research at the University of Manchester (Daniel is a founder member of this group).

Introduction

Being gay is difficult in the UK; being gay and having a learning disability is even more difficult. This chapter explores some of the issues facing gay learning disabled men and how one group of such men set up a peer support group in the hope of supporting each other to challenge and overcome some of these difficulties. Before we look at these issues we will explore the process of writing/researching together and some of our thoughts on partnership research.

Who we are

Craig has been a full-time lecturer and academic at the University of Manchester for nine years. He teaches a variety of courses relating to disability but his interests lie specifically in the areas of sexuality and identity. His doctoral research was about the experiences of 12 disabled gay men who spent time in Manchester's gay village, so he has lots of experience of undertaking research alongside gay disabled men (see Blyth 2009).

Daniel helped develop the Partnership Steering Group at the University of Manchester in 2002 and until recently was a very active member of the group.

---

1   There is a voice recording of Daniel presenting this paper at www2.open.ac.uk/hsc/ldsite/ audios/Sexuality%20conf%20audio%20MP3s/Daniel%20-%20Disk2.mp3

Daniel has published widely about his experiences as a learning disabled man (see Carson and Docherty 2002) and has lectured on a variety of courses at the University of Manchester.

Both Craig and Daniel identify as gay but they have had very different experiences of how this affects their lives. They have known each other for nearly ten years both professionally and as friends. Daniel identifies as having a learning disability and Asperger syndrome. Craig does not identify as a disabled person but he does have a physical impairment.

Writing in partnership?

You will see that this chapter was written *by* Craig Blyth *with* Daniel Docherty and the reason we have decided to use this approach to the authorship is that we want to be open and honest about how it was written. It would have been very easy to have claimed that the chapter was written 'inclusively' or fully 'in partnership' but we think it is important to be clear about the process and enable the reader to understand how this knowledge was created. (This issue is also covered in Chapters 1 and 22.) We both have substantial first-hand experience of being involved in 'partnership' or 'inclusive' work that was less than transparent in relation to the actual involvement of each partner and which failed to acknowledge the more complex issues involved in joint work or projects. As McClimens (2008, p.273) states, 'I felt that some of the grittier and messier aspects of collaboration were being glossed over or perhaps ignored…the collaborative research process was no more taxing than a walk in the park.' We were keen not to 'gloss over' these challenges as it is important to acknowledge that Craig did the writing involved in the production of this chapter but much of this was based on previous work with Daniel and in particular his presentation for the Open University SHLD conference (see Chapters 1 and 2).

Personal lives and stories

We both have lots of experience of writing about issues relating to sexuality, sex and relationships. However, there is one big difference between what Daniel writes about and what Craig writes about. This difference is that Daniel tends to write about himself (with a non-disabled co-author) whilst Craig writes about other people (usually gay disabled men). This approach is quite typical of 'partnership' work where the disabled co-researcher/author often reflects on their own life and experiences alongside a non-disabled academic who, in general, remains silent on the subject of their personal life. For example, Daniel wrote a chapter in 2002 in partnership with a non-disabled academic where he talked about his experiences of sex and relationships (Carson and Docherty 2002) but there was nothing in it about the non-disabled author's relationships or sexual experiences. Similarly, Craig has written about the very personal experiences of some disabled gay men (Blyth 2009; Blyth 2010) but he has written very little about his own experiences of relationships and sex. We think this is a really important and complex issue and suggest that there are a number of reasons why this happens.

First, it is important that learning disabled people can use partnership research as a vehicle for telling their stories, as often they are not listened to in other areas of their lives. Goodley (1996, p.334) has written about this saying that it is important as it can act as 'an agency through which historically marginalised individuals may account for their own lives'. This is a really important element of partnership work but it should not be used as an excuse for non-disabled academics to 'exploit' the lived experiences of their disabled co-researchers and lots of attention should be given to the potential consequences that revealing personal stories can have.

Second, non-disabled academics may feel like they cannot reveal personal details of their own lives as it might change how other academics view them and affect their chances for promotion and so on. This is a difficult issue and individual researchers need to make decisions on how much of their own experiences they reveal. Whatever individuals decide it is really important the research is not labelled as 'participatory' simply as a way of producing 'one-sided' research that enables the non-disabled researcher to 'dissect' the experiences of the disabled co-researcher; we think this is really just traditional research that is done 'on' disabled people but that is called 'participatory'.

In this chapter, we are focusing on Daniel's story as he has made the decision to tell it to as many people as possible in order that things might improve for others. Craig does talk about some of his experiences as a young person as a way of exploring the differences between individuals who rely on support and those who don't.

As explained in the introduction, the writing below is taken from presentations that Daniel gave at the Open University (UK) and also at the Society for Disability Studies conference in Philadelphia (USA).

Daniel's story
Family and services
When I first knew that I was gay it was difficult for me in relation to my family but also the services I received. Lots of staff think it is their job to pry into learning disabled people's private life; because of this I pretended to be straight. They seemed to feel it was *wrong* to be gay – they would not accept it and I was told I was better off with a girlfriend; they thought homosexuality was dirty. It's hard being an adult with learning disabilities, but it is even harder being gay. The staff who supported

me at home tried to put me 'back in the closet'. Staff told me to take down pictures of men from my flat wall and put up pictures of women.

It was difficult with my family. My foster Dad was an ex-policeman and he didn't approve of people being gay. He said if I didn't become straight that he would cut me out of his will. My foster Mum was more accepting; she said, 'I can't choose your destiny', but when my foster Dad was around she had to go along with him. I felt like I had to be the way my family wanted me to be.

Being excluded from the gay scene

It felt like there was no place to go for me; I experienced bad attitudes and even the members of the non-disabled gay community didn't want me. Bar staff didn't want me in the bars; they said I was disabled and belonged in a day centre. I was also told I 'wasn't gay enough', but straight people went into the bars. I had problems with bouncers – they wouldn't let me in some of the bars. They were not trained in disability awareness. A lot of the bars that would not let me in on my own would let me in when Craig came for a drink with me – this showed that they knew they were wrong stopping me from going in as they never tried to stop me if Craig was there. Some of the bouncers had really bad attitudes.

A lot of the bars are very busy so even if you got in, it was difficult to meet people. There was a real thing about image; it seemed you had to be slim and good-looking or you didn't fit in. If you looked at all different you were made to feel like an outsider. I have described this to Craig before and it's like you're not a member of that club and you never will be.

Something needed to be done

So there was no access to most of the gay scene in Manchester if you were a person with a learning disability, and learning disability service providers were very negative about being gay. Even if staff aren't actively telling you to pretend to be straight, a lot of them ignore the sexuality of the people they support; I think this is a huge problem (see Blyth 2010; Carson and Docherty 2002). I was treated as if I was asexual. I felt isolated; there were no opportunities to go out socially with gay men. I tried to go to groups for gay men with physical impairments but they did not include me either as my disability is hidden. I knew that if I wanted to spend time with other gay learning disabled men I would need to do something.

Good As You 2 (GAY2)

I decided set up a group to provide a network for other people like me. At the start we only had three members. It was for lesbian, gay, bisexual and transgender people with learning disabilities.

We put out leaflets to try to get more members but the group didn't work at first because the volunteer we had behaved like a service provider and expected to control the group with his ideas. This was bad support. For example, the volunteer filled out application forms for funding and we were not included. He did a lot of things without telling us and behind our backs, so we ended up sacking him; the right support is vital.

I was approached by Iain Carson. Iain was at that time a lecturer at the University of Manchester. In the group we talked it through about the type of support we wanted and needed. We needed a support that did not take control and who kept in contact with us. Iain was ideal in this way. After a few months Craig joined Iain as a volunteer supporter and this meant we could do more activities.

Once Iain and Craig started to work with us, things changed for the better. I felt my existence had been acknowledged. For example, I got invited to take part in mainstream gay organisations. The Chief Constable invited me to a meeting to talk about the needs of gay men with learning disabilities in Manchester – and they kept in touch with us. BBC Radio wanted to do a programme about the group and they took us seriously. We also spent time in Manchester's gay village and although lots of the bar and door staff were not great, the more we went there the better it became. It shows that once learning disabled people can access places people start to get used to them and become more accepting.

Improvements started to be made

Learning Disability Services started to take us seriously. They referred 13 people to the group to find support. I was also involved in a national research group with the Norah Fry Research Centre, in which people who were gay and lesbian talked about their experiences. I started doing research with Iain Carson about the way services respond to gay men with learning disabilities. I stopped feeling so socially isolated.

We went to the bar with the volunteers and they supported our right to be there. Some members of the group told me that the group was a lifeline to them – it was the only support they got. One member of our group stayed in his bedroom at the residential service he lived in and only really came out to come to the group or when he went to a day centre! I was asked to do training for learning disability service providers about sexuality issues and people gave us money to produce posters.

GAY2 made me and other learning disabled people feel included in the gay village. I think the group was unique because it was controlled by people with learning disabilities and gave us the control over how to get on with what we wanted to do. We were lucky as we found two volunteers who did not try to tell us what to do but supported us to do the things we wanted to do. They never told us who we could and could not be. Some members of the group started relationships with each other and at least one couple now live together; this would never have happened without GAY2.

Sadly, the group is currently suspended because we need to find more money. This has really made me realise how important the group was to my life.

Craig's story

I have known I am gay for as long as I can remember. In some ways I had a similar experience to Daniel when I was young as I had to pretend I was the same as everyone else (I assumed everyone else was straight). However, as I got older (15 or 16) I was able to start to go to gay bars without my friends and family knowing and this was very different to Daniel's experience, as I didn't need support to do this. I think this is a big issue for disabled young people who need support, as they have to turn their private lives into public property in order to receive appropriate support; I know if I had needed support to go to a gay bar at 15, I would never have asked for it.

When I was 18, I moved into my own flat and it was then that I told my parents and the rest of my family I was gay. Their reaction was, again, pretty similar to Daniel's but as I lived on my own I wasn't reliant on my family (or staff) for the same level of support and thus I was able to carry on with my 'gay life' regardless of what my family thought. My parents, and the rest of my family, slowly got used to the idea and they totally accept me for who I am now.

For me, being gay has never really caused me any problems. People I have worked with have always accepted me and the people in my life. When I have come across people who have reacted badly, I have felt able to challenge them and, if necessary, not have them in my life. This is very different to Daniel and other learning disabled gay people who rely on support staff and who have very little control over who they receive support from; Daniel has, over the years, been supported by some very good staff but also some very bad staff who have tried to control what he does.

Volunteering

When I first started volunteering for GAY2 it took me some time to get used to being a supporter and not a member of staff (I used to manage residential services for learning disabled people). I had to learn to support people in the way they wanted to be supported and not to impose my views on them. This was difficult at times as, on occasions, I worried that some members were potentially going to get emotionally hurt, but I soon learned to 'butt out' and just to be there to support people if things did go a little wrong.

We spent a lot of time in Manchester's gay village. As Daniel has explained, the reactions of the bar staff to members of the group were very different when Iain or I were with the group to when they were on their own. On one occasion, I was late and arrived to see two members standing outside a bar because the bouncer would not let them in; I supported one of the guys to tell the doorman we would be spending our money somewhere else and his pub was rubbish anyway!

I remember the night when a new guy came to join the group and was excruciatingly nervous and shy; it was great to watch him relax over the next few months and to really start to feel part of a circle of friends. Better still, he developed a relationship with one of the other members and eventually they moved into a house together (despite both their families objecting strongly). GAY2 received very little funding and we met in one small room of a local gay support service, but it made a real difference to the lives of a lot of gay learning disabled people; I often wonder how much difference could be made if there were GAY2s in lots of cities.

The group do not meet any more as we struggled to keep the little funding we had but also both Iain and I have busy academic jobs and we could not keep dedicating the time needed. I hope at some point in the future we can secure a more significant amount of funding so that the group can restart but, this time, with a paid support worker (gay of course!). GAY2 taught me a great deal about living life as a disabled gay man, to the point that I went on to focus on disabled gay men's experiences for my doctoral research.

Summary

This chapter has looked at how it can be really difficult to be learning disabled and gay. A lot of the issues that face disabled gay men are the same as those that face non-disabled gay men but the difference is often related to the provision of support. It is important that support staff are trained to support people in appropriate person-centred ways if the way services run are to get better for people who identify as gay. Staff need to be supported to understand that they are entitled to hold whatever personal views they like, but they cannot impose these views on the people they support.

GAY2 has highlighted that, with the right support, learning disabled gay men can lead the lives that they want to and that they can become part of a wider community. Although still far from perfect, Manchester's gay village has changed as a result of GAY2 as people are more used to seeing gay learning disabled men in the space. The only way things will change in the village is if more learning disabled gay men are supported to spend time there.

References

Blyth, C. (2009) 'Commercial Gay Space and the Regulation of Disabled Bodies.' In A. Sparkes (ed.) *Auto/Biography Yearbook 2009 71–88*. British Sociological Association. Nottingham: Russell Press.

Blyth, C. (2010) '"Members Only": The Use of Gay Space(s) by Gay Disabled Men.' In R. Shuttleworth and T. Sanders (eds) *Sex and Disability: Politics, Identity and Access*. Leeds: The Disability Press.

Carson, I. and Docherty, D. (2002) 'Friendships, Relationships and Issues of Sexuality.' In D. Race (ed.) *Learning Disability – A Social Approach*. London: Routledge.

Docherty, D. (2007) 'Good as You 2.' Paper given at The Learning Disability, Relationships and Sexuality: Past and Present conference, Open University, Milton Keynes, 5 July.

Goodley, D. (1996) 'Tales of hidden lives: A critical examination of life history research with people who have learning difficulties.' *Disability and Society 11*, 3, 333–348.

McClimens, A. (2008) 'This is my truth, tell me yours: Exploring the internal tensions with collaborative learning disability research.' *British Journal of Learning Disabilities 36*, 271–276.

CHAPTER 17

'I HAVE BEEN BLESSED TO HAVE A VERY GOOD SUPPORT WORKER'

Experiences Related to Ethnicity and Diversity

Jackie Downer MBE with support from Linnette Farquarson

Overview

- Jackie Downer lives in London and is a Black woman with learning disabilities.

- She has a very high award, an MBE, for her services to the community.

- She talks about her memories of going into special school and how people treat people with learning disabilities.

- She also talks about her parents being from Jamaica and how Black people with learning disabilities are discriminated against.

- Relationships are important to Jackie and she describes examples of how people with learning disabilities can get hurt and taken advantage of.

- Jackie also tells us how important good support is, especially when people understand your culture.

The writing process

Jackie wrote this chapter over a period of time facilitated by her supporter, Linnette Farquarson. Her preferred choice of terminology is 'people with learning disabilities'.

Jackie's story: early actions – being assessed

One of the things I will never forget was when the psychologist came to my school to assess me. I remember the teacher saying, 'Jackie can you come with me please?' All my friends were mumbling and asking me what I had done wrong. On the way I saw my mother, which meant that something was definitely wrong. When you were taken out of your class during a lesson and your parents were at the school, you knew you had done something wrong!

We were taken to a room and introduced to a man who wore a suit; he was white and he sat behind the desk and to me; this meant that he was powerful.

The psychologist

The man was a psychologist and he brought lots of things with him like building blocks and a timer. I can never forget the timer; this meant speed and it is clear now that I could never do some things fast enough. This affects me to this day as someone who has a learning disability and who doesn't think and do things fast enough; people leave us behind. Even when I am in working groups looking at policies, you hear some people say, 'We don't have the time we need to get the document in for the deadline', so our inclusion is still limited.

The psychologist hardly spoke to my mum; he asked me lots of questions and also gave me tasks to do. I was scared of him. I had to do things like show him how I eat. In my culture we often eat with spoons and so I showed him how I ate with a spoon. There were no questions that allowed the difference of our cultures; what people like him said, went. Rice is a common food that Black and Asian people eat; children are allowed to eat rice with a spoon because it is more practical, until they learn how to eat with a knife and a fork.

My mum's background

Although my mum was there, I knew she couldn't understand the situation and she thought that he would know better. We never had advocates. The language he used was a barrier and my poor mother was in his hands. My mother came from the countryside area in Jamaica, where some children could not afford to go to school. When my school advised her that they were helping my education, my mum would say 'yes', to most things as she felt that they knew best. You have to understand that most Jamaican parents believe in education and the education in Jamaica is good, but when you don't have it you just don't have it.

The discrimination that our parents faced in this country made them say 'yes', most of the time, as they would be punished if they got things wrong. You have to remember that for my mother the psychologist was like a doctor and he would help me, her daughter, to get better. He never said 'goodbye' and we never saw him again, yet he changed my life in a very big way.

Into special school

Because of this assessment I had to change my school and leave all my friends behind. The new school was a special school and the teachers told me how I was special and that I was going to a lovely school, that was special for me, and that I would get more attention. My mother and I never understood that my school years were about to change. My special school didn't feel special, especially because it was next to a so-called 'normal girls school'. The children from my school were teased because they knew we were different, because we went to school in a special bus. They called us names like 'backwards', 'idiots', 'dunce', 'stupid', and many other names which sometimes to this day I am still called. At times, even if it is not said, people treat you as though you are stupid and find ways of not including you.

Let me give you an example. Sometimes in my jobs, I know that some workers are upset that people with learning disabilities are now being included in the workplace, but you can see at times where we do not mix. We have no contact outside work and at meetings the 'normal managers' still always stand together. It really hurts me because these are the same people who tick funding boxes and say they have full inclusion. My lead support worker always says that attention must be paid to the wheel of inclusion as it has phases and it doesn't happen overnight.

Support

When I look back, my mum was my first supporter, she believed in me. My mum used to tell me stories about how the family told her to give me away when I was small, because I would be slow and would draw her back. My mum could not believe it and she said, 'You come from my belly and you were mine, how could I give you away?'

When my mum met my lead support worker she was happy because she was Black and she could speak my mother's language, because although Jamaican people speak English it is funny and we call it patois. Sometimes you can't understand it, especially when it is spoken fast. My support worker says that she had to believe in the rights of people, because when she was small she had lots of views as a child and remembers feeling hurt when she wasn't given choices. She also has a brother with a learning disability who she loves and she remembers that when the green bus came to take him to school it hurt her. He never ever looked happy when he went in the bus and it was then that she felt that he changed – up until then he was 'normal'.

She loves him and she says he has rights and choices, but that it just takes longer for him to learn.

Now in life I find it very important to have a Black support worker, because I travel throughout England. There are some places that I travel to and there are hardly any Black people. Very often I have been to places where, when we walk into the pub, my support worker and I are the only Black people. It is strange that they just stare and they never say 'hello'. You can imagine how it feels when I am on my own. I feel settled that there is somebody like me with my colour and I don't mean to be horrible (because it doesn't feel good) but who feels the way I do when I am in isolation?

My support workers are my lifeline and they help to keep me on track in my home life and with my work. Even though I got my MBE,[1] I know that my support workers helped me to get there. I now live a life where I have a bank account, I live in my own home and I have my own friends. My support staff are like my interpreters; they have many skills and they have made the world a better place for me to live in.

I have had white support workers, but they never felt the way I felt when I went to places that are out in the sticks, because people would stare at us, but I knew that this was because of me being Black and being in their surroundings. When I turn to my white supporters and I say, 'I don't feel comfortable here', they always say, 'Don't worry, you are with me.' Then I realise that they cannot possibly know how I feel. One of my white female support workers did say that she feels funny when she is the only woman with all men and I guess it is similar.

Sometimes I get scared when I hear of race attacks and I look back at things like slavery and the Nazis. I hope things like that never happen again, but I'm not sure if people really understand these things – like what happened to Nelson Mandela. He fought for the rights of Black people.

There are places that are like this in London, but it is so very mixed that I don't experience it as much in London, which has many more cultures. There are some attacks, but I pray to God it will be a nice world; but some people in it are not nice.

My culture and discrimination

In my own culture, having a learning disability can go against me; sometimes people are not nice, because I do not talk in a certain way. Sometimes a nice person can be Black or white. What can I do? I cannot force people to like me, but some people

---

1   This award, *Member of the Order of the British Empire,* is put forward by senior civil servants and then agreed by the Prime Minister and the Queen. The MBE is for a significant achievement or outstanding service to the community.

just feel uncomfortable and they do not know how to approach people with learning disabilities.

When I first started to work with the Black Friendly group, lots of horrible things came out, like people bleaching their skins to be whiter. It may sound silly, but when you are white you get more things and when you are Black and disabled it is worse. Let me explain, I live in a country where there are many people with different colours. But even on the television adverts, lots of things that we use as Black people, simple things like shampoo, cereals and soaps do not show us in the adverts. It hurts, but it is getting better. I was happy when the Halifax advert came out because the man in it was Black and he wore glasses and it let everyone know that we are here and that we use banks too.

I remember when I was little I used to watch the TV a lot, because my brothers and sisters didn't want me to play with them much; I made the games too slow and boring and I couldn't keep up. There weren't lots of Black people on the TV and definitely not disabled people. I remember the cartoons of Michael Jackson and I loved it, it had songs and Black characters. I remember 'Ironside' because he was in a wheelchair, I am not sure if he could walk in real life, but he still solved crimes as a disabled person. I think the most popular Black person on the TV was Muhammad Ali. When he was fighting we were allowed to watch, even if it was late, and when he won our parents would make a lot of noise. I realised that they were proud of him, so I liked him too. I realise now that he too was fighting for the rights of his people and that he was actually boxing. To this day I have found out that he has done many things for young people and charity and that we must all fight for each other's rights.

Black people have come a long way on TV and so have people with disabilities.

Sometimes my Black supporters can talk to me about how they struggle when people do funny and horrible things to them because they are Black and it helps because they can relate when it comes to being Black women. I am so passionate about good support that I am now designing my own training package. I have been blessed to have a very good support worker (Linnette Farquarson) who is a person who simply believes in everyone having a right, and she has been good support for me and is working in partnership with me to produce a training package.

Because of the good support I have, I do many things in my life such as having a bank account, paying my bills, living on my own, having a circle of friends, helping at church, having a job and just feeling like the other normal people. I know I am normal, it's just that many people don't treat me as normal.

My views on relationships

I would love to have a boyfriend and I talk to my friends and my personal support worker about it. Once I met someone but he turned out to be a bit tricky, I believed him because he said things like, 'You can do what you like with me.' My brother was angry when I told him, because he said that I needed to be clear about what things he wanted me to do with him. My brother said that he reminded him of a paedophile, because I sometimes look at things in a simple way like a child and my brother was feeling that this man wanted that part of me and that he would have done many things to me. I was sad because I liked him but I knew he wasn't good for me. When I told him that my support worker and my brother wanted to meet him, he was angry and I never really saw him again.

I like someone again now and he is a bit nicer and my brother, my friends and my support worker know of him and some of them have met him. I am getting some support to have a relationship, but we will see how it goes. I think the man that I like thinks I'm OK, but I know I get on his nerves, because I am too simple in the way that I talk and do things. He says things like, 'Why do you always repeat the things that you say?' I try to stop, but that is who I am, my learning will always have a disability to it. I would like to hug him and kiss him and sometimes I do have sexual feelings for him. We do hug and that's when it feels nice, but I must take time. I always tell him that I am not a fool. What I do like about him, is that if I say he has to go home now, he always leaves, but I'm not sure if this will be the same if I kiss him and have sex with him.

When you have a learning disability you have to be very careful, because people know that we take things the way it is said, so you can be tricked. Let me give you an example. I have a friend who has a learning disability. She wanted to have a boyfriend and she wanted to be married, and when she met a nice guy his family were happy for her because he had a learning disability too, but he was an illegal immigrant. The family tried to get them married. My friend was happy to have a boyfriend and she was happy to get married, but her family had to step in because they realised what was actually happening and that they were forcing the marriage so that their son could get what they call 'his stay' and there was lots of arguing.

My friend realised in the end that she was being used. It makes me even sadder because now I know that she is sleeping with lots of men and I feel like she may be doing prostitution, but getting cigarettes and not much money. When I see this friend I feel sad and she says she lives in a hostel and I feel like this is not the person I knew, yet it is her. I know that all the men that are having sex with her know that she has a learning disability. I sometimes wonder why people do not understand that we have all the feelings that others have but we may not be clear about boundaries and recognising danger when it is around or near.

At the moment I am not running any groups or facilitating them, but I do remember that women who come from the Black or Asian communities and who have a learning disability dated the type of person that was a reflection of the type of workers that run the groups. Therefore, if a group was run by Mencap and (white staff), a lot of the women who were Black would date white men. Yet for the Black Friendly group (Black staff) a lot of the women dated Black men. I am not saying that this is the solid truth but I did notice it.

One of my friends used to talk to me about his girlfriend, but once the staff heard that his girlfriend was pregnant, they gave him hell. They needed support and if they had given them a chance things would have worked better for him, but the girl's mother took over and this is in the Black community. My friend was so angry because he said that she interfered too much and she didn't welcome him. It broke his heart and he just wasn't given a chance to be a father to his child because he had a learning disability. But there are people around me who have grandchildren and none of the parents have a learning disability but they are supported, so what's the difference? My friend had to leave London and he was never the same.

Don't get me wrong, I have friends with learning disabilities and who are married and all the relationships are different. I even have friends who are parents. Having a learning disability is a barrier for us when we want or have relationships, there are many 'do's and don'ts'. A lot of people with learning disability are very huggy and will say 'you're my boyfriend' yet they do not know them. There are people who will take advantage of my hugging and my extra touching, but we don't realise. I think sometimes we need relationship training.

There are lots of children in Social Services who have been taken away from parents with learning disabilities. They constantly tell us that we are not capable of looking after our children, yet I see many people who do not have learning disability who have had their children taken away and they never looked after their children well. I know it is about getting the right support.

Sex is a big issue and people with learning disabilities do actually have a lot of sexual contact, more than people would want to believe. I have seen many people who have attended my groups in the past do many sexual things and sometimes out in the open, where they have had to be guided.

In the end, for myself, I would like someone to love me and I to love them, but sometimes in life you don't get what you want. I know that if people gave us a chance and some support then we could overcome some of our barriers.

When I was at school, we did have some sex education, but it was more about having periods and the boys and the girls were in separate rooms, because I think teachers felt that we shouldn't have sex. Some of our parents think we shouldn't have sex, much less the wider part of society. I am blessed and I fight for my rights and I was lucky to work with a doctor on the 'Books Beyond Words'[2]. I helped with the book that was called *Keeping Healthy Down Below* (Hollins and Downer 2013) because people with learning disability find it hard when they have to deal with sexual health matters. This was an interesting thing for me and I enjoyed it. In the work that I am doing now, I have to look at the quality of life that people receive and one of the things that came up was about them being healthy 'down below'. The support worker told me that the people who came to that organisation need to know this. She knew of the books and thought that they were great. So I will keep on pushing.

Summary

I will always push for the rights of women, children, Black people and people with a learning disability, because I have the experience of all of these things and at times it disables my life. My support worker always says, 'Concentrate on your abilities and dis the disability.' In Jamaica nearly every time we say 'dis' we mean to not regard it, so in my language it is not a good word; to talk about ability is better than *dis*ability.

Reference

Hollins, S. and Downer, J. with illustrations by Webb, B. (2013) *Keeping Healthy Down Below.* London: St Georges University (see www.booksbeyondwords.co.uk/home).

---

2   Books Beyond Words use pictures to engage and empower people who find words difficult to understand. See www.booksbeyondwords.co.uk

CHAPTER 18

THE FINAL FRONTIER

Young People with Learning Difficulties and Sex Education

Ruth Garbutt with an introduction by Lyndon Strickland

Overview

- This chapter talks about sex education for young people with learning difficulties.

- It talks about laws about sex education and what schools should be doing.

- It talks about a research project undertaken by CHANGE[1] that tried to find out more about this topic.

- The research project found that most schools provided sex education. Some schools had sex education classes but other schools only gave sex education to one person at a time if they needed it.

- The project found that different people provided sex education, such as nurses, teachers and social workers. Parents also provided sex education. Sometimes it was a mixture of different people. This could be confusing. Teachers felt that they needed more training to teach sex education. Parents wanted more help too.

- The project found that young people with learning difficulties couldn't always get the information they needed in a format they could understand.

---

1   CHANGE is a National Human Rights Organisation, run by disabled people in Leeds, UK (www.changepeople.org).

- The project found that many parents wanted their sons and daughters to have relationships but they didn't know the best way of talking to them about this.

- The workers on the project have made some recommendations that have come from the project.

- It is a difficult area to talk about and more needs to be done to help young people with learning difficulties.

The writing process

Ruth Garbutt wrote this chapter about the project she had been involved in. Afterwards she explained to Lyndon Strickland, a man with learning difficulties, what was in the chapter, and asked him add a section on his thoughts. Lyndon is a young person who helped on the research project about sex education undertaken by CHANGE. As part of the project a group of young people undertook drama workshops relating to sex, relationships and sex education. This added to the other parts of the research (the interviews, survey and focus groups). Lyndon describes his involvement in the project and says what he got from it and what still needs to be done for young people with learning difficulties. The preferred terminology used by Lyndon and Ruth is 'people with learning difficulties'.

Introduction

LYNDON

It was four or five years ago when I started in the sexuality project. When I first went to the project I didn't know anyone else. I didn't know who was going to be on the project. I was a bit nervous about it and was worried about the questions and the activities. I thought I wasn't going to stick with it. I liked the talking and the information. I thought I wasn't going to fit in but something pulled me toward the group. We did a drama project and we acted out someone going to a chemist to buy condoms. Some of us had a go at playing this. Everyone thought I did brilliant and good. I thought 'this is good'. Sometimes I stayed behind afterwards and helped out at CHANGE.

We produced leaflets about how people can meet with other people who have a learning difficulty and about other sex stuff. It helped people to see if they could get a bond going with others. I thought the leaflets were good and interesting too, I've still got some. I can read them and know what to do in the future. If we hadn't done the leaflets and shown them to the group, none of us would know what to do or what to believe.

I didn't get any sex education at school, none at all. It was a strict school. We did all the other lessons but nothing about sex lessons. There was no feedback on things like that. My mum told the project worker at CHANGE that I would like to come on the sexuality project. She thought I could learn more about it. I was 25 when I started it I think. All that time and effort mum and the project worker gave me I took on board. I feel more prepared now. I have more confidence now.

Sex education still needs improving. If I was still at school we could have a sexuality project and set one up. People get information from TV and the internet which isn't the best. We still need to get a load of information and activities for young people with learning difficulties. If it hadn't been for the sexuality project I'd have been really stuck. I might not have a girlfriend. The project helped me understand things a bit better. It was a good project. I thought it could have gone on a bit longer and we could have got more out of it.

We went to a sexuality conference in Birmingham. I got more information from that. We talked to other people about the project. We did the play about going to the chemist, which was a really good scene. We thought we wouldn't get many people at the presentation but we did – a big group of people and they all took something from it.

If we had the time, chance and money I'd like to do that again – to see what we've learnt and what else could be done, and finish the project completely.

I now work in a resource centre. I've mentioned the sexuality project and they've all talked about it and want to know about it and where I've been.

Introduction

Ruth

This chapter provides an overview of some of the issues experienced by young people with learning difficulties in the UK around sex and relationships education. It will draw on the findings of a recent research project that looked at these issues.

People with learning difficulties in the UK are now able to live more independently in the community. This can include choices about where to live, education, employment and leisure. People with learning difficulties also have rights to relationships that are enshrined in law (e.g. The Human Rights Act 1998, Article 8, The Disability Discrimination Act 1995 and the Mental Capacity Act 2005) and in policies such as *Valuing People Now* (2009). Since the UK policies on community care and the deinstitutionalisation of the 1980s, it could be argued that opportunities for people with learning difficulties to meet other people and get into intimate relationships have greatly increased, and recent articles have also argued that concern about risk, safeguarding, pregnancy and vulnerability has increased the scrutiny of this intimate area of their lives. However, Shakespeare *et al.* (1996) suggest:

> People with learning difficulties face some of the biggest restrictions in terms of availability of sex education. Whereas in other areas of life the trend is towards 'normalization', in other words, fitting people with learning difficulties into the roles and values of the rest of society (Wolfensberger 1972), this does not seem to prevail in the area of sexuality. (Shakespeare *et al.* 1996, p.25)

Given this context, this chapter will particularly look at the need for sex education for people with learning difficulties. Although it will focus on young people with learning difficulties, it is interesting to note that non-disabled young people only gained access to statutory sex education in the 1940s with a focus on 'hygiene', 'modesty' and 'self-control'. It wasn't until 1988 that the Education Reform Act (Section 1) stated that all pupils should be offered the opportunity of receiving a comprehensive, well-planned programme of sex education during their school careers through a curriculum which:

(a) promotes the spiritual, moral, cultural, mental and physical development of pupils at school and of society; and

(b) prepares such pupils for the opportunities, responsibilities and experiences of adult life.

Following this, the 1996 Education Act stated that sex education should include discussions about marriage and should 'encourage pupils to have due regard to moral considerations and family life'. The 1996 Act also stated that parents could withdraw their child from sex education if they chose to do so. Although this legislation equally applies to young people with learning difficulties, this chapter will draw on research that suggests that there are numerous issues that might limit the extent to which these young people access sex education.

Research into this area has included the following aspects: sexual behaviour (Lesselliers 1999); staff attitudes (Grieve *et al.* 2009; Murray *et al.* 1999); parent attitudes (Johnson *et al.* 2002); effectiveness of information (Barber and Redfern 1997; Cambridge 1999; McCarthy and Thompson 1995); sexual knowledge (McCabe 1999; Simpson *et al.* 2006); women with learning difficulties (Gillespie-Sells *et al.* 1998; McCarthy 1999); men with learning difficulties (Yacoub and Hall 2009) and gay, lesbian and bisexual relationships (Abbott and Howarth, 2005). By reviewing the literature it can be seen that little had been reported in relation to young people (defined for the purposes of this chapter as aged 16–25) with learning difficulties around sex and relationships. In response to this gap in the literature, in 2007 CHANGE, a national organisation that fights for the rights of people with learning difficulties, collaborated with the Centre for Disability Studies at Leeds University to set up a three-year research study looking at the views and experiences of young people with learning difficulties in relation to sex and relationships.

Findings from the project indicated that many parents and professionals acknowledged that people with learning difficulties needed increased opportunities to develop relationships and explore their sexuality, if they chose to do so. However, findings also indicated that many of the young people lacked knowledge around sex and relationships. The findings highlighted that there was insufficient sex education and limited availability of accessible information. The responses raised concerns about a lack of support for young people and also for their parents and this was particularly so for young people from Black and Minority Ethnic (BME) communities. The project highlighted the negative attitudes and stereotypes that young people with learning difficulties faced around sex and relationships.

The research highlighted many key messages for practitioners and policy makers, and publications were written with the research team highlighting some of these messages (Garbutt 2008; Garbutt 2009; Tattersall 2009; Tattersall, Roy and Zulu 2009). For the purpose of this chapter, one key aspect of these messages will be discussed: the need for provision of sex and relationships education.

What is currently provided?

A national survey of special schools, focus groups with teachers/governors and interviews with parents were undertaken as part of the research. As a result of the national survey of 200 special schools it was found that, of the 76 schools/colleges that responded to the survey, most of them (90.3 per cent) said that they provided some kind of sex education to their students. For the remaining schools that didn't provide sex education, the reasons included:

- the students were not at a level to understand or had profound disabilities

- teachers hadn't been told they needed to do it

- governors hadn't approved it

- religious ethos

- it was not seen as being important as other topics.

Although most schools/colleges who responded to the survey stated that they provided some form of sex education, only 69.2 per cent of the schools/colleges had it as a compulsory subject, despite legislation (Education Reform Act 1988) to the contrary. The issue of sex education as a compulsory subject was then also discussed in the four focus groups with teachers (about eight to ten in each group) from special schools in a Yorkshire city. The discussions in these groups highlighted some of the difficulties teachers experienced around sex education with pupils with learning difficulties, such as: not being trained or feeling confident to teach it; not knowing about relevant resources; worries about reactions from parents and worries about the vulnerability of the pupils. The teachers in these focus groups indicated that, quite often, sex education was provided in schools, but mainly on an 'as-and-when-needed' basis with individuals rather than following an approved curriculum. The research indicated therefore that sex education, in general, is being provided to young people with learning difficulties, but the level and amount varies depending on the needs of individual pupils.

Who should teach sex education?

Tackling sex and relationships for people with learning difficulties can be difficult for professionals; at the same time, staff attitudes can greatly influence the experiences and rights of people with learning difficulties in this area (Murray *et al.* 1999). Teachers of individuals with learning difficulties have been reluctant to become involved in sex education due to moral beliefs, attitudes, lack of confidence in their abilities to provide adequate sex education and the lack of availability of sex education materials (Howard-Barr *et al.* 2005; Murray and Minnes 1994; Smigielski and Steinmann 1981). Diamond (1984) states that, 'While they [professionals]… generally wish the sexual concerns to be ignored; they want them to sort of "go away", since they are ill at ease dealing with them, and don't really know how to handle the issues' (Diamond 1984, p.210).

The research undertaken by CHANGE found that there were variations in who actually delivered sex education. This, in turn, meant that young people could miss out on receiving information as there was no clear guidance on who should be providing the information. From the national survey within the research it was found that the main group delivering sex education was school teachers and college lecturers (93.9 per cent). A smaller percentage of educational institutions used a school nurse (27.3 per cent), a specialist sexual health worker (19.7 per cent) or someone else (30.3 per cent) such as care staff, counsellors or support staff. Further in-depth questioning in the focus groups found that there were mixed views around who *should* be teaching sex education to young people with learning difficulties. The suggestions varied between community nurses (who were seen as best placed because they networked between school and home); specialist staff from outside (who could be specially trained); teachers (as they would know the young person and have a good relationship with them); teachers and parents together (so there was continuity between home and school); or two people at once (such as a specially trained member of staff with a teacher, so that there was the trust and also the specialist input). This quote exemplifies some of the comments: 'I don't think it's just resources, I think it's professional input, it's trained input as well. We've all got teacher training but we don't have specific sex education training in this field. I think it's a specialist field.'

The research found that those teachers who did actually have a level of confidence around delivering sex and relationships education (which was only a small handful) tended to be those who had been given previous training and had been teaching sex education for several years.

The research also included interviews with 20 parents and these interviews generated further discussion on the area of who should deliver sex education. The parents in the study stated that quite often they ended up giving their child information about sex and relationships as the child either wasn't getting it from anywhere else, or the information hadn't been presented to them in a form that they could understand. One parent stated:

> At the end of the day…no one is going to give her [my daughter] that information except for me, I would think. There's no other source for her. She wouldn't dream of going looking for it. My daughter has only just started making her own hair appointments so she isn't going to go to a family planning clinic.

Many of the parents suggested that professionals could be doing more within this area, particularly community nurses, as the following quote from one of the parents implies: 'I think there should be more work done in partnership. The community nursing team has all those resources, they are experienced professionals… They [community nurses] should be going into school as part of PSHE (Personal, Social and Health Education).' Similarly to the teachers, many parents felt that there could be more than one person responsible for sex education, for example:

> It should be provided by parents like me, school and to a certain extent through the social services… So really wherever, as many places as possible, as many opportunities as possible…social workers. Support workers. Anybody who is involved with these young people.

The findings of the research indicated that there was no one specific person who was responsible for teaching sex education. This was found to be confusing for parents and it meant that young people could fall through the net as there could be an assumption that another professional was doing this work. The parents in the study were indicating that they would welcome more help in this area and the chance to work together with professionals to achieve a good outcome for their sons and daughters. The teachers in the study indicated that they would also welcome more guidance and direction and to work with trained professionals.

Although the research focused mainly on the experiences of young people, teachers and parents, throughout the course of the research, the role of sexual health clinics and sexual health workers came under scrutiny. By networking with clinics/workers in the local area, it was found that, although the clinics/workers had policies that their service was for all, they did not always have adequate information in accessible formats and hadn't made due consideration for the needs of people with learning difficulties. They welcomed the chance to talk with the research team about this and indicated that they were very willing to consider making changes to their services in order to support people with learning difficulties better. In this way the project has begun a pathway to impact by improving support in local areas.

Experiences in mainstream schools and special schools

The Department for Education's guidance is that schools have a duty to ensure that children special educational needs, including those with learning difficulties, are properly included in sex and relationship education (DfEE 2000). 'Special schools' have broadly the same duties and responsibilities as other schools, in that they must apply the National Curriculum and carry out its assessment procedures, for example. However, the findings of the research by CHANGE indicated that young people with learning difficulties could have differing experiences of sex education, depending on whether they were in a mainstream school or in a special school.

Some of the teachers in the focus groups indicated that they felt that some young people with learning difficulties could miss out on sex education if they went to a mainstream school as the sex education classes were often not at a level that they could understand. However, they suggested that these young people might be more aware of relationships and sexuality because they would be more integrated with other young people. In this way, therefore, they might have a fuller awareness of puberty and of their own sexuality but if they were unable to understand the information they were being taught, they could potentially end up being more sexually vulnerable.

Many of the teachers said that special schools could potentially respond to the needs of the students more and it could be done in a more sensitive way. They also said that in special schools it is easier to have small groups, that information can be adapted more easily, that teachers know the students better and that a young person could undertake a sex education programme again if they missed out on it or didn't understand it. However, as suggested earlier, sometimes special schools only taught sex education on an 'as and when needed' basis and often the teachers didn't feel confident to teach it.

The findings from the study indicate that schools play an important role in teaching sex education to young people with learning difficulties. However, the study shows that there were benefits, and also difficulties, within both mainstream and special schools. The important message arising from the study is that young people with learning difficulties should have sex education in a format that they can understand.

Summary

The research found that many parents were positive about the possibility of their sons and daughters having relationships. 17 (out of 20) parents interviewed within the research said that they wanted their young people to have relationships because it was a right, as the following quotes show:

> I don't think we can just leave them, I think we owe it to them really to help them. (Mother)

> [It] comes down to equal rights really, doesn't it, I don't see why just cos they've got learning difficulties why should they…be penalised..?(Mother)

> I really hope that my son has the opportunity to have a full sexual relationship, get married and have children. (Mother)

However, the main areas of concern for parents were around the lack of information and the lack of proactive support from professionals. They also indicated that they worried about the vulnerability of the young person and they did not always know the best way of tackling the subject: there was no clear guidance from professionals and no standard resources.

This chapter has touched on some of the issues involved, such as the background legislation, the extent of provision, the professionals and the issues around both mainstream and special schools. As a result of the research on which this chapter is based, the final report for the research (CHANGE 2009) made the following recommendations about sex education for people with learning difficulties:

- Young people with learning disabilities should have a human right to sex education.

- There needs to be more accessible information and support.

- There should be more places for young people with learning disabilities to meet each other and spend time together.

- Sex education should be improved through giving teachers access to more resources and more training.

- There needs to be better training for teachers, sexual health professionals and learning disability nurses about delivering sex education.

- Negative attitudes of professionals, parents and other people…need to be challenged.

These recommendations are a starting point for moving forward on such a complex issue.

The area of sex and relationships education for young people with learning difficulties would benefit from further research and the messages need to be fed into policy and practice in this area. There is a long way to go. As Shakespeare *et al.* (1996) suggested, this area has not been 'normalized' yet. As the title of this chapter suggests, for people with learning difficulties, getting access to a fair and accessible service to support their sexual and relationships needs could be seen as the 'final frontier'.

References

Abbott, D. and Howarth, J. (2005) *Secret Loves, Hidden Lives? Exploring Issues for People with Learning Difficulties who are Gay, Lesbian or Bisexual.* Bristol: The Policy Press.

Barber, F. and Redfern, P. (1997) 'Safer Sex Training for Peer Educators.' In P. Cambridge and H. Brown (eds) *HIV and Learning Disability.* London: Routledge.

Cambridge, P. (1999) 'Considerations for informing safer sex education work with men with learning disabilities.' *British Journal or Learning Disabilities 27,* 123–126.

CHANGE (2009) *Talking about Sex and Relationships: The Views of Young People with Learning Disabilities, Final Report.* Leeds: CHANGE.

DfEE (Department for Education and Employment) (2000) *Sex and Relationship Education Guidance.* 0116/2000. London: DfEE publications.

Department of Health (2009) *Valuing People Now: A New Three-year Strategy for People with Learning Disabilities.* London: The Stationery Office.

Diamond, M. (1984) 'Sexuality and the Handicapped.' In R.P. Marinelli and A. Dell Orto (eds) *The Psychological and Social Impact of Physical Disability.* New York: Springer Publishing.

Garbutt, R. (2009) 'Barriers to relationships and sexuality for young people with learning disabilities.' *Community Living Magazine,* December.

Garbutt, R. (2008) 'Sex and relationships for people with learning disabilities: A challenge for parents and professionals.' *Mental Health and Learning Disabilities Research and Practice 5,* 2, 266–277.

Gillespie-Sells, K., Hills, M. and Robbins, B. (1998) *She Dances to Different Drums.* London: King's Fund publishing.

Grieve, A., McClaren, S., Lindsay, W. and Culling, E. (2009) 'Staff attitudes towards the sexuality of people with learning disabilities: A comparison of different professional groups and residential facilities.' *British Journal of Learning Disabilities 37*, 1, 76–84.

Howard-Barr, E.M., Rienzo, B.A., Rienzo, R.M., Pigg, Jr. and James, D. (2005) 'Teacher beliefs, professional preparation, and practices regarding exceptional students and sexuality education.' *The Journal of School Health 75*, 99–104.

Johnson, K., Frawley, P., Hillier, L. and Harrison, L. (2002) 'Living safer sexual lives: Research and action.' *Tizard Learning Disability Review 7*, 3, 4–9.

Lesselliers, J. (1999) 'A right to sexuality?' *British Journal of Learning Disabilities 27*, 4, 137–140.

McCabe, M.P. (1999) 'Sexual knowledge, experience and feelings among people with disability.' *Sexuality and Disability 17*, 2, 57–170.

McCarthy, M. (1999) *Sexuality and Women with Learning Disabilities.* London: Jessica Kingsley Publishers.

McCarthy, M. and Thompson, D. (1995) 'No More Double Standards: Sexuality and People with Learning Difficulties.' In T. Philpot and L. Ward (eds) *Values and Visions: Changing Ideas in Services for People with Learning Difficulties.* Oxford: Butterworth-Heinemann.

Murray, J.L., MacDonald, R.A.R. and Levenson, V.L. (1999) 'Staff attitudes towards the sexuality of individuals with learning disabilities: A service-related study of organisational policies.' *British Journal of Learning Disabilities 27*, 141–150.

Murray, J.L. and P.M. Minnes (1994) 'Staff attitudes towards the sexuality of persons with intellectual disability.' *Australia and New Zealand Journal of Developmental Disabilities 19*, 45–52.

Shakespeare, T., Gillespie-Sells, K. and Davies, D. (1996) *The Sexual Politics of Disability: Untold Desires.* London: Cassell.

Simpson, A., Lafferty, A. and McConkey, R. (2006) *Out of the Shadows: A Report of the Sexual Health and Wellbeing of People with Learning Disabilities in Northern Ireland.* London: FPA.

Smigielski, P.A. and Steinmann, M.J. (1981) 'Teaching sex education to multiply handicapped adolescents.' *The Journal of School Health 51*, 238–41.

Tattersall, J. (2009) 'Let's talk about sex.' *Our Say Magazine*, May/June.

Tattersall, J., Roy, D. and Zulu, P. (2009) 'Letter.' *Disability and Society 24*, 6, 673–674.

Yacoub, E. and Hall, I. (2009) 'The sexual lives of men with mild learning disability: a qualitative study.' *British Journal of Learning Disabilities 37*, 1, 5–11.

CHAPTER 19

'WOMEN LIKE SOAPS AND MEN LIKE FOOTBALL'

The Men's Room: Intellectually Disabled Men Talking
About their Views on Women, Relationships and Sex

Bill, Peter and Alan with Niall McNulty

Overview

- A group of men talked together about their views on women, relationships and sex.

- There are different types of relationships.

- Some relationships can be good but some are bad.

- It can be very hard to meet women and get to talk to them.

- Meeting people in public spaces, such as parks, or through dating agencies seemed to give a more accessible route.

- Some did not agree with this.

- There were differences of opinion about looking at women and admiring them.

- Some people have negative views of people with learning difficulties.

- It can be hard to feel accepted and included.

The writing process

Five men took part in a series of discussions about men's issues around relationships and intimacy. The small group met over a series of four sessions to answer some questions, share some of their own experiences and look at relationships from a male perspective. The group was made up of three men who had been labelled as having a learning difficulty; Bill, Peter and Alan, plus two support workers. One of the support workers, Niall McNulty, facilitated and wrote up the conversations. The Men's Room is situated in a large rural county in the North of England.

In order to keep the names confidential, because of the nature of the conversations, the chapter has been written as a discussion between four people, Bill, Peter, Alan and Niall. This could mirror any group of men sitting around a table talking over a few drinks.

The initial sessions were quiet and we talked a lot about what the word 'relationship' meant. Apart from some minor editing, we have kept as near as possible to the words actually used. Alan used fewer words but was very much part of the conversation. Interestingly, in regard to terminology, the men did not use any specific label, although 'difference' was mentioned.

Relationships

Bill said relationships were about people getting together, *'There are different types of relationships; like with your friends, or a girlfriend or boyfriend.'*

Peter thought that relationships were about when two people wanted to be together or wanted to live together and share things. But, as Bill said, there are different kinds of relationships, and this includes good ones and bad ones.

There's always a need to find a place to start; relationships are a difficult thing to talk about, but most people have something to say about them. The group talked about what they thought might be a good or bad relationship: *'There are good and there are bad relationships. That much I know, and sometimes the people who are in them don't even know it. You see it on TV and with others; sometimes there is nothing good about it'* (Peter).

Bill thought that abusive relationships would include beatings and fighting, which would be *'doing the wrong thing'*. Peter added that staying out late, bringing home bottles of wine and drinking alcohol all the time, would be wrong.

Bill had been married and divorced and had been struggling to start a relationship over the past few years. He said, *'I don't understand why people would do this, we are on this world to be in a relationship, to have a good time with girls, to take them out...not to fight, have wars and things.'*

Peter said that a good relationship was about going out and having a laugh, talking, smooching, going to the cinema or having a meal out. At the end of the night you would have a happy feeling after a date, like a *'thumbs-up feeling'*.

Physical closeness was important. Bill thought that going home with the other person, watching TV, making tea and *'putting an arm around her and cuddling'* were ideal.

'In a relationship there may be some of the same things that you do with your friends, like going to see a film or having a drink, but it is different with a girlfriend or partner, it's a different kind of thing. I like my friends and being with them is a good laugh, but I don't want to kiss them' (Peter).

He added, *'Sometimes I really like being with my friends, I like that we know each other and that we do things together. But I really like to have a girlfriend; it's like having a friend only more…like you can say more and be together more.'*

Why would anyone want to be in a relationship?

'I would love to be in a relationship, not just in a relationship but to be in love and be loved by someone. Being with someone and knowing that you will be together for the rest of your life; that would make me happy' (Bill).

Peter thought that appearance was important. He and Bill and Alan agreed that a girl should have a good complexion, a nice body and walk in a good way.

Talking about sex

Niall asked the men what they thought on the topic of sex.

Bill set out that, *'This can come later after meeting someone.'*

Peter argued that, *'There's more to a relationship than just sex…you have to find out what each other wants, and wait until people are ready'*. He added, *'Years ago disabled people couldn't have a child. Now people have safe sex and they should always use a condom. Some people don't use them, but they should.'*

He also thought that if a couple argued it would probably be about when to have a baby: *'She might be upset and crying and rush out the door because he doesn't want to get into it, when she does.'*

Alan added, *'This is when it goes pear-shaped.'*

Talking about pornography

Bill talked about pornography.

'When you're with your (men) friends and you're watching something which has adult material in it; it would be different with a woman. It would be uncomfortable with a lady…whereas with your friends it's just a laugh…but it does depend on what men it would be with, like it would be different with Prince Charles.'

He added, *'Some of the TV shows I watch are on the Playboy channel and there's nothing wrong with that.'* But Peter disagreed and said, *'I think it's not right.'*

Niall questioned what they would do if their partner thought that men who looked at porn were perverts?

Bill said, *'I would think she was wrong, and I would tell her so as she probably has to accept me the way I am. We all have our likes and dislikes. She probably likes soaps and I don't. I wouldn't be nasty to her, but just let her know what I like.'*

However, there were other things to consider: *'The hardest thing is to even start a relationship. There's nowhere to go, or people who would help you.'*

Issues around meeting women

Peter thought that if people went to mainstream schools then it would be easier to grow up knowing how to talk to women. He also thought that parents could be a barrier to relationships later on when adults were still at home with their parents, but if people were living on their own, then it would be up to them.

Bill said that he had never talked to his parents about relationships, but that some people's parents were more open. He thought this was strange because obviously his parents had sex.

Bill, Peter and Alan agreed that no one should get in the way of people having relationships.

Peter said he used to go out into town on a Saturday night because there were lots of people, especially women around. *'But,'* he said, *'they wouldn't talk to me or when I looked at them they wouldn't smile… It's really hard to meet someone, to start talking to them. Some places are too noisy and then if you did get to talk to a woman then some bloke would get in the way, or think you were bothering her. I don't like going out in town any more, it's just too rough and not friendly.'*

He added that he had been to seminars about relationships and to speed-dating as well as dating agencies.

Niall asked, was it really hard to meet people?

Bill said, *'It's how we are. I could meet someone when I'm out but it depends on how they look at you. You have to keep smiling, and they will be smiling, and then you talk to each other.'*

But Peter interjected, *'If that happens there's always someone with them, or they have a boyfriend or someone comes along and gets in the way.'* He said he wanted to try to go on TV dating shows like *Take Me Out*.

Niall wondered if that was a good thing and he said, *'I don't think I would be confident enough to do that. They seem to judge people on what they look like and it's all in front of an audience – plus it's on the tele.'*

Peter replied, *'But, at least you are able to meet people and talk to them. At least you get the chance to try and talk to them before someone else interferes. I have also registered on dating sites in the newspaper but sometimes they are difficult to manage, it would be good to get help to do all these things.'*

Niall asked how else or where else can men meet women?

Bill responded, *'I meet different types of women, but it's hard to find the right one. Somebody out there is my type... but that's the thing, it's not easy to meet them. It's not right to say but I would like someone normal; a normal woman, and that's why I used to go out to clubs and pubs, but then some of them are just not nice.'*

Peter said, *'When I go out I ask someone if I can buy them a drink. If they say yes I will buy them what they want and talk to them.'*

Bill replied, *'I think that there's not enough time to talk to them so when I have been out I've gone up to women and said "I love you, do you want to come home with me?" They will either smack you or not.'*

Peter was surprised. He said, *'I think that is wrong as it can put people off us, that way of talking. The way you talk to women is different to talking to men friends. You can have a good crack and joke with your mates.'*

Bill remembered, *'In the old days you would just tell them that you want to go out with them... "Give us your number and I'll ring you later"!'*

Peter replied, *'But you wouldn't demand it, you would ask in a nice way... I would write a letter or something, or ask for a phone number. It would be easier than talking or going up to someone.'*

Peter had met someone when he was in long-stay hospital (an institution for intellectually disabled people). He said, *'The men and women were on separate wards and the women would come to us. That's how it should be. It was just organised by the staff and there were no worries about what would happen as there was always staff around. There used to be dances in the hospital and we would be able to meet up.'* He added, *'I remember hearing stories from someone who lived there about patients sneaking off together and having sex. One of my friends did it. He just met up with a girl from the other ward that he knew and then they were having sex. He only told me he said, because he didn't want the matron to find out…it wasn't allowed but people did it…we're all human.'*

Alternatives: where is it best to meet people?

In contrast, Bill thought the best place to meet someone would be in the park, *'I could say "hello" to someone I like and then if they say "hello" back I would talk to them more… I would follow them and talk to them if I liked them… This is a better way to meet people, better than in town. In town there's a lot of people watching you. In the town girls don't want to talk to you because there are so many other people about. They are not friendly and other people are watching them so you can't talk to someone or say "hello". I think it's because of the way we are. It feels like other people are watching you all the time.'*

Peter agreed, *'I think it's safer talking to people in the park, more friendly and nicer.'*

Niall questioned if it might be that talking to women in the park could lead to trouble. Was it predatory behaviour? He asked if it might be a bit scary for someone who is walking through the park, especially if you then started walking after them.

Peter replied, *'This is what I hate…you are not just standing there looking at them, but you are admiring them. It's not exactly staring at them…its admiring. I've done this before and I've been caught, it's just looking, but other people don't like it. It's not offensive, but other people think it is and it can get you into trouble; there's cameras in the park and they record what you are doing.'*

Bill thought that some people might find it a bit weird, *'But it all depends on the type of woman…it all depends on whether they are a miserable woman or a happy woman and I don't want to be with a miserable woman.'*

Peter agreed, *'The parks are nicer places to be, nicer to talk to people, especially when it's good weather. But people think because we are different that we are staring at women and that's not right. It's more like admiring them and then maybe talking; it's no more than that and it's difficult to be able to do that in a club or pub.'*

Niall was concerned, *'But the way people see it, it might be seen as dangerous, they might judge what you are doing?'*

Bill asked Niall, *'But where else is there that's safe and nice for us to meet people?'*

Peter said, *'That's why I talk about going on TV dating shows or to a dating agency. At least it's doing something, and then other people aren't so worried.'*

Niall added, *'Usually people meet a husband or wife on a night out, or through friends or mainly, it seems, at work.'*

'There you go,' replied Bill. *'There's not a lot of places to go for nights out that I feel happy to go to. I've stopped going out to clubs because I don't enjoy it. There's nothing fun about people looking at you. Where I work it's all different and separate. There are women to talk to but they're more like in charge and it's a different set of rules where I work.'*

'There are women in the Centre, but it's not like that where I work,' added Peter.

Bill continued, *'And also I don't really like it there. It's difficult to meet women, and so it's difficult to get into a relationship. Then once you have met someone it's about talking to them and knowing what to say.'*

Peter replied, *'Just be yourself I think. If not, how are they going to get to know you?'*

Bill mused, *'But you've got to be funny first…otherwise they won't talk to you.'*

Peter added, *'I will only talk to people I think are nice, who are smiling. You know then that you can be yourself.'*

Learning about relationships

Niall pondered on this, *'No one tells you this stuff though. No one tells you how to talk to women, what you should say, how to say it. How do you know?'*

Bill said, *'You just have to try it. Try and say something; sometimes it'll work and sometimes you might get a slap!'*

Peter confided, *'I wouldn't know what to say. Sometimes I can't think of things. It's a hard thing to do when you're talking to someone. Trying to say what you want to and then if you feel so much for them…it's hard…where do people learn how to do this stuff?'*

Previous relationships

Bill had previously been married to Annette. They were introduced by a social worker. He talked about the wedding day, that it was sunny and he felt good. His brother was his best man.

He was asked why the relationship had not worked out. Bill replied, *'After we were married she started to go out drinking. She changed, she would stay out late and we had lots of arguments, slamming doors, and in the end we went our separate ways. She kept telling me, "this is not going to work out". In the end she found another partner, it put me off…now she is married to someone at work.'*

Peter added, *'This is a problem when people are in a relationship and one person wants to do one thing and the other wants to do something else, it's not easy, it's hard. You need to wait until the girl is ready and she likes you. You have to wait for the person to come to you.'*

Looking towards the future

Alan talked about a woman he knew and said, *'I just need to say "hello" and "how are you doing?"'*

Bill said he would really like to be in another relationship but that he wouldn't get married again.

Peter thought that he wouldn't have children or pets but would like to be living with a woman: *'We would spend time together, watch TV and enjoy life.'* However, he also warned, *'It all starts nicely and then it goes bad. It's hard because I have a job and you need to have time and patience. Relationships are hard and difficult and there are other things that need doing.'*

Summary

NIALL

The conversation will carry on in pubs, snooker halls and anywhere men get together. It might not always be so honest, but relationships are something everyone has an opinion on, or questions about.

It is hoped that conversations with this men's group will continue as they can share what they think and feel. They can support each other and talk to each other, which is more than some men's groups might do. The difficulty that they have is feeling accepted and included in the traditional routes and methods of starting a relationship and meeting a potential girlfriend. The parks, TV shows and dating agencies seem a more acceptable and accessible route.

Graphics

These images are created by KIRSTY LIDDELL (Yarrow).

FIGURE 19.1 YEARS AGO DISABLED PEOPLE COULD NOT HAVE A CHILD

FIGURE 19.2 PUTTING AN ARM AROUND HER AND CUDDLING

FIGURE 19.3 FOUR MEN SITTING AROUND
A TABLE HAVING A FEW DRINKS

CHAPTER 20

INTELLECTUALLY DISABLED PEOPLE WHO SELL OR WHO ARE SOLD FOR SEX IN THE UK

An Exploration

Craig Blyth and Rohhss Chapman with an introduction by Louise Townson

Overview

- This chapter is about a hidden activity that needs to be researched in further depth.

- We already know that people with intellectual disabilities may access prostitutes to buy sex.

- We already know that some intellectually disabled people may commit sexual offences.

- What we know far less about are intellectually disabled people who sell sex or are sold for sex by others in the UK.

- There are some researchers who have mentioned this in the past.

- Some comments have been made indirectly when academics are researching other topics.

- We are planning to research the topic but we are only at the start of the work.

- It will be very difficult to find people to be included in the research.

The writing process

This chapter was written by Craig and Rohhss, based on a presentation they did together in Finland in 2013. This was an initial study to obtain funding for a further project. As it is such a hidden area of research they were unable, at this stage, to write together with an intellectually disabled researcher or colleague. Louise read the paper and made her comments as an introduction. She did emphasise that it was a hidden topic which she knew very little about. The aim, eventually, is to access intellectually disabled men and women who sell or are sold for sex to put forward their own narratives. We are using the term 'intellectual disability' as it is the preference of the publishers.

Introduction

LOUISE

We talk a lot about relationships and the lack of knowledge that people with intellectual disabilities have about them. Prostitution is a very complex issue. I think that many people with intellectual disabilities might not have even heard of the words 'prostitution' and 'exploitation', let alone understand the meaning of them.

This is totally wrong. They are just as likely to have a sexual relationship and be at risk of catching a sexually transmitted disease as anyone else, so they should be educated in all matters regarding sex.

I do feel that the reason staff, parents and carers don't talk about prostitution and exploitation is because they think people with intellectual disabilities don't need to know about that. I have never come across a prostitute or working girl or anything like that, but it doesn't mean it doesn't happen. Some disabled people are supported to spend time with prostitutes so that they can have a sex life.

This chapter looks at something a bit different – Rohhss and Craig have written about the hidden issue of how people with intellectual disabilities may be sold by others or sell themselves for sex. It is an area where not much is written and because of that we have placed it near the end of the book. We know that further research needs to be done.

Introduction

CRAIG AND ROHHSS

We want to begin this chapter by acknowledging it is a sensitive area of research and is, more often, an area of the social world that is ignored or believed not to occur. We had been working on a review of literature to help us put in a funding application on this topic. We found there was clear evidence that within the UK there are intellectually disabled people either selling sexual services or, in some cases, being sold for sex. This concerns us because we know it is a largely hidden topic and we are very concerned about sexual health.

The main body of the chapter looks at the gaps in our current knowledge and at some of the themes arising from previous research and literature. We conclude by looking at the implications of these findings for intellectually disabled people who are active in the sex industry and for those people and services that support them.

Background

CRAIG

Both Rohhss and I have had a long-standing research interest in issues related to disability and sexuality.

As I mentioned in Chapter 16, I have undertaken qualitative research with disabled gay men exploring their experiences of commercial and alternative gay spaces (Blyth 2009, 2010). As a result of this work, I was made aware of the lack of access that intellectually disabled gay men had to commercial and social gay spaces and how, for many, this resulted in them accessing alternative spaces such as public toilets or cruising grounds. Whilst this work did not bring me into contact with disabled gay men who were selling sexual services, it highlighted how a lack of access to commercial and social gay spaces was resulting in many of the men accessing the more 'risky' spaces. For example, all of the men who participated in my study accessed public toilets and other 'cruising' grounds to meet other gay men. The use of these spaces is well documented (Blyth 2009; Cambridge 1999; Thompson 1994) as are the risks associated (such as the risk of sexual violence, gay bashing and sexually transmitted infections). In addition, whilst reviewing literature relevant to the project, I was becoming aware that others were acknowledging (often in fleeting ways) that there were intellectually disabled men selling sexual services. Finally, as someone that spends a lot of time in the second largest commercial gay space in Europe (the Village) I was aware from my own observations that there was a group of young men who were obviously selling sexual services and, at the time, I suspected that a number of these young people were intellectually disabled.

ROHHSS

My interest in this area comes from working closely as an ally with intellectually disabled women in the self-advocacy movement over the past 24 years. Part of our work had been to create space for women to talk and discuss issues personal to them, which led to engagement in a number of funded projects focused on women in a northern county of the UK. At our initial conference organised and run by intellectually disabled women, narratives around relationship experiences resonated with research by McCarthy (1999). She found that 14 of the 17 women she interviewed in her study had experienced sexual abuse of one kind or another and that some had experienced several acts of abuse. Later research (Chivers and Mathieson 2000) corroborates these findings.

The anecdotal evidence of the women we worked with suggested a complex situation. Some talked of acts that had taken place without their control or consent and until they had the space to discuss it with others, they had little idea this constituted abuse. Yet many of these women wanted to continue in their relationships and resented the interference of relatives or others interrupting their situations.

Furthermore, it had been noted in our women's work that some of the women had linked up with much older men in the community, where they 'stayed overnight' in exchange for 'meals out' and other 'rewards'. Whilst this would perhaps be seen as on the fringes of 'selling sex', there is much anecdotal evidence from the old long-stay institutions that women engaged in sexual favours in exchange for cigarettes and other commodities as a means of barter (see Chapter 13).

It is well recorded that intellectually disabled people may feel very isolated, and that 'it is the primacy of a relationship that is often more important that what is happening within it' (Landman 2010). Landman worked on a UK project about mate crime safety where an intellectually disabled woman was being persuaded by her boyfriend to have sex with his mates as a way of obtaining money.

Issues arising from our work in the north of the UK led to a focus on sexual health, promoting activities such as engaging with the Josephine Project (see Chapter 11) and individualised work with support from Women's Aid. What was learned was that constructing women as victims who needed to be rescued was felt as patronising rather than helpful and undermined women's volition and self-confidence. Unsurprisingly, there is a plethora of literature upholding social stereotypes of disabled women as passive and helpless (Hassouneh-Philips and Curry 2002).

So the message from this work was to understand the complexities of women's relationships through their own narratives and interpretations (Bryman 2004), and that where notions of victimisation are imposed it becomes very difficult for women to empower themselves and may lead to ever more unwelcome control by others.

Additionally, my work in inclusive research (Chapman 2006), working in partnership with intellectually disabled colleagues, sets out the type of research approach we feel necessary; we want to hear directly the narratives of those involved. Again this influences the approach to further research.

Overall, the combination of both of our interests in relation to sexuality and disability have, for us, created what Ravetz (1971, p.135) described as the seeds of any research project and that is simply an 'awareness that there is a question to be asked'.

Terminology in this area of research

Equally contentious and theoretically driven is the use of words such as 'sex worker' or 'prostitute'. The feminist movement has divided opinion over those who interpret prostitution as violence against women (Labour Left Review 2007), and those who hold a more neoliberal perspective that prostitution is sex work, like any other form of work, that sex workers may enact individual choice over whether to be involved and further, that the state should not interfere (Pataniak 2002 and Lisborg 2002, cited in Jeffreys 2008). However, most people are agreed that anyone exploited in the name of prostitution or sex work has a right to protection and support.

It is clear from the literature reviewed that exploitation, abuse and trafficking are rife; moreover, that prostitutes/sex workers are particularly vulnerable and that desperate choices are made in their lives. To this effect, women in prostitution in the UK are 18 times more likely to be murdered than the general population (Jarvinen *et al.* 2008). Even so, it could be viewed that much analysis is overlaid by a particular standpoint.

We are against exploitation and criminalisation of sex workers but we are equally averse to binary assertions over the intentions of people involved in sex work/prostitution (at least until we research further). We need terminology that includes men and women in a variety of relationships rather than the topic being typically constructed within a heteronormative framework.

Contrasts between conservative and liberal morality are rife. In short, a conservative view would hold there is something intrinsically wrong in sex work, that it is a threat to society and its institutions and that if the threat is proved, it should be banned. However a liberal approach does not focuses on the inherent characteristics of the act but rather on whether there is more harm committed by banning it (Mahoney 1984). The Nordic approach[1] calls for decriminalisation of those exploited in prostitution and the criminalisation of demand, which is much the same as is being called for by parts of the UK feminist movements. Taking all of these factors into account, we are currently using the term 'sex work'.

Method

We have undertaken a literature review covering databases and electronic journals using keywords such as intellectual disability/ies, learning disability/ies, prostitution, sex, sexuality, sexual offending, sex work/ers, exploitation and abuse. We significantly increased the range of years of publication to expand our findings.

---

1   Sweden understands prostitution as a form of violence against women and a symptom of inequality. In its 1999 Act, it also committed to tackling global sex trafficking. (This works alongside funding for harm ministration and exit services.)

However, it quickly became apparent that the range of literature we accessed fell into a number of strands:

- sex education

- sexual health

- HIV and intellectually disabled gay men

- intellectually disabled men accessing or being supported to access prostitutes or sex workers

- violence and abuse against (intellectually disabled) women and issues of identity

- abuse and safeguarding – as victims of sexual abuse

- intellectually disabled men as perpetrators of sexual abuse regarding offending.

Specific research and literature related to intellectually disabled people selling or being sold for sex was very limited. This parallels the findings of Jeffreys (2008, p.330) who commented, 'Evidence about the exploitation of girls and women with disabilities in prostitution is anecdotal at present. No research has been conducted into the percentage of prostituted women who fall into this category.'

In fact, there were only a handful of articles related to disability and sex workers and of those only two – the study by Kuosmanen and Starke (2011), in their work on prostitution in Gothenberg, Sweden, and the work of Paul Cambridge (1995) in the UK – deal directly with people labelled as having intellectual disabilities. There are, however, a number of media articles particularly related to Australia that also point to intellectually disabled women as prostitutes, recorded by Jeffreys (2008).

General construction of intellectually disabled people's sexuality

Before detailing the findings of the review specifically in relation to intellectually disabled people working in the sex industry, we want to outline the dominant ways in which intellectually disabled people's sexuality is constructed and understood within the literature, but also within the services designed to support them.

It is widely recognised that one dominant view within western society (and raised throughout this book) is that intellectually disabled people are 'asexual' and often considered to be 'eternal children' (Ryan and Thomas 1987). This construction not only denies people their rights to a sexual life but contributes to services becoming 'blind' to their needs in relation to sexual issues.

There is a myriad of literature that details how intellectual disability services both implicitly and explicitly deny people support in this area. For example, Blyth (2009, p.117) described how one intellectually disabled men had been told to 'stop being dirty' when he asked questions relating to sex or sexuality. Whilst this lack of appropriate support is clearly unacceptable and can lead to people being left feeling confused and unsupported, research carried out by Carson (2002) highlighted how services' inability to conceptualise intellectually disabled adults as sexual beings can be, as he puts it, 'paramount to preparation for death'. He justifies this statement by exploring how a young man was told by his support staff that he didn't need to know about condoms when in fact he was having unprotected sex on a daily basis with other men in public toilets.

Similarly, according to Fitzgerald and Withers (2011, p.8) in their interviews with ten intellectually disabled women regarding sex and sexuality, the women felt sex was something that should not be talked about and further they were 'not allowed' to have sex, that if they 'got caught' they would be 'in trouble', that is, they believed other people prohibited them from engaging in sexual activity. Further, according to the authors (Fitzgerald and Withers 2011, p.9), they appeared to live in a state of 'suspended adolescence' evidenced by the participants being unable to identify themselves as women: 'One woman said she felt like a "grown teenager" even though she was 56 years old'. They, and a number of other authors, discuss this infantilisation and denial of women's sexuality.

So to summarise, it is clear from the literature that, currently, within the UK many intellectually disabled people are left with little or no support in the area of sex and sexual relationships as a result of the dominant construction of being viewed as non-sexual beings.

Overview of findings

Despite the hidden nature of our topic, there is, without doubt, evidence that intellectually disabled people are selling sex and sexual services within the UK.

However, the fact that this issue has not attracted the attention of the academic world is evidenced by our identifying only one small-scale piece of UK research that specifically investigated the issue. This study was led by Cambridge (1995) at the Tizard Centre at Kent University. It is telling that the only specific piece of research was undertaken nearly 20 years ago.

The project was an evaluation of an eight-month sexual health outreach programme targeted at intellectually disabled women who worked as prostitutes. The project was operated by the UK sexual health organisation Respond. The evaluation consisted of interviews with a range of professionals working within the project, case studies of users of the service and the analysis of activity and contact records.

The project also included women who, whilst working in the sex industry, were also victims of domestic violence and some who were pregnant and living within support services. The project, whilst modest in size and timescale, clearly established that these women were working on the streets of a London borough as prostitutes.

In addition to doing direct work with project staff and users, the authors met with key professionals working within a range of learning disability support services across London. Cambridge (1995) reported that staff across these services were aware that people were involved in providing sexual services which included the following situations:

- intellectually disabled women's partners 'selling' them for sex

- a young intellectually disabled man being sold for sex for as little as 20p

- intellectually disabled people exchanging sex for favours or 'friendship' within services

- an intellectually disabled woman who was assaulted by her partner and who encouraged his friends to have sex with her

- a women who would wander up and down a high street and exchange sex for cigarettes or for as little as 50p

- family members using 'sweets' to encourage intellectually disabled relatives to engage in sexual activities.

Whilst this project was geographically limited it evidenced that vulnerable young people were also selling sexual services on the streets in other large urban UK cities as well as being exploited and sold for sex from within both family homes and learning disability support services.

Whilst Cambridge (1995) is the only paper that reports on this specific issue in the UK, the review of literature did reveal a range of studies that indicate there are significant numbers of intellectually disabled people involved in the sale of sexual services (either 'voluntarily' or through being forced) throughout the UK. We will now provide a brief overview of the overall situation.

In a later paper exploring issues related to gay intellectually disabled men, Cambridge (1999) identifies how intellectually disabled men who work as prostitutes are less likely to have the skills required to ensure that customers use condoms. Additionally, he states that this group are more likely to experience financial disadvantage, which can act as a significant disincentive to insisting that customers practise safer sex.

Lindsay *et al.* (2004) undertook a study looking at referral patterns and outcomes following interventions with 111 male intellectually disabled sexual offenders. Of the 111 men, 8 per cent had been charged (or dealt with under the Mental Health Act) with the offence of prostitution.

Again, Lindsay *et al.* (2011; 2012) reported that in their study exploring the sexual and physical abuse history of offenders with intellectual disabilities, 14.5 per cent of female offenders had been arrested for prostitution. This would indicate that a significant number of intellectually disabled people who are entering the criminal justice system have been working in the sex industry.

General discussion

Overall, we have established that there are, clearly, indications that sex work is happening and that it potentially involves significant numbers of individuals. The available literature has raised two themes that we feel are worthy of further discussion and which may offer useful insights or starting points for the next stage of our project. These themes are *classification* and *discourse*.

1 Classification – how would a researcher be able to access sex workers?

Of the projects reported in the literature, classification is problematic. There appear to be three main approaches to identifying sex workers who are intellectually disabled.

The first is accessing individuals through general sexual health/sex worker outreach projects. It would appear that participants are identified based upon the judgement of staff as to whether an individual has an intellectual disability or not. For example, in Cambridge's (1995, p.6) study women were included in the project if they 'were suspected by staff to have mild learning disabilities'. No further information was provided by Cambridge as to whether the women went on to self-identify as intellectually disabled or not. Clearly, basing inclusion/exclusion criteria upon the 'suspicions' of general sexual health outreach staff is problematic and raises a range of questions in relation to the overall validity of the research.

Second, in a number of the studies referred to, individuals were identified as part of larger projects related to sexual offenders. All the participants were identified through disability offenders' services or through forensic mental health services. For example, Lindsay *et al.* (2004) restricted inclusion to those individuals who accessed a specialist ten-bedded forensic unit. Due to the nature of the service, individuals were asked to undertake IQ tests and only those scoring below 70 were included. This approach to inclusion criteria would appear to guarantee the inclusion of people who, according to 'conventional' medical criteria, have an intellectual disability. However, this is problematic for two reasons. One is that we question the very notion of applying labels to people as a result of using IQ tests. The socially constructed nature of intellectual disability is well explored within the literature (see Anyon 2009) and we find ourselves rejecting the notion of 'testing' individuals by using an arbitrary scale in order to label them. Furthermore, accessing intellectually disabled sex workers through offender services would clearly only lead to those individuals who have been detained being included and thus, it is reasonable to assume, will exclude significant numbers of individuals who have not been identified or dealt with by statutory services.

A third approach is accessing information regarding individuals from social work/social services staff who are aware (or suspect) that they are working within the sex industry (see for example, Kuosmanen and Starke 2011). Whilst this appears potentially to identify individuals known to learning disability services, previous research utilising this approach (Kuosmanen and Starke 2011) has sought to gather data only from professionals (using focus groups, interviews, etc.) and thus the data gathered is not primary data and is clearly subject to interpretation.

However, this is also a more generalised problem. Difficulties of classification are not restricted to sex work study. In an English national project by Emerson *et al.* (2005), which was the first survey of intellectually disabled people in the UK, researchers also grappled with the issue of discovering who was intellectually disabled to include in their research. They developed a validation exercise to identify potential participants. This covered questions such as, 'Did they have difficulty in learning things?'; 'Did they have difficulty as a child?'; 'Does this make life difficult for them now?' Clearly these again seem to be rather arbitrary questions, but how else can we separate intellectual disability as a category away from other facets of identity? The problem is complex but needs to be solved as much evidence about intellectually disabled people selling sex or being sold for sex is probably already within the literature but we have no means of extracting it.

For example, Harding and Hamilton's study (2009) of homeless 'working girls' in Nottingham found their 26 participants through charity houses that supported homeless women. The study arose from concerns of support workers about the perceptions of 'working girls'. Information about the project was made available in advance and the women could choose if they wanted to be involved. Not all of the women were 'working' but this gave essential material for understanding why some women became working girls and others did not. Harding and Hamilton state that, 'the research did not include questions about ethnicity, class, family, background or local authority care history' (p.1126). However, neither did it ask about *intellectual disability*.

The approaches to recruitment that we have identified in the literature all have their own set of problems and offer only limited usefulness in relation to gathering primary qualitative data directly from intellectually disabled people working in the sex industry. As we move forward with this project, a significant challenge is the identification of participants in this ethically complex field. Our commitment is to enable the voices of intellectually disabled people to be heard and to enable people to self-identify.

Blyth (2010) is experienced in the recruitment of 'hard to reach' groups who self-identify as disabled. However, the sensitive and, frequently, hidden nature of this group of individuals will present a unique set of challenges.

The second of our themes is around *discourse*.

2 Discourse – how are intellectually disabled people who sell sex viewed?

During our review of the limited literature available, it became apparent there were two dominant textual constructions relating to intellectually disabled people working in the sex industry. The manner in which the individuals were constructed largely depended on the scope and purpose of the research reported. Research such as that carried out by Lindsay *et al.* (2011) clearly discusses individuals in the context of *sexual offending*. This is a logical decision given that all the participants were accessing forensic services.

The second construction is that of *victim or exploited vulnerable person*. For example, Kuosmanen and Starke (2011) report how the professionals they interviewed often talked about people as being 'victims' who traded sex in return for closeness or a 'relationship'. Cambridge (1999) refers to intellectually disabled men selling sex in the context of their being vulnerable to violence, sexual transmitted disease and coercion. In an earlier paper, Cambridge (1995) explored how intellectually disabled people are exploited and 'rented out'.

The construction of intellectually disabled people as 'victims' or 'perpetrators' is, for us, too simplistic. Clearly, the line between victim and perpetrator can be blurred and there is a wealth of literature exploring this issue in relation to sex workers in general. So, for example, in the UK study by Harding and Hamilton (2009) of *Working Girls in Nottingham*, there is an overarching discourse of abuse and vulnerability. We know the women they worked with were young and homeless but we know very little else about them. All of the working girls had been exposed to various incidents of abuse and they felt there was some degree of coercion in their decision to become a working girl (see p.1132). Even so, they stood by their decision to engage in sex work and insisted that they had made a free choice. Their statements could be viewed as contradictory but Harding and Hamilton encourage us to think that victimisation is neither a universal nor a static concept.

The issues of vulnerability, exploitation and agency are exceedingly complex when considering intellectually disabled sex workers. We do not, in any way, suggest that many intellectually disabled sex workers are not 'victims' of exploitation (as are many sex workers in general); however, we think there are complexities that the currently available literature overlooks.

For example, we explored earlier how intellectually disabled people are often considered 'asexual' or as 'eternal children' and how there is a wealth of evidence to suggest that families, services and society in general consider intellectually disabled people to be non-sexual. With this is mind, it could be suggested on a more theoretical or conceptual level, that intellectually disabled sex workers are resisting this form of discursive or, from a Foucauldian perspective, 'disciplinary power' (Foucault 1980) by not only engaging in sexual activity but receiving a financial 'reward' for the provision of sex acts. From this perspective, it is possible to view the simplistic binary of victim/perpetrator as failing to consider how power is never permanently won (perpetrator) or lost (victim) but is continually negotiated through forms of resistance and regulation. It is quite possible that for some intellectually disabled sex workers, the option to sell sex is an active choice and to deny this possibility is to deny that individuals can exercise agency in relation to their own lives and bodies.

Summary

Clearly, the two main issues we have explored in this chapter are highly sensitive, complex and, put simply, constitute an ethical minefield. However, what is apparent is that the only way we can begin to gain an insight into the experiences of this group of people is to hear from them directly. In all of the literature reviewed, the voices of academics, medics, social workers, psychiatrists and other professionals are central to the current discourse. However, the next step in gaining insights into this issue is to gather narrative data from interviews with intellectually disabled sex workers themselves with the aim of, as Riessman (1993, p.8) stated, 'giving voices to previously silenced groups of women' (and men in this case).

References

Anyon, Y. (2009) 'Sociological theories of learning disabilities: understanding racial disproportionality in special education.' *Journal of Human Behavior in the Social Environment 19*, 44–57.

Blyth, C. (2009) *'Disabled gay men and Manchester's Gay Village: the socially and spatially constituted gay body.'* Unpublished EdD thesis, University of Manchester.

Blyth, C. (2010) '"Members Only": The Use of Gay Space(s) by Gay Disabled Men.' In R. Shuttleworth and T. Sanders (eds) *Sex and Disability Research: Sexual Politics, Identity, Access and Policy.* Leeds: Disability Press.

Bryman, A. (2004) *Social Research Methods*. Buckingham: Open University Press.

Cambridge, P. (1995) Respond Outreach Research Project, unpublished final report, Respond (a copy of the report is available from the applicants).

Cambridge, P. (1999) 'Considerations for informing safer sex education work with men with learning disabilities.' *British Journal of Learning Disabilities 27*, 123–126.

Carson, I. (2002) 'An Inclusive Society? One Young Man with Learning Difficulties Doesn't Think So!' In P. Farrell and M. Ainscow (eds) *Making Special Education Inclusive*. London: David Fulton.

Chapman, R. (2006) 'The role of the self-advocacy support worker in UK People First Groups: developing inclusive research.' Unpublished PhD thesis, Faculty of Health and Social Welfare, Open University.

Chivers, A. and Mathieson, S. (2000) 'Training in sexuality and relationships: An Australian model.' *Sexuality and Disability 18*, 1, 73–80.

Emerson, E., Malam, S., Davies, I. and Spencer, K. (2005) *Adults with Learning Difficulties in England, 2003/4*. London: National Statistics/NHS Health and Social Care Information Centre.

Fitzgerald, C. and Withers, R. (2011) 'I don't know what a proper woman means: What women with intellectual disabilities think about sex, sexuality and themselves.' *British Journal of Learning Disabilities 41*, 1, 5–12.

Foucault, M. (1980) *Power/Knowledge: Selected Interviews and Other Writings (1972–77)* in C. Gordon (ed.). New York: Pantheon Press.

Harding, R., and Hamilton, P. (2009) 'Working girls: Abuse or choice in street level sex work? A study of homeless women in Nottingham' in *British Journal of Social Work*, Vol 39, pp.1118–1137.

Hassouneh-Philips, D., Curry, M.A. (2002) 'Abuse of women with disabilities: State of the science.' *Rehabilitation Counseling Bulletin 45*, 96–104.

Jarvinen, J., Kail, A. and Miller, I. (2008) *Hard Knock Life: Violence Against Women*. London: New Philanthropy Capital.

Jeffreys, S. (2008) 'Disability and the male sex right.' *Women's Studies International Forum 31*, 5, 327–335.

Kuosmanen, K. and Starke, M. (2011) 'Women and men with intellectual disabilities who sell or trade sex: Voices from the professionals.' *Journal of Social Work in Disability and Rehabilitation 10*, 129–149.

Labour Left Review (2007) *Prostitution is Violence Against Women*. Available at http://finnmackay. wordpress.com/articles/prostitution-is-violence-against-women-labour-left-review-nov-07, accessed on 25 September 2014.

Landman, R. (2010), Mate crime fears for people with learning disabilities.' *The Guardian*, 14 September 2010. Available at www.theguardian.com/society/2010/sep/14/learning-disabilities-mate-crime, accessed on 05 August 2014.

Lindsay, W., Steptoe, L. and Haut, F. (2011) 'Referral patters for offenders with intellectual disability: A 20-year study.' *Journal of Forensic Psychiatry and Psychology 22*, 4, 513–517.

Lindsay, W., Steptoe, L. and Haut, F. (2012) 'The sexual and physical abuse histories of offenders with intellectual disability.' *Journal of Intellectual Disability Research, 56*, 3, 326–331.

Lindsay, W., Smith, A., Law, J. Quinn, K. *et al.* (2004) 'Sexual and nonsexual offenders with intellectual and learning disabilities.' *Journal of Interpersonal Violence 19*, 8, 875–890.

Mahoney, K. (1984) *Obscenity, Morals and the Law: A Feminist Critique.* Available at www.commonlaw.uottawa.ca/index2.php?option=com_sobi2&sobi2Task=dd_download&fid=498&Itemid=842, accessed 24 May 2013.

McCarthy, M. (1999) *Sexuality and Women with Learning Disabilities.* London: Jessica Kingsley Publishers.

Ravetz, J.R. (1971) *Scientific Knowledge and its Social Problems.* Oxford: Clarendon Press.

Riessman, C. (1993) *Narrative Analysis.* London: Sage.

Ryan, J. and Thomas, F. (1987) *The Politics of Mental Handicap (revised edition).* London: Free Association Books.

Thompson, D. (1994) 'Sexual experience and sexual identity for men with learning disabilities who have sex with men.' *Changes 12,* 4, 245–263.

WORKING IN PARTNERSHIP

The Editors' Story

Rohhss Chapman, Louise Townson and Sue Ledger

Overview ————————————————————————

- This chapter discusses the process of writing together.

- We explain how the book has built upon life story and partnership working developed by the Social History of Learning Disabilities Research Group at the Open University.

- We discuss issues of confidentiality and how people decide to be named as authors or not.

- Louise explains how her involvement in co-writing started.

- We set out a table of different models of collaboration in writing used in the book.

- We talk about the length of time it might take to work together well.

- Louise presents ten points on how to work together well.

The writing process

Rohhss took the lead on writing the chapter after talking with Louise and Sue and after Louise had sent in her part of the chapter. Later Sue added her sections and it was sent to everyone to add or agree changes. There were many phone calls between the three editors. We use the term 'intellectual disabilities' in our writing.

Introduction

SUE

In her book about inclusive life history approaches, founder member of the Open University SHLD Research Group, Dorothy Atkinson (1997, p.1) reflected, 'There is, and has been silence on the part of people with learning disabilities... One consequence is that much lived history in the form of personal experiences of people with learning disabilities has gone unrecorded.' Our belief that this continues to be the case in terms of sexuality and relationships for people with intellectual disabilities was the driving force for this co-edited publication. As Louise said in Chapter 1, we were all committed to getting it – the word, message – 'out there'.

Yet the process of how we got from our initial ideas – excitedly formulated, as described in Chapter 1, at the inclusive conference back in 2007 – to the completed publication, has a story of its own.

Between 2005 and 2007 Melanie Nind and Jane Seale brought together people with intellectual disabilities, support workers, researchers and practitioners to examine issues of access in relation to people with intellectual disability. Discussions included access to ideas, knowledge and research. Funded by the Economic and Social Research Council, these inclusive seminars identified storytelling as a highly effective approach 'to making content accessible and validating everyone's experiences'. This included stories of conducting research projects alongside life stories, such as the ones in this collection: 'Each story had a narrator and central actors and through this we could relate to the ideas. These stories encouraged other participants to tell their own stories of big or small battles and victories' (Nind and Seale 2009 p. 276).

Encouraged by this group's endorsement, in this chapter we, as editors, share the stories behind our co-edited and co-authored book. These include the experiences that shaped our approach, our reflections on the process and our learning of the differences between co-authoring and co-editing. As editors we acknowledge that many of the contributors to this book have been brave in coming forward and telling their story. 'Being brave' – not always playing it safe – has a key contribution to make in breaking down the many barriers that exist for people with intellectual disability (Cooper 2011). In this chapter we aspired to be brave in being as transparent as possible about what we did – including difficulties alongside successes – and our thinking about ownership, equality, ethics and confidentiality. We have also tried hard to reflect honestly on the journey we have made together to bring the book to completion in the hope that it will encourage others to take forward partnership projects of their own.

Establishing partnership approaches

ROHHSS

From the 1990s onwards the SHLD group hosted a range of PhD students, including Sue and myself (involving Louise), who have worked on developing inclusive research. This work has focused on recovering and recording the voices of those who often find it harder to be heard and studying power processes within the advocacy movement.

The partnership approach was established and the work of SHLD has been far reaching: a development of co-working, conducting inclusive research, reconstructing and recording missing life stories and facilitating co-writing by intellectually disabled people alongside academic partners (Chapman 2014). This has become a hallmark approach, to which we are all committed. However, it also has its drawbacks.

Writing a book alongside many other people takes a lot of time. There are also potential tensions around how a chapter has or could have been produced. I think we would all agree that there is no one set way for doing this and that we are all learning from each other. For myself, I know the best way I learn a new approach is to observe it happening and try and emulate the way it is done. When I started working in the self-advocacy movement I was at times really inspired by the specific, thoughtful approaches that particular people took. This included Niall McNulty (Chapter 19), whose support appeared very much in the background, yet filled people with confidence to be themselves.

In my view, much of the approach to partnership working also aligns to issues of (ideal) advocacy support. It is important for supporters and allies to *stand back* to allow other people's thoughts and ideas to develop. With a history of people with intellectual disabilities not being listened to alongside not being heard, a lot of preliminary work, as in any minority movement, needs to go into raising consciousness and developing self-confidence: respecting people as equals.

This initial 'stand back' approach has been demonstrated in many self-advocacy studies (see Aspis 1997; Goodley 2000; Tilley 2006). However, people and groups develop and move on and new members join. The initial approaches can usefully be remembered and used, but where relationships and ways of working are established, other more flexible methods may become even more useful. Even then, critical reflection needs to be taking place, a constant 'parrot on the shoulder' (Chapman 2014, p.50) to check people who are supporting or facilitating are not 'taking over'. Suggestions around vigilance can be found in Chapman (2006) as demonstrated by different advocacy groups across the UK.

However, even if this is a starting point, I do not believe we used a 'stand back' approach in this venture; it was more of a dialogue, a topic we will return to later.

Getting involved in writing together

LOUISE

I was involved in work with the Open University and helped develop the collaborative methods used for OU courses. For example, Rohhss and I had draft chapters for courses sent to our homes where we read them individually. We then got together on a weekly basis to go over our comments and discuss our findings, usually at her house in Carlisle whilst eating bacon sandwiches for breakfast. We looked at the content of each chapter and the suggested exercises. It was important to do this initial work separately so we were not overly influenced by each other's ideas, before bringing them together. These ideas have carried on into other work.

I have been working in collaboration for the last 21 years. This has been in teaching, reviewing and research as well as writing. Often we have used a PATH[1] approach to writing or research where we all have a say about what we want to do and how we want to do it. We try out different methods (see Townson *et al.* 2004). At the start of my co-writing, Rohhss asked me if I would be interested to write a piece in partnership with her about 'consultancy' in *Community Living* (Chapman and Townson 1999, later published as Chapman and Townson 2002). This was based on the experiences we had in a local adult centre, where consultancy about moving premises took place but decisions had already been made. The management were more interested in getting people with intellectual disabilities to choose the colour of curtains than where they would be living.

We both sat down and thought about what needed to be included in the article and took it from there. We discussed the issues. I think the collaboration works well because we have been colleagues and friends since I joined People First 21 years ago and we both understand how each other works.

Since then, I've been involved in lots of different collaborations with Rohhss and with other people. Some of these include reviewing books and articles for different academic journals such as the *British Journal of Learning Disabilities* and *Disability and Society*. We do this by reading the book or the article separately and putting down our own views and opinions. I meet or email Rohhss and then she includes my words and gives or sends it back for my approval and any changes. It was a similar approach to collaborative working for this book, it is something we are used to doing.

---

1 PATH is a creative planning tool developed by Pierpoint, O'Brien and Forrest (2001). It uses graphic facilitation to enable groups or teams to put forward their views and ideas in planning a project. PATH starts with what the outcome is to be and then works back to define the process.

Finding a publisher

ROHHSS

We related earlier how we had conceived the idea of the book in 2007, but although we were keen and energetic and had the support of allies and colleagues, it was not an easy road to find a publisher. In some respects the book did not fit their criteria – it was an academic book but it was not classically academic because it was also written with people with intellectual disabilities. Another publisher explained it was an edited collection which some publishers avoid. Thankfully Jessica Kingsley Publishers recognised the value of what we aimed to do and have been very patient with us.

Being an editor for this book

LOUISE

After we got the contract, Daniel, Rohhss and I met at the University of Manchester. I would get the train down from Carlisle and be met at the station. Usually I'd stay over, and Rohhss and I would share a hotel room so we could catch up too. With Daniel, we recorded discussions of what we thought about sexuality and relationships and the experiences and issues that were important to us. Sometimes Rohhss joined in and sometimes she just prompted the conversation with additional questions, 'Why do you think that? Tell me a little more about what happened there.'

I transcribed the tapes so we could use the material later. Afterwards, Rohhss and I would meet at my house in Carlisle and work through the transcriptions and the chapters sent in from authors. My mum made us sandwiches and we could have a catch-up at the same time.

I would sometimes email the authors back to ask questions or let them know where we were up to. Towards the end, Sue, Rohhss and I met in London and also in Carlisle to work out the emerging themes and what we wanted to write in our editorial chapters. Throughout the time we spent on the book, I got copies of each of the authored chapters to read through and make editorial comments about. I've also written quite a few of the introductions to the chapters.

The authors involved all worked in different ways. Some of them directly included or supported people with intellectual disabilities and some did not. A few were just written mostly by people with intellectual disabilities themselves. The chapters that didn't have the voice of a person with an intellectual disability I would read and then write a 'lead in' to their chapters, setting out my views on the subject. The whole point of the book was that it was very important to include the views of people with intellectual disabilities.

I think it does take time to properly include people with intellectual disabilities, but the main reason why it doesn't happen is because either the academic doesn't know anyone or the people they do know may not want to share their stories on what is a very sensitive and personal issue.

Warts and all!

LOUISE

There have been some unforeseen issues along the way. These have been hard and stressful at times. For example, we were sometimes not able to get in touch with people, or people did not respond to us because they had moved jobs or had changed email addresses and we didn't have their new one. Some of the original authors dropped out because their workloads or jobs changed and they no longer had time to devote to it, or in one case, sadly because they had become very ill. These are issues that we as co-editors have found out for ourselves along the way and dealt with it the best way we could through discussing together what to do.

A lot of things happened in our own lives, too. For example, I was waiting to go into hospital for an operation which took forever to organise; I then moved house; one of the original editors had a baby; another person found it really hard to commit to meetings because of difficult things happening in their life. We have all been away ill at various times! Being an editor isn't a paid role (well, not unless we sell enough books to get royalties!); it has to fit into other commitments and people's nine to five jobs have had to come first. This means you cannot always get on with the work even when you want to.

Another factor was that as co-editors we live at different ends of the country. Myself and Rohhss live in Cumbria so we could meet when time allowed; Daniel lives in Manchester and Sue lives in London, so we have met less frequently.

Over the last few months as the book was nearing its completion, I found it hard to keep up with the amount of emails that came through, especially as I was having trouble with my eye. But one of the most positive things for me was getting to know people that I've known for many years, but haven't worked with very much.

I have learned a great deal in co-editing this book. The main thing I've learned is hearing about what relationships are like in other parts of the world and how advanced some places are at including people with intellectual disabilities. Some are still very much in a learning phase of how to do this. Overall, I do feel that collaborative working is the way to go forward because it can enhance knowledge on both sides. It is good to involve experts by experience because we are the ones who know what it is like to have an intellectual disability.

Coming in towards the end

SUE

My involvement with the book changed over time. I was at the 2007 SHLD conference, where the idea of the book originated. Later I was at the SHLD research group meeting when Rohhss presented the book proposal to the group and asked me to co-author a chapter. Through my involvement with SHLD and my work on the chapter I maintained regular contact with Rohhss, Daniel and Louise as editors and was aware of progress with the book. In the later stages one of the original editors was no longer able to continue due to family commitments and I was asked if I could step in. I immediately said 'yes' and was soon in a position of commenting on first and second drafts of a range of co-authored chapters. We very quickly sorted out a way of working together as a team. Initially we did this through email messages. As the volume of chapters and editor reviews rapidly grew we soon arranged to meet up at the British Library in London to discuss our ideas and compare our thoughts on each of the chapters in person. This meeting really moved things on in terms of how we worked together. I think one of the reasons it was so helpful to meet and spend a day on the project together was that we got to understand each other's approach and way of working much better.

Practically we used a collage method to get our views on individual chapters down on paper before using coloured pens to make links between various themes. As we worked on this together we had time to talk about our respective ideas and experiences in relation to the subject of the book. We also had time to learn a little about each other's backgrounds, including where we lived and worked and our families and friends. In addition to making our day together much more interesting and enjoyable, taking the time to build our team-working relationships also served an important purpose. In the final stages of the book, as deadlines loomed and editorial chapters had to be drafted and re-drafted, often under considerable time pressure, the investment of time in our earlier face-to-face meetings paid off enormously. If any one of us was stuck it felt very comfortable simply to phone each other and resolve any concerns there and then. In this way we worked closely together and relied on each other to get the job done. Working in this interdependent fashion made it an effective and genuine partnership in which we each brought different expertise; none of us could manage without the other, and power issues in relation to disability could be openly discussed and dealt with as they arose.

Partnership working across the broader spectrum of contributing authors also felt very comfortable. Chapter 2 outlines how authors were drawn from our existing networks and this made the process of clarifying and questioning issues about the co-authoring process straightforward. It felt comfortable to ask questions about how individual chapters had been constructed and to raise important questions about ownership of voice and ideas. In working with a highly sensitive subject a sense of shared purpose and enthusiasm from all our contributors supported a spirit of openness in the project. In turn this enabled a more honest picture to be told in relation to the process behind the various stories.

Collaborative writing: roles can develop and change
ROHHSS

The approach to collaborative writing in my and Louise's experiences and with the Carlisle People First Research Team Ltd (CPFRT) has been explained in detail elsewhere (Chapman 2014; Townson *et al.* 2007). In these publications we (the CPFRT team) have variously talked about the importance of recognising people's abilities and playing to their strengths, of working in ways that people choose for themselves and learning from each other's strong points. Definitive roles were not needed as we each developed our approach as we proceeded. People learnt new skills which opened up fresh ways of approaching the task. We found that working together is something that can move and shift, not a process that can be set up and adhered to in isolation of other aspects of people's lives. For example, when we first set out on fieldwork, I was the 'research supporter' and took on particular roles (taking dictation of fieldnotes, transcribing tapes). As we developed, Louise took up those tasks as well, which changed the dynamic of working. Louise could support as well as research. Likewise, this new venture has been an interesting journey because, through the contributing authors, we have seen many different methods and approaches that have developed and that we could try and use ourselves.

In 2012, The Partnership Steering Group of Learning Disability Studies at the University of Manchester produced a world first; this was a Special Issue for the peer-reviewed *British Journal of Learning Disabilities*. The theme of the issue was the 'Research and work of people with learning disabilities and their allies and supporters'. This was an opportunity for peer reviewing and editorial work undertaken by a collaborative team, made up of two academics (myself and Craig Blyth), five colleagues with intellectual disabilities and a research supporter. Apart from this being a collaborative project (the process of which is written about in the article, Blunt *et al.* 2012), what proved very interesting were the different approaches and interpretations of what made up 'collaborative' work. Apart from our own process (discussed in the Special Issue) we found that many of the articles sent in for the journal disguised the process of partnership writing through using terms such as 'we', where it was too hard to distinguish who 'we' were. Sometimes the notion of 'we' would change but without any signposting. We (The Partnership steering

Group) wrote back to some of the contributors and asked them to explain in more detail what exactly had taken place.

Walmsley and Johnson mention this importance of detail in their *Inclusive Research* book (2003). The significant factor in any collaborative work is the *transparency of the process*. Craig picks up this point in Chapter 16, saying that we need to say exactly what has happened, otherwise how can the process be improved upon? Likewise, in some of the chapters of this book we have asked authors for more clarity.

There are many issues to consider in a co-edited book about sexuality and relationships which invited contributions predominantly co-authored by people with intellectual disabilities. We have had people's individual knowledge and experiences to present and think about; gender differences; ethical questions; matters around language, culture, law and policy; approaches to abuse, risk and protection; and, importantly, power.

There are individual voices represented here, as well as partnership writing, dictation, art, poetry and group pieces. For continuity, each chapter included an accessible overview, an explanation of process, terminology and cultural context where required, a summary and, finally, references, where used.

Issues around confidentiality and representing the person
ROHHSS

As mentioned earlier, people are courageous in telling their stories and sometimes it is easy to forget how uncomfortable we might be if it were asked of us (see Chapter 16). I did specifically ask Craig Blyth to write about his experiences of 'coming out', to counteract this silence in regard to academic partners and it is an interesting comparison, not least because it demonstrates how far apart people's experiences may be. I was able to ask him because we have worked together for a long time and we get on well. This reinforces the notion of having time to form and sustain relationships and to embed trust in partnership working.

Sexuality and relationships are private and are not usually discussed in any intimate detail. The fact that we were publishing material that focused on such a private area of people's lives was of particular concern to us. There have been many conversations about the ethics of confidentiality (or not) of authorship between our editorial team and more importantly the teams involved in writing chapters. We have checked that authors are comfortable; all the people involved want this information to be published.

In terms of authorship, on the one hand it makes sense for people to have their hard work attributed to them. Writing or co-writing a chapter for a book is a time-consuming and challenging activity, so if an author is not recognised for this, then where is the reward? Having such a chapter attributed and published, with the promise of a wide readership, could be viewed as a valued activity. Indeed, some of our contributors have insisted they want their real names to be used.

However, having real identities presented can place people in difficult situations where others find out about their private experiences, or may strongly object to their views. Additionally, authentic authorship may allow others to be identified who are tangental to the story. Is it really fair to other people to be taking that risk, especially where we cannot ask, or simply do not know where they are now? In this respect a great deal of care has been taken to anonymise information where necessary, but getting the balance right, with such a sensitive subject, is not always easy. In other chapters, authors have specifically asked to be named because the subject is so important to them (Chapters 5 and 15); or not named, because they would feel vulnerable if they could be identified (Chapters 6 and 19). We asked the groups to have this discussion (most had already done so) and come to a decision as to whether or not they wanted to be named. Interestingly, we had to positively encourage one author to consider a pseudonym because of the material presented.

As editors, we therefore explained how the process of co-writing or representing people's voices was approached and how decisions about authorship were made.

The editorial process of the authored chapters

ROHHSS

In overseeing the authored chapters, I identified six different models of co-writing (see Table 21.1). These models are in no way exhaustive; there are many approaches in the developing area of collaborative writing around life stories (Goodley *et al.* 2004). The models here relate to the chapters of this book. What the table demonstrates is that there is no one specified approach that works for everyone, and what is more important is to consider how groups come to their own decisions, as the approach taken clearly needs to be influenced by the preferences of individuals involved (Chapman 2006, 2014; Townson *et al.* 2004).

Overall, in this book some chapters are more heavily reliant on the voice of academics (see Chapter 7) whereas others (see Chapter 5) weave in (see Chapter 4) or cite much more of the voice of people with intellectual difficulties. A premise of the book was to include people's voices in every chapter, which proved to be very challenging in some of the cultures we approached. We had some discussion over whether or not there should be a lead-in for some chapters (Chapter 3, for example), but decided to strive for a continuous approach.

With regards to Chapter 7 from Japan it was made clear by the authors from the start that it would be very hard to co-write with colleagues with intellectual disabilities, doubly so because of the subject content. Despite this, the chapter does make reference to some self-advocacy by people with intellectual disabilities. When Chapter 7 is read it will become clear that there are strong cultural influences to understand. For example, there is a very pervasive familial element to relationships in Japan, where adults in any case tend to live for much longer in their parents' home and under their influence, with or without intellectual disabilities. So the Japanese authors, in finding ways to prioritise authenticity, rely heavily on interviews conducted with a man and woman whom they have established relationships with and who know and trust each other. The authors took that decision and Louise was asked to make some introductory comments.

Transparency
SUE

Transparency of researcher activity may be of increased significance in co-writing with people with intellectual disabilities where there is a risk that people may not be in a position to speak up for themselves or to question or comment upon the interpretation and telling of their stories. The use of 'thick description' (Geertz 1973), reflexive accounts and an ongoing commitment to making the part played by the co-writer as 'transparent' as possible were approaches we adopted in response to these concerns.

Getting back to the authors
ROHHSS

Most authors sent in a number of drafts of their chapter. These would be printed out and/or emailed to the other editors who would read through and make comments. These comments were drafted into another email to be sent back to the author/s, mostly by myself or Louise. Authors were very responsive to the comments and would discuss the comments and send a further draft. This would go on until it was felt the chapters were ready for critical review. One chapter went through eight drafts.

Writing about the process in this way makes it sound as if everything went smoothly. It didn't always go smoothly! Louise picked up on this in her 'warts and all' section earlier.

TABLE 21.1 MODELS OF CO-WRITING

	Style	Detail	Example chapters	Advantages and challenges
1	**Full authentic voice**	Where the author writes their own story or the story is recorded and transcribed by others with little editorial input	14	+: enables the story to be told with minimal editorial influence or interpretation −: method may be restricted to people who can communicate easily through written or spoken word
2	**Authentic voice with support**	Where the article is authored by a supporter/ally but focuses on authentic voice and weaves sections together, i.e. minimal skilled background support	4, 6, 15, 17, 19	+: enables participation of people who use fewer words to communicate but very much highlights their input −: confusion over whose voice if it is not clearly marked
3	**Shared voice (explicit)**	Where article is an amalgamation of academic and person/people with intellectual disabilities voice, where sections are clearly defined	5, 9, 13, 16 1, 2, 10, 11, 21	+: good for two people co-writing or can include many people/a team −: careful attention to signposting to ensure separation of voices
4	**Shared voice (hidden)**	Where article is co-written but specific areas of voice are not defined	Many joint articles by academics 20, 22, 23	+: easy to read as one overall voice −: cannot distinguish who said what; danger of 'we'
5	**Academic voice reporting on direct research of intellectually disabled participants**	Where academic is writing alone about lives/research of intellectually disabled people/where lead-in by intellectually disabled author has been requested	7, 8, 12, 18, 20	+: still able to gather a story where circumstances may be limited or difficult, i.e. sensitivity of topic/distance of authors Can add an introduction to this but usually by someone outside the situation/more distanced −: will not hear directly about impacts
6	**Academic voice reporting on secondary research**	Where there is no direct inclusion of person with intellectual disabilities		Typical of academic research – we have tried not to use this approach

273

The editorial process of our own chapters

ROHHSS

We have tried to be as collaborative as possible in writing the editorial chapters but we are aware, especially towards the end of this experience, of ways in which we can develop and improve to make co-writing easier. Time is an issue which haunts any collaboration: *if only we had more time.* Accepting that we often don't, it is better to think about doing the very best we can rather than giving up or not embarking on partnership work in the first place. So we approached the challenge of time by openly acknowledging it between ourselves, talking about the risks that it presented in terms of non-disabled editors taking over and trying to ensure that we kept to our team approach, where we each played to our strengths.

Usually, after meeting and discussing the progress of the work, one person would take the lead on a chapter (either Rohhss or Sue, reflected in the order of authors at the start of each chapter) and begin the writing process. The other two would be writing and would then deliver their own sections, often interspersed with phone calls or emails. The lead author would then 'weave' or 'knit' the work together. These words came to be used between us as we were engaged in the project. Afterwards the chapter would be sent around by email for further comment and changes to be made.

Early on, after a variety of styles were trialled, we made a decision to write our editorial chapters in a way that reflected, as transparently as possible, the way we were in conversation, talking and writing together. It is hoped that this would not only make the reading more accessible but importantly would also demonstrate who was saying what. We did not want the work to meld into an undefined 'we'; rather let us take responsibility for our own words and allow the reader to capture differences in style and opinion. However, in the two concluding chapters we made so many additions back and forth as the book came together that in the end it became impossible to separate the voices as we were sharing paragraphs and sometimes sentences. The editors would be interested to hear how readers have found this and whether it is useful for their own work or not (email rohhss@yahoo.com).

Graphics and lessons learned

SUE

The original contract made provision for the use of graphics to accompany the text in both editorial and co-authored chapters. However, in practice, we found that we would have preferred to include a lot more visual material than could be accommodated in the final edition. In Chapter 19, The Men's Room, for example, the editing team felt that the content would be enhanced by the text being accompanied by some visual signposting of key points. We wanted to achieve this by commissioning a series of drawings from intellectually disabled artists. The artists were identified and pictures were drawn but the number of graphics included in the text was limited by space and production costs.

A further learning point was the selection of an image for the front cover. We had all, quite early on, agreed on two photographs that we felt would work really well. However, the publishers informed us that the quality of photographs (taken in the 1990s) was not good enough. Our immediate alternative was a poster about sexuality by learning disabled artist Clare Miller, co-author of Chapter 15; but here too the format presented problems for reproduction. We then agreed on a romantic painting by the artist Marc Chagall only to find out that the royalties were prohibitive! In the end we all sat down again and selected what we felt was the best fit from an online 'free copyright picture bank'. Although we were reasonably happy with the result there was no getting away from the fact this was a compromise in terms of our initial vision of how the finished book would look and our ideal of a cover presenting material directly from people with intellectual disabilities.[2] For many people with intellectual disabilities graphics have a key role in publications and this experience was valuable learning in terms of the need to address graphics at the proposal and early drafting stage of the publication process.

Critical review
ROHHSS

The next stage was to find critical reviewers. We had the assistance of the SHLD group and Sue identified an 'outside' pool of people who could give us critical feedback on each of the chapters; these were people who were involved in writing or publishing, but not familiar with intellectual disability studies or services. This proved advantageous as we could explore where we had made assumptions and taken background knowledge for granted. These 'outsider' reviewers pointed out areas where more explanation and better signposting were required. They were also very helpful in highlighting sections where ownership of voice had drifted and become unclear.

---

2   Happily just before going to press Jessica Kingsley Publishers were able to change the front cover to feature the photograph we had originally selected. As a consequence the photograph of Eyglø Ebba Hreinsdøttir and Sigurjøn Grétarsson (Jonni) (authors of Chapter 4) appears on the cover. Thank you JKP!

Critical review: the practicalities
SUE

As we worked together on writing the editorial chapters I took the lead in making arrangements for each to be critically reviewed. As we were all keen for the book to influence research, policy and practice it was important to check that our ideas could be easily understood by a range of readers. We identified critical readers for each of the editorial chapters and as soon as we agreed each chapter was complete we sent it to reviewers for feedback.

In addition, after we had edited one or more drafts of the authored chapters we agreed together on their running order. As described in Chapter 10 we then used our team of critical reviewers to read each of the chapters and to identify what they felt were the three key themes from each. Again, as described in Chapter 10, this provided a helpful check to make sure that as editors our own views were not over-influencing our interpretation of the chapter content.

In developing the timeline we sought feedback from a self-advocacy group. Their input (as explained in Chapter 2) was critical in terms of inserting pictures to make the timeline more accessible. Our critical reviewer feedback was an extremely helpful part of the process; as a result of their insightful comments and feedback, changes were made and new questions raised which again, fed back into revisions of our own editorial content. As editors we would recommend building in time for this process and also extending it to include critical review from people with intellectual disabilities.

Ten points on how to work together well
LOUISE

Based on my experiences, here are my top ten tips for collaborative working:

1. Working with someone who you trust is of vital importance because you both may be sharing very sensitive information.

2. Find out each other's working needs at the start.

3. Work on ground rules and boundaries at the start so then there will be no misunderstandings later on.

4. Make sure that any problems you may face are talked about. Be honest about them so then they don't escalate.

5. Confidentiality is a vital part of working collaboratively.

6. Always be honest; if you can't make a meeting let the person know in advance.

7. Listen to each other and take views on board from all sides.

8. Don't be tokenistic.

9. Learn from each other and enjoy it.

10. Celebrate achievements and build in social time.

There are many good points to working together and finding out knowledge from each other. I've worked in collaboration with many different people for many years. It has been helpful because I have a visual impairment and I need to use certain equipment like a reading monitor, so the print needs to be of a decent size to be able to read it. Because I have worked with people over the years, they have become familiar with my needs.

Sometimes collaborative working can have its downsides. By this I mean when we were working on this book, myself and Rohhss could make a meeting but Daniel couldn't or if Rohhss and Daniel could make a date I couldn't, or vice versa. So because of the distance, finding a date when we could all meet could be problematic. We overcame that by Rohhss and myself meeting anyway. Geographical distances could be a problem at times so email and phone were a good way of contacting each other.

Summary

ROHHSS

This chapter has discussed the story behind the writing of the book. We have endeavoured to lay out the process of our editorial partnership approach clearly and transparently. We have discussed some difficult issues around ethics and confidentiality. Whilst we have only scratched the surface of different approaches, table 21.1 of different collaborative approaches should be useful in the work of others. Links to theory and further critiques can all be found in the references we have provided. The focus of this chapter was to discuss partnership working in relation to this specific book.

References

Aspis, S. (1997) 'Self advocacy for people with learning difficulties: does it have a future?' *Disability and Society 12*, 4, 647–654.

Atkinson, D. (1997) *An Auto/Biographical Approach to Learning Disability Research.* Ashgate: Avebury.

Blunt, C., Blyth, C., Chapman, R., Frost, L. *et al.* (2012) 'Special issue on the research and work of people with learning disabilities and their allies and supporters.' *British Journal of Learning Disabilities 40*, Issue, 2 83–84.

Chapman, R. (2006) 'The role of the self advocacy support worker in UK People First groups: developing inclusive research.' Unpublished PhD thesis, Faculty of Health and Social Welfare, Open University.

Chapman, R. (2014) 'An exploration of the self advocacy support role through collaborative research; "there should never be a them and us".' *Journal of Applied Research in Intellectual Disabilities 27*, 1, 44–53.

Chapman, R. and Townson, L. (1999) 'Consultation: Plan of action or management exercise?' *Community Living Magazine.*

Chapman, R. and Townson, L. (2002) 'Consultation: Plan of Action or Management Exercise?' In Reynolds, J., Seden, J., Henderson, J., Charlesworth, J., and Bullman, A. (eds) *The Managing Care Reader.* London: Routledge.

Cooper, M. (2011) Personal Communication on May 5 2011.

Goodley, D. (2000) *Self Advocacy in the Lives of People with Learning Difficulties.* Buckingham: Open University Press.

Goodley, D., Clough, P., Lawthom, R. and Moore, M. (2004) *Researching Life Stories: Method, Theory and Analyses in a Biographical Age.* London: Routledge Falmer.

Nind, M. and Seale, J. (2009) 'Concepts of access for people with learning difficulties: towards a shared understanding.' *Disability and Society 24*, 3, 273–287.

Pierpoint, J., O'Brien, J. and Forrest, M. (2001) *PATH: Planning Alternative Tomorrows with Hope: A Workbook for Planning Possible Positive Futures.* Toronto: Inclusion Press.

Tilley, E. (2006) 'Advocacy for people with learning difficulties: the role of two organisations.' Unpublished PhD thesis, Faculty of Health and Social Welfare, Open University.

Townson, L., Macauley, S., Harkness, E., Chapman, R. *et al.* (2004) 'We are all in the same boat.' *British Journal of Learning Disabilities 32*, 2, 72–76.

Townson, L., Macauley, S., Harkness, E., Docherty, A. *et al.* (2007) 'Research project on advocacy and autism.' *Disability and Society 22*, 5, 523–536.

Walmsley, J. and Johnson, K. (2003) *Inclusive Research with People with Learning Disabilities: Past, Present and Future.* London: Jessica Kingsley Publishers.

CHAPTER 22

EMERGING THEMES FROM PART 2

Rohhss Chapman, Sue Ledger and Louise Townson

Overview

- This chapter identifies the key themes from Part 2.

- It identifies that supporters, family and staff play a key part in enabling (or not enabling) relationships and sexuality.

- Supporters are often in a position of significant power and high-quality support can make a real difference in people's lives.

- Many people with intellectual disabilities feel 'outsiders' in terms of sexuality and relationships.

- There is a constant struggle in services to balance rights to relationships and sexual expression with risk.

- Comparing life story narratives with the legal and policy framework shows that there are gaps between policy and what is happening in people's lives.

- We suggest that in many circumstances it is the attitude of family, front line staff and managers rather than the legal and policy framework that determines outcomes.

The writing process

As editors, we met together and worked on the emerging themes in Part 2 using the large art board Sue described in Chapter 10. Whilst keeping in mind our research questions, we discussed what had really struck us about the chapters in Part 2 and delved further for commonalities. Together we identified four themes and then compared them with themes suggested by our peer reviewers. Many of the themes are interconnected and writing about each theme separately may suggest somewhat artificial splits between them, so please bear this in mind.

As in Part 1, we grouped the emerging themes into four clusters. We refined the headings to reflect the material in the themes and this is how we present them in the chapter.

1. the crucial role of supporters

2. the outsider: being badly treated and being ignored

3. balancing rights against risk

4. gaps between policy and practice.

Rohhss started writing the chapter; it was then circulated to Sue and Louise who added in their comments. These were emailed back and forth to tie the sections together and add in further thoughts along the way. As the chapter developed it became harder to attribute particular sections to individual authors (see the previous chapter); this is why we have described this chapter as 'joint writing'.

Introduction

This chapter brings together themes from Part 2 chapters.

The varied experiences in Part 2 highlight that whilst acknowledgement of the rights to sexual relationships has broadly followed wider social trends (Chapter 12) for many people with intellectual disabilities this has been complicated by increased awareness of sexual abuse and an ongoing dependence on services for support.

Discussion of themes

1. The crucial role of supporters

In Chapter 16 Craig Blyth says: 'A lot of the issues that face gay disabled men are the same as those that face non-disabled gay men but the difference is often related to the provision of support.' In the Part 2 narratives, the power of positive, skilled and sensitive support from families, paid staff and other allies to make a real difference to the way in which people experience relationships and sexuality is a recurrent theme.

FAMILIES AS ALLIES

Jackie Downer (Chapter 17), when talking about her own mother's commitment to her well-being, said, 'When I look back, my mum was my first supporter, she believed in me.' Having a family member who understands you, who believes in you and will stand by you was identified by people with intellectual disabilities as very important. In Chapter 15, Clare describes her mother's positive reaction to her coming out as a lesbian. Lyndon (Chapter 18) explains how his mum helped him to find out more about sex and encouraged him to get involved in the CHANGE project.

The commitment of many parents to supporting their adolescent children to find out about sex and develop relationships is reinforced in findings reported from the CHANGE sexuality project. 'I really hope that my son has the opportunity to have a full sexual relationship, get married and have children' (mother, quoted in Chapter 18).

In contrast, the narratives also provide insight into situations where family support was problematic: in the case of Alice (Chapter 14), for example, whose relative could not accept her transgendered identity and wish to live as a woman, and Daniel (Chapter 16) whose foster father rejected his gay sexual identity.

Both stories reveal the hurt caused by the rejection of sexual identity by a close family member. They also show how the threat of rejection can leave people with intellectual disabilities facing a difficult choice: trying to change to please, belong and retain their family support or being themselves.

THE POWER OF SUPPORT STAFF

In Chapter 17 Jackie Downer reflects:

> My support workers are my lifeline and they help to keep me on track in my home life and with my work. My support staff are like my interpreters, they have many skills and they have made the world a better place for me to live in.

Jackie explains that 'a learning disability is a barrier for us when we want or have relationships, there are many 'do's and don'ts'. Many people with intellectual disabilities are reliant on staff support to develop relationships and express their sexuality. In this respect the narratives show how supporters like Jackie's who 'believe in the rights of people', treat people with respect and take steps to proactively support people play a key part in enabling relationships and supporting sexuality.

The impact of positive staff support is evident in Chapter 15 where Adam noticed a poster Clare was working on about her ideal girlfriend. He started a discussion that led to Clare forming the Rainbow Fairy Group. Following Clare's idea, Adam supported her to set up and run a group for people who were, or thought they might be, gay. Again, in Chapter 16, Daniel explains how he decided to set up a network for gay men with intellectual disabilities like himself. He describes how, following involvement from his supporters Iain and Craig:

> things changed for the better…we went to the bar with the volunteers and they
> supported our right to be there. Some members of the group told me that the group
> was a lifeline to them – it was the only support they got… GAY2 made me and
> other learning disabled people feel included in the gay village.

By contrast, Daniel's description in editorial conversations about staff who badgered
him to take down his posters of men and put up pictures of women instead,
powerfully brings home the impact of staff who abuse their position of power by
seeking to impose their own views rather than adhere to good practice. The insider
perspective drives home that the values and approach of individual staff are critical
in determining how policy guidance is translated into practice.

In focusing on the role supporters play, key questions arise: are they knowledgeable
about law and policy regarding the sexuality of people with intellectual disabilities?
Are they forward thinking and do they hold a human rights perspective; or crucially,
do supporters and staff 'other' people with intellectual disabilities or discriminate
against additional identifiers such as ethnicity, gender, class or homosexuality?

As we can see through the development of the stories, in some respects people
receiving support are at the hand of fate, or *luck of the draw*. Similar to dangers of
a 'postcode lottery' in access to health and social care (Linkage Community Trust
2013, p.14) it can be a lottery as to where they are placed and by whom they
are supported.

2. The outsider: being badly treated and being ignored

Sadly, being ignored, anticipating or experiencing poor treatment, both generally
and in relation to sexuality and relationships, recurred time and again through the
stories. Jackie Downer describes being called 'stupid' as a child because she attended
a special school and emphasises that this name calling continues on occasions even
though she is an adult.

Insider accounts provide insight into a spectrum of painful experiences: from the
psychologist who assessed Jackie as suitable for special school without even saying
goodbye, to Daniel Docherty's description of feeling doubly rejected as a gay man
with intellectual disabilities, to the abusive hate-crime as described in Alice's story:

> People would [also] throw rubbish at me, like I was a piece of rubbish. I had people
> run me off the road. I also had death threats, threats to be burnt out of my home.
> Some people exposed themselves in front of me, not once but a few times over the
> years.

Distancing, ignoring and rejecting are all acts that are keenly felt by people with
intellectual disabilities (Williams and Evans 2013). Anticipation of rejection (see, for

example, Bill from The Men's Room in Chapter 19) can curb people's behaviour and make people wary of taking steps towards developing relationships. In this way the stories show how a consciousness of being 'different' and anticipation of difficulty not only cause concern but limit people's actions through self-regulation. In the men's group Peter, talking to his support worker, highlights the unfairness of this difference between intellectually disabled and non-disabled people: 'But, at least you are able to meet people and talk to them. At least you get the chance to try and talk to them before someone else interferes.' In this way narratives reveal how people with intellectual disabilities are often left feeling like an outsider: a person destined to miss out on what other people can do and experience and some accept it as their lot. In terms of developing relationships and expressing your sexuality, it does nothing for developing self-confidence and self-esteem.

3. Balancing rights against risk

In Chapter 1 we asked readers to hold in mind the question of how practices designed to protect people are impacting on the relationships and sexuality of people with intellectual disabilities. Part 1 narratives highlighted the impact of 'rules and regulations' on relationships. In Part 2, the struggle to balance rights to relationships and sexual expression with risk is clearly evident.

In her introduction to Chapter 12 Louise points out that relationships can go wrong for anyone, regardless of whether they have an intellectual disability. In her view, within services and amongst many supporters, there is a tendency to focus on the negatives of having a relationship rather than the positive effects. In accord with this, Rachel Fyson's chapter identifies a pressing need for more thinking, analysis and guidance on how to provide opportunity for people with intellectual disabilities to develop consenting relationships whilst protecting themselves from abuse.

Walmsley et al. (Chapter 13) highlight that much of the sex in institutions was exploitative. Yet their testimonies demonstrate how in the 1960s some individuals respected residents as adults and appreciated the positive impact a sexual relationship could have on their lives. These authors question whether people in the old long-stay institutions had more opportunity to develop sexual relationships than modern community living where, as highlighted in Part 1, lives are often closely regulated. In contrast, the Chapter 15 and 16 accounts from Clare and Daniel explain that supporters took risks and enabled people to express their sexual identity. Although we do not hear about how these decisions were made by supporters, in Chapter 15 we learn that Yarrow's sexuality policy was developed *with* people with intellectual disabilities and endorsed the rights of individual to have relationships, including same-sex relationships.

The narratives continue to emphasise just how important relationships are to people. People emphatically want to develop relationships and this desire will not go away. We know people with intellectual disabilities are already having sex as revealed in Jackie's story (Chapter 17):

> Sex is a big issue and people with learning disability do actually have a lot of sexual contact, more than people would want to believe…and… I have seen many people who have attended my groups in the past do many sexual things and sometimes out in the open, where they have had to be guided.

There is a danger that if we continue to manage risk by discouraging or preventing relationships developing, then we will only succeed in driving people underground and making the situation more covert and potentially unsafe.

The use of life stories provides insight into the fact that that people with intellectual disabilities themselves are often aware of the concerns generated by their sexual vulnerability. Jackie Downer says, 'There are people who will take advantage of my hugging and my extra touching, but we don't realise,' and goes on to add, 'I think sometimes we need relationship training.' In the next chapter when we identify the implications of our findings for policy and practice we suggest this use of life stories as a key way forward in shifting the balance away from preoccupation with risk to effective and personalised sexuality support.

As highlighted in our first theme, families and support workers are key to enabling this to happen. Building their skills and confidence to undertake this work is also crucial in moving forward, perhaps even more so as services become increasingly individualised and there is less of a pool of staff experienced in this work to draw upon (McCarthy and Thompson 2010). In addition, it is vital that managers and senior managers within services feel confident to promote the value of relationships for all people with intellectual disabilities and to implement skilled and confident practice that capitalises on the supportive aspects of the current legal and policy framework.

As Ann Craft (1987) said nearly three decades ago, 'To be a human being is to be a sexual being…sexuality is not an optional extra that services should be choosing to bestow or withold.' Taking away opportunities for relationships can jeopardise people's future happiness and well-being, yet all too often the narratives tell how bureaucracy in services presents barriers to relationships. In 2009, a Department of Health consultation on current safeguarding policy (DH 2009) highlighted the importance of achieving improved balance between intervening to prevent possible harm and promoting the independence and choice associated with the personalisation of adult social care.

In England, the introduction of the Mental Capacity Act 2005 has brought to the fore issues concerning the capacity of vulnerable people with intellectual disabilities to consent to sexual relationships. Case law from before and after this legislation has now evolved giving further guidance on the management of risk in this area.

Curtice *et al.* (2012) provide an in-depth review of advice to emerge from recent case law and in doing so consider the human rights issues in trying to balance the right to sexual relationships as part of an individual's private life, whilst managing concerns about potential abuse. This informative review quotes what we consider to be extremely valuable guidance from the High Court in 2007:

> The court must be careful to ensure that, in rescuing a vulnerable adult from one type of abuse, it does not expose her to the risk of treatment at the hands of the state which however well intentioned, can itself end up being abusive of her dignity, her happiness and indeed of her human rights…the emphasis must be on seeking a proper balance and being willing to tolerate manageable or acceptable risks as the price appropriately to be paid to achieve some good – in particular to achieve the vital good of the vulnerable person's happiness. (Ruling cited in Curtice *et al.* 2012, p.287).

Narratives in Part 2 highlight the danger of this central happiness being overlooked as organisations focus on implementing policy initiatives, ironically often introduced to improve practice.

4. Gaps between policy and practice

The use of an historical approach enabled the lived experience of people with intellectual disabilities and staff to be considered against the backdrop of an evolving legal and policy framework in relation to sexuality and relationships. A key point to emerge from the juxtaposition of real life with official policy was that a direct relationship between enlightened thinking/progressive policy initiatives and people's experiences (in terms of sexuality and relationships) cannot be assumed.

Paradoxically testimonies from nursing staff (Chapter 13) show how a greater awareness of rights resulted in greater control of sex:

> When we set the sexuality policy up they said, 'You don't allow this sort of thing to go on, do you?'… So we ended up limiting people in effect. That was a consequence. And I wish we'd never started doing it, because less sex went on after we'd given guidelines than before… When we really started to get to grips with the law we realised that sex was illegal.

This provides a clear example of how policies intended to improve practice can serve a different purpose as they are operationalised.

In her introduction to Chapter 12, Louise raises a critical question: when rights to a sexual relationship are overridden, is this due to the law and policy or to the way in which law and policy are being interpreted? In Chapter 18, Ruth Garbutt, states that tackling sex and relationships for people with intellectual disabilities can be difficult for professionals. At the same time, staff attitudes can greatly influence people's experiences and rights and staff have the power to ensure better experiences for people with intellectual disabilities in this area.

The first theme emerging from Part 2 stories was the crucial role of supporters. For example, if a member of staff is saying it is okay to be gay, or sharing that they are gay (Chapter 16), it can powerfully challenge any perceptions that a person with intellectual disabilities may have that being gay is intrinsically wrong. Alternatively, staff who impose heterosexual conduct present a significant barrier in the translation of policy into practice.

The fact that difficulties with understanding and interpreting the law seem to have persisted (Chapter 15) highlights that as laws and policies are approved, staff need effective and timely training in order to understand how to utilise the imperatives placed upon them in a way that continues to support, rather than restrict, relationships between people with intellectual disabilities.

Themes across Parts 1 and 2

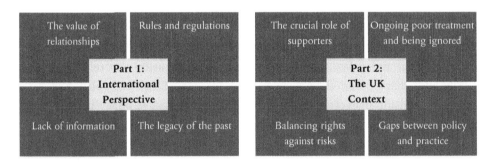

FIGURE 22.1 THEMES FROM PART 1 AND PART 2 FOR COMPARISON

There were many themes that overlapped from Part 1 into Part 2 of the book. When the two are placed alongside each other interconnections become increasingly apparent (see Figure 22.1).

In Part 2, as in Part 1, the importance of relationships to people with intellectual disabilities comes through time and again. In Chapter 19, Peter says that:

a good relationship was about going out and having a laugh, talking, smooching, going to the cinema or having a meal out. At the end of the night you would have a happy feeling after a date, like a 'thumbs-up feeling'.

In Chapter 15, Clare talks about her girlfriend and how happy she is with their relationship.

For people not in a relationship, meeting someone is often in their thoughts. Jackie (Chapter 17) talks about how she 'would love to have a boyfriend' and talks to her support worker about this. Bill (Chapter 19) echoes this sentiment: 'I would love to be in a relationship, not just in a relationship but to be in love and be loved by someone.'

Many people live in settings where their sexuality is 'under surveillance' and, as highlighted in Part 1, 'rules and regulations' apply to people's lives. In the Part 2 narratives we come to understand connections between rules and regulation intended to improve and protect and how they translate into practice in the way rights to relationships are balanced with risk. Docherty and Blyth highlight that people with intellectual disabilities have to turn their private lives into public property to receive support; all too often whether the support is forthcoming is dependent on which staff are responding and the extent to which they are committed to supporting relationships.

Part 1 highlights that there is a tremendous lack of information for people with intellectual disabilities about sex and relationships. In Part 2 we see how this lack of information also extends to staff, including managers (Chapter 15), who are uncertain of the legal and policy framework, particularly in relation to groups who may be perceived as 'different', that is, lesbian women and people with high support needs.

Summary

People with intellectual disabilities are often not aware of their right to support with sexuality and relationships. In addition, we hear how people often do not understand the legal and policy framework and have low expectations of what can be aspired to, often founded on multiple experiences of poor treatment and being ignored. In these circumstances it is very hard for people to participate in making their own choices and decisions, even though this is now a legal requirement under the Mental Capacity Act 2005.

We suggest that people need to be empowered by information and good, skilled support so that they can play a more active part in balancing rights against risk for themselves rather than being reliant on others to do this on their behalf. We also suggest that the complex task of balancing rights with risks must give centrality to the wishes and potential happiness of people with intellectual disabilities themselves.

We contend that the process of doing this in a way that genuinely respects the person/people involved is at an early stage in many services. We feel this area requires more open debate and honesty about the genuine complexities involved. Such dialogue should include problem-solving *in partnership* with people with intellectual disabilities and their families. This in turn would increase opportunities for services to learn from this experiences rather than simply resorting to the rhetoric of rights versus risk.

In the final chapter we draw the book to a close by re-visiting our initial research questions and identifying a number of recommendations for practice.

References

Craft, A. (1987) 'Mental Handicap and Sexuality: Issues for Individuals with a Mental Handicap, their Parents and Professionals.' In A. Craft (ed.) *Mental Handicap and Sexuality: Issues and Perspectives.* Costello: Tunbridge Wells.

Curtice, M., Mayo, J. and Crocombe, J. (2012) 'Consent and sex in vulnerable adults: a review of case law.' *British Journal of Learning Disabilities 41,* 280–287.

Department of Constitutional Affairs (2007) *Mental Capacity Act Code of Practice.* London: The Stationery Office.

DH Department of Health (2009) *Safeguarding Adults: report on the consultation on the review of No Secrets.* London: Crown publications.

Linkage Community Trust (2013) *Learning Disability Today.* Available at http://www.learningdisabilitytoday.co.uk/learning_disability_charity_calls_on_government_to_clear_up_ordinary_residence_rows.aspx accessed on September 11 2014.

McCarthy, M. and Thompson, D. (2010) 'Introduction.' In M. Carthy and D. Thompson (eds) *Sexuality and Relationships.* Brighton: Pavilion.

Williams, P. and Evans, M. (2013*) Social Work with People with Learning Difficulties.* London: Sage.

CHAPTER 23

RE-VISITING THE RESEARCH QUESTIONS AND RECOMMENDATIONS

Rohhss Chapman, Sue Ledger and Louise Townson

Overview

- In this final chapter we return to the five research questions set out in Chapter 1.

- Review the major lessons learned and identify key implications for policy and practice.

Introduction

In this final chapter we return to the research questions identified in Chapter 1. We devised these as a skeleton framework to guide us through the writing of the book. Answering these questions enabled us to consider the implications for policy and practice. In the light of this we highlight four priority areas for future work.

The writing process

After we had identified key themes from Parts 1 and 2 we began work on answering our initial research questions. We approached this by discussing the research questions together and then mapping evidence from each chapter across the five research questions – again using a large art board. As this was our final chapter and each of us had a lot to say we put our thoughts together in joint writing (see Chapters 21 and 22).

Answering the research questions

1 Does history help us to understand people with intellectual disabilities' experiences of sexuality and relationships today?

In editing this book we aimed to contextualise narrative accounts with an historical overview of the treatment of people with intellectual disabilities in relation to sexuality across the twentieth and early twenty-first centuries.

It has been argued that any social movement has a fundamental need for its members and those it is seeking to influence to understand its roots and history (Bersani 1998). This is arguably as true of the self-advocacy movement for people with intellectual disabilities as it is of the Black Civil Rights movement and Women's movement.

To date, in part as a result of limited access to education, many people with intellectual disabilities are unaware of their history. For example, Louise, after reading the timeline in Chapter 2, was amazed that thousands of people with intellectual disabilities had been sterilised around the globe.

The book demonstrates how acquiring *an understanding of history can be of considerable value to some people with intellectual disabilities.* Knowing what has happened in the past, in view of societal attitudes and norms, can help to de-personalise difficult events, making it easier to understand past abuse of rights and to recognise and challenge these as they re-occur in current practice. Ebba (Chapter 4), in relation to her own sterilisation whilst living in an institution in Iceland, reflected on the value of knowing this history: 'I understand now that this was a historical phase… I understand that this was not my fault; it was the government that decided to do such things to people.'

This connects to C. Wright Mills' (1959, p.8) classic idea of how individuals, through taking an historical and sociological view, can begin to understand their own 'private troubles' as ' public issues', allowing a connection between an individual's experience to be viewed from a wider social perspective. Thus Ebba's comment above demonstrates that when she came to understand the impact of historical events upon her own sterilisation, she saw that the upset and anger she felt was not about deficit within herself or being let down by her mother, but that events had actually happened out of the reach of her own or her family's power. Understanding this crucial point and being able to forgive is evidently cathartic.

Consideration of the historical context also supports understanding of how the legacy of the past continues to influence current attitudes and practice. In this book analysis enabled recognition of two major historical typologies of people with intellectual disabilities in relation to sexuality – that of *sexual menace* and *asexual/adult child.* Several chapters make reference to this paradoxical legacy and how it still continues to exert influence on people's lives under the mantle of 'rights and protection'.

Further discussion within our editorial team raised the question of whether these typologies are applied differently according to the level of impairment of the individual – with people described as having moderate or mild intellectual disabilities being regarded as more of a *sexual liability* whose fertility must be controlled (historically reflected in the fact that increased numbers of women of child-bearing age were admitted to long-stay institutions). People with more complex disabilities, on the other hand, may be more likely to be perceived as *eternal children* in need of protection and screening from sexual contact. *We strongly suggest that further exploration of these stereotypes would be of value* – the use of an historical perspective enabled greater appreciation of their continuing impact upon the lives of people with intellectual disabilities today.

Placing insider stories against their evolving backdrop of legal and policy changes challenges the traditional 'textbook' picture that charts a positive continuum of development from the past to the present (Chapter 13).

Importantly, the stories point to pockets of good and poor practice that reflect the values of different support staff, rather than a steady change towards a rights-based approach. This history, told largely by people with intellectual disabilities and their allies, reveals that progress is often uneven – with the values of supporters, managers and services often determining people's experiences of relationships to a greater extent than policy and legal frameworks. In this manner, the use of life histories allows official history to be challenged and a new history owned by people with intellectual disabilities themselves to emerge.

2 What have people's own experiences been?

A resounding message in this book is that relationships can be very positive and are given great priority by many of the people with intellectual disabilities who have spoken here. Yet, in the early twenty-first century across the globe many people continue to lead lives that vary from the rest of the population in terms of opportunities to meet people and become involved in relationships. Many people lead lives that are isolated and lonely. Possibly as a result, people with intellectual disabilities are considering the internet and television dating as possible routes to find a partner (Chapters 6 and 19).

A key area of 'difference' emerging from the narratives is that people often find themselves reliant on support staff and managers to develop relationships and to express their sexual identity. In Part 2 the *crucial role of supporters* in making relationships a reality for people with intellectual disabilities is brought to the fore.

For people often reliant on families or services, it is seen that the quality of direct support, rather than policy, makes relationships and sexual expression a reality.

Many negative experiences have been shared and, as the testimonies demonstrate, people with intellectual disabilities all over the world, are leading somewhat 'atypical' lives. As a result, people with intellectual disabilities have had far fewer opportunities to live a life of their choice, to live with people they choose, to develop relationships and to have experiences around risk and exploration that their non-disabled peers have. Many people are living 'regulated' lives and have little opportunity to act spontaneously. Linking this to a general lack of sex education, understanding of relationships and resistance to and from services (and sometimes families), people could be said to be living very restricted lives. These are lives of limitation in regard to sexuality, which fly in the face of current legislation and policy.

Not all testimonies are negative or limiting. Some stories (particularly Chapters 4, 9, 15 and 16) pick up on resilience, strength and tremendous innovation – however this is often, but not exclusively, narrated in opposition to prevailing attitudes. *We strongly suggest that these positive stories need to be heard by a wider audience.* The book suggests there is much value in these positive stories being shared by people with intellectual disabilities themselves, providing role models (Chapter 9) and champions for others.

3 How do allies effectively support people in their aspirations around sexuality and relationships?

Chapter 15 highlights that many staff admitted they did not understand the law and were unable to explain the approach of their organisation to supporting gay relationships. Many front line staff were sympathetic to providing support but said they did not know where to go for information or guidance. In order to be effective, allies also need information, training and support themselves.

Importantly, given the positive impact of family support, Garbutt (Chapter 18) identified this as an area where parents want more help and the chance to work together with professionals to achieve a good outcome for their sons and daughters. Similar findings were reported from an earlier FPA study on the sexual health and well-being of people with intellectual disabilities in Northern Ireland (FPA 2006). Accounts in this book provide further evidence for the value of investing in supporting families in terms of positive outcomes in the lives of people with intellectual disabilities. Positive stories of relationships and sexuality shared by people with intellectual disabilities themselves, including the narratives in this collection, could make a useful contribution to such support.

One of the highlights of this project is realising that good practice can be identified and replicated. Ebba and Jonni (Chapter 4) demonstrate how relationships with supporters develop over time and how trust is such an important component of the support relationship. As supporters or allies we are reminded that *listening to what people are saying is crucial*, as is following the lead from what we are hearing.

The writing process sections within the chapters provide insight into how collaborations are formed and maintained to raise awareness of sexuality issues and to seek change. People with intellectual disabilities, peers and friends are described throughout as helpful or inspirational. *We urge professionals and supporters to be far more ready to acknowledge the power of peer support.* These reflections are particularly captured in Chapters 4, 5, 6, 7, 9, 13, 14, 18 and 19.

4 What can partnership working and life story methodology contribute to this field?

In Chapter 4 Ebba Hreinsdøttir says:

> We think it is of a great importance that people all over the world tell their stories and learn from each other. It is also important that the government and people without disabilities know that we are not different from them. We want to live a good life, have a partner, get married, have enough money... We should be in control of our lives. People should understand that.

Through adopting a life history approach we have heard directly about the thoughts and experiences of people with intellectual disabilities and their allies. In this way, 'insider' accounts have allowed an alternative, and often a hidden perspective, to emerge: the voice of those whose lives, relationships and sexuality are on the receiving end of legal changes and policy initiatives. Without this material we are reliant on 'professional experts' and their interpretations of people's lives. Our material for this book values 'experts by experience'; we can reflect on first-hand accounts and understand far more about personal experiences, about how it *feels* to be *standing in the shoes* of other people. Without this knowledge it is much harder to appreciate the ethical and moral questions underlying practice, to identify and challenge oppression when it happens and to spread stories of what people with intellectual disabilities are saying works well.

In Chapter 9 Janice Slattery talks about her involvement in partnership work in the Living Safer Sexual Lives project: 'All the women in the project team brought different skills, experiences and had different impacts on the programme. I was a project worker, a peer educator trainer and a peer educator and was involved in the evaluation.' It is important that partnership in the field of sexuality and relationships is not confused with the idea of adding on the views of intellectually disabled people later, when decisions have already been made. The term as we use it in the book is *collaboration* to gain the contribution of an essential perspective – expertise on sexuality and relationships that would otherwise be missing. In a subject as central to people's lives as sexuality and relationships we argue that *it is imperative to include that perspective at the core.*

Writing at this time of economic recession we are all too aware of the risks attached to reliance on profit-making institutional and segregated care (see Chapter 11). Chapter 15 details how staff can provide positive support and the difference this can make to people's lives. We have written in Chapter 21 about the pitfalls of working in partnership, and *we encourage realistic and open debate in this area, making practices as transparent as possible so they can be replicated or critiqued.*

In relation to sexuality and relationships, what has been very encouraging for us are the programmes around sex education and advice, where both life story and partnership approaches have been adopted (see especially Chapters 5, 9 and 18). As Goodley *et al.* (2004, p.107) argue, 'the hallmark of life story research is that it should prompt positive social change'. We need to take this message forward to policy and practice.

5 What are the implications for policy and practice?

One of the key motivations in gathering the stories for this book was to consider their application to current policy and practice: to make it useful. This required consideration of our findings in the light of a move towards increasingly personalised support for adults with intellectual disabilities. Inevitably limitations exist in the generalisations that can be drawn from a relatively small number of experiences, yet their content raises many issues for policy and practice. As space is limited we chose to focus on four key implications that people with intellectual disabilities identified as important. We suggest that taking action in these areas has the potential to make an immediate difference to people's lives. These are:

(a) improved access to information, training and support for people with intellectual disabilities and their allies

(b) greater recognition of the potential of sexuality and relationships to bring happiness in the lives of people with intellectual disabilities

(c) greater attention to enabling people to socialise and develop relationships

(d) promotion of more open and honest debate at all levels of the health and social care system about how to practically achieve translation of a rights-based policy framework into best practice through supporting sexuality and relationships.

Key implications

(a) Improved access to information, training and support for people with intellectual disabilities and their allies

People with intellectual disabilities require information about sex, sexuality and relationships. The information provided needs to be non-judgemental and include information about homosexuality. It should include clear legal and policy information that can inform understanding of rights and build individual capacity to recognise and self-protect (Hollomotz 2011) from abuse.

People with an intellectual disability have a rightful and essential place at the table as partners in planning and running sexuality and relationship programmes. The collaborative Living Safer Sexual Lives project (Chapter 9) demonstrates the importance of involving people in roles such as project workers, programme and research advisors and peer educators. These roles recognise and use experiential knowledge about sexuality and relationships.

Similarly the potential value of life story material in delivering relationships and sexuality training has been highlighted. As peer educators and project team members, people can use their own experiences to support key messages about positive, safe and happy relationships, as well as how to deal with some of the negative aspects of relationships. The sharing of positive stories about relationships, partnership and parenting can assist others to 'aim high' in terms of their own aspirations and to recognise and challenge when their support is falling short of policy intention.

(b) Greater recognition of the potential of relationships and sexuality to bring happiness in the lives of people with intellectual disabilities

There has been a clear message from people with intellectual disabilities across the globe that relationships are highly valued, recommended and sought after. Taking away opportunities for relationships and sexual expression can jeopardise people's future happiness, well-being and mental health. *This risk of harm must be equally taken into account.* All too often the experiences of people with intellectual disabilities reveal how bureaucracy in services presents barriers to relationships and instances where providers often elect to prioritise the management of risk over rights.

People with intellectual disabilities often have few friends and as adults continue to live with family or in communal settings with little knowledge about sex and with little or no experience of having a boyfriend or girlfriend. Given the importance of all of these things to most people without intellectual disabilities, *we need to view the issue of personal relationships and the tackling of loneliness as a key priority in the delivery of support.*

Where people want to form partnerships and develop relationships, either same sex or heterosexual, they must be helped to do so. In this respect we argue for greater priority to be given to sexuality and relationships issues within the design of personalised support. This can be achieved within existing systems of person-centred planning, review and quality regulation.

In the evaluation of services greater emphasis should be placed on exploring the outcomes wanted in terms of relationships and sexuality by individuals with an intellectual disability themselves. Exploring these issues and expressing what is wanted may require the support of a 'known' and trusted keyworker, family member, friend, advocate or peer supporter.

Some people may well have little interest in forming deep emotional or sexual relationships; others may want to explore casual sexual relationships or the use of prostitution; others may have a degree of impairment that makes it very hard for them to understand the concepts and consequences of marriage, civil partnership sex, pregnancy and parenting. That said, this book has highlighted that for many people opportunities to consider these options continue to be restricted. *For everyone there is a need as a minimum to acknowledge and explore the potential value of sexuality and relationships in the design and delivery of their support.*

(c) Greater emphasis on creating opportunities for people to socialise and develop relationships

It is still the case that people with intellectual disabilities most commonly develop relationships and meet potential partners through opportunities to socialise with other people with intellectual disabilities. In the past, when building-based services predominated, these opportunities were arguably more common as relationships were often developed within residential homes, day services or social clubs (McCarthy and Thompson 2010).

Now that support is rapidly moving to a more individualised model (where people are increasingly supported on a one-to-one basis by staff in their own homes and local communities) there is a risk that support may increasingly become more acutely focused on domestic practicalities such as shopping, cooking, cleaning and bill paying (McCarthy and Thompson 2010). Under these circumstances there is a real danger that creating opportunity for relationships is overlooked or dismissed as non-essential.

We emphasise that individuals who wish to meet new friends or a potential partner need to be taken seriously and should be supported to access shared community leisure, work and education spaces (Chapters 6 and 16). *This should be a priority area when recruiting staff with compatible interests, designing rotas and evaluating support.*

Innovative approaches need to be taken. The internet is increasingly available to people with intellectual disabilities. 'Stars in the Sky', a London-based dating agency for people with intellectual disabilities, was launched in 2005. In addition to introducing people with intellectual disabilities and providing social events, it provides a screening and chaperoning service. Similar schemes are now spreading throughout the UK and other countries, and merit further development. Younger people with intellectual disabilities in particular are increasingly using Facebook and other social media networking sites as a means of making and maintaining contact. *Access to these alternatives needs to be further explored.*

d) Promote much more honest and open debate about the genuine complexity of enabling people with intellectual disabilities to enjoy intimate relationships whilst keeping as safe as possible from harm

This book has repeatedly highlighted how a rights-based approach is diluted and sometimes subverted as it is translated into everyday support.

Accounts in this book shed light on how barriers to relationships arise through the bureaucracy of service systems. Examples included a requirement for management authorisation if couples with intellectual disabilities wanted to spend private time together, and staff rotas dictating whether or not people could meet. Equally, staff did not understand the legal framework in which they operated and were anxious about the legality of sex and relationships.

Supporting people with sexuality and relationships is undoubtedly a complex area. The fact that staff are increasingly working on a one-to-one basis rather than in teams also means there may be less chance of people working alongside others who are experienced and skilled in supporting people in this area. However, its importance to people with intellectual disabilities means it can no longer be ignored or dismissed under the rhetoric of weighing rights against risks. *The importance of sexuality and relationships would benefit from increased attention at all levels from ministerial speeches and policy-making to committed support at local level.*

For people with more complex needs there may be issues of capacity, but it does not mean their sexuality should be denied or ignored (Mallett and Stewart 2010). Although the need to protect people from sexual abuse is very real there are also significant mental health risks in denying people what they really want. To counteract this, *more local support and skills-sharing groups* where issues can be openly raised and jointly discussed may be of real value, both in encouraging skills development and tackling inconsistency of staff support both within and across services.

The FPA (2006) suggest setting up local networks of people interested in championing good practice in relation to sexuality and relationships. *Networks would involve people with intellectual disabilities, family carers, practitioners, service providers and managers meeting regularly to share information and plan joint events* with the intention of ensuring continuity across services and providing mutual support and problem-solving. They could also provide an important opportunity for leading on promoting sexuality and relationships, peer support and for collaborative local policy-making.

The narratives in this book reveal that many rules affect people with intellectual disabilities in terms of sex and relationships. The legal and policy framework has to interact with other factors such as religion, family expectations and cultural norms which can also have their own rules attached. For people with intellectual disabilities and staff, the situation can soon start to feel overwhelming. In this respect it is no wonder that in practice settings people sometimes find it simpler to discourage relationships from developing.

In editing the book we found the model developed by Fanstone and Andrews (2009) in Appendix 3, to be very helpful in exploring various rules that might be exerting influence in people's lives. *We suggest it may be a useful tool in supporting individuals to explore their own circumstances and staff to take forward person-centred support and policy development in relation to sexuality.*

Summary

We would like to end on the words of two contributors with intellectual disabilities. First, Jackie Downer MBE, who reminds us of the reasons for writing this book:

> In the end, for myself, I would like someone to love me and I to love them... I know that if people gave us a chance and some support we would overcome some of our barriers.

Second, Ebba Hreinsdøttir reminds us why we decided to adopt a life story approach:

> What people can also learn from our stories is that we are not victims. We have overcome barriers and challenges we have faced in our lives and managed to be independent together. If you believe in yourself you can do anything, but sometimes you have to fight for it.

Sharing the stories of people with intellectual disabilities and their allies has aided understanding of the value that sexuality and relationships can bring and the difficulties many people face. Our next project as an editorial team is to put together more accessible information and deliver training based on the material in this book. This will include a programme of peer support, mentoring and partnership training for people and organisations interested in moving the agenda forward for sexuality and relationships in the lives of intellectually disabled people.

Our intention is that the narratives shared through this book will play a part in enabling barriers to sexuality and relationships encountered by people with intellectual disabilities around the globe to be recognised, addressed and eventually overcome.

References

Bersani, H. (1998) 'From Social Clubs to Social Movement.' In L. Ward (ed.) *Innovations in Advocacy and Empowerment.* Lancashire: Lisieux Hall Publications.

Fanstone, C. and Andrews, S. (2009) *Learning Disabilities, Sex and the Law.* London: FPA.

FPA (2006) *Sexual Health and Wellbeing in Northern Ireland: Factsheet.* Belfast, Family Planning Association publications.

Goodley. D., Lawthom, R., Clough, P., and Moore, M. (2004) *Researching Life Stories: Method, Theory and Analyses in a Biographical Age.* London: Routledge Falmer.

Hollomotz, A. (2011) *Learning Difficulties and Sexual Vulnerability: A Social Approach.* London: Jessica Kingsley Publishers.

McCarthy, M. and Thompson, D. (2010) 'Introduction.' In M. Carthy and D. Thompson (eds) *Sexuality and Relationships.* Brighton: Pavilion.

Mallett, A. and Stewart, D. (2010) 'Sexuality support for people with profound and multiple disabilities' In M. Carthy and D. Thompson (eds) *Sexuality and Relationships.* Brighton: Pavilion.

Wright Mills, C. (1959) *The Sociological Imagination.* New York: Oxford University Press.

APPENDICES

EXAMPLES OF PUBLICATIONS FROM THE OPEN UNIVERSITY SOCIAL HISTORY OF LEARNING DISABILITY GROUP

Atkinson, D. and Williams, F. (1990) *Know Me As I Am: An Anthology of Prose, Poetry and Art by People with Learning Difficulties.* London: Hodder and Stoughton.

Atkinson, D., McCarthy, M., Walmsley. J., Cooper. M. *et al.* (eds) (2000) *Good Times Bad Times: Women with Learning Difficulties Telling their Stories.* Kidderminster: BILD.

Atkinson, D., Holland, C., Humber, L., Ingham, N., Ledger, S. and Tilley, E. (2010) *Developing a 'Living Archive' of Learning Disability Life Stories: Project Report.* Milton Keynes: Open University.

Blunt, C., Blyth, C., Chapman, R., Frost, L., Hayward, D. *et al.* (2012) ' Editorial.' *British Journal of Learning Disabilities, Special Issue: The Research and Work of Learning Disabled People with their Allies and Supporters 40.* Vol 40, 2, 83–84.

Central England People First with Walmsley, J. (2012) *21 years of CEPF 1990–2011: A Journey and a Celebration.* Kettering: CEPF.

Chapman, R. (2014) 'An exploration of the self-advocacy support role through collaborative research: 'There should never be a them and us.' *Journal of Applied Research in Intellectual Disabilities, Special Issue: New Directions in Inclusive Research 27,* 1, 44–53.

Chapman, R. (2006) 'The role of the self-advocacy support worker in UK People First groups: developing inclusive research.' Unpublished PhD thesis, Milton Keynes, Open University.

Chapman, R. (2006) 'Devolved Policy for People with Learning Difficulties in Scotland, Wales and Northern Ireland.' In Welshman, J., and Walmsley J. (eds) *Community Care in Perspective: Care, Control and Citizenship.* London: Palgrave Macmillan.

Chapman, R. and Townson, L. (2012) 'Researching Together: Pooling Ideas, Strengths and Experiences.' In Davies, C., Flux, R., Hales, M. and Walmsley, J. (eds) *Better Health in Harder Times: Active Citizens and Innovation on the Frontline.* Bristol: The Policy Press.

Chapman, R. and McNulty, N. (2004) 'Building bridges? The role of research support in self-advocacy.' *British Journal of Learning Disabilities 32,* 2, 77–85.

Chapman, R., Spedding, F., Harkness, E., Townson, L., Docherty, A. and McNulty, N. (2002) 'The Role of Self Advocacy: Stories of a Self Advocacy Group through the Experiences of its Members.' In Gray B., and Jackson R. (eds) *Advocacy and Learning Disability.* London: Jessica Kingsley Publishers.

Chapman, R. and Townson, L. (2002) 'Consultation: Plan of Action or Management Exercise?' In Reynolds, J., Seden, J., Henderson, J., Charlesworth, J. and Bullman, A. (eds) (2002) *The Managing Care Reader.* London: Open University Press.

Cooper, M. (1997) 'Mabel Cooper's Life Story.' In Atkinson, D., Jackson, M., and Walmsley, J. (eds) *Forgotten Lives: Exploring the History of Learning Disability*. Kidderminster: BILD.

Dias, J., Eardley, M., Harkness, E., Townson, L., Brownlee-Chapman, C. and Chapman, R. (2012) 'Keeping Wartime Memory Alive: An oral history project about the wartime memories of people with learning difficulties in Cumbria.' *Disability and Society 27*, 1, 31–49.

Docherty, A,. Harkness, E., Eardley, M., Townson, L. and Chapman, R. (2006) 'What They Want, Yes! But What We Want, Bugger Us!' In Mitchell, D., Traustadóttir, R., Chapman, R., Townson, L., Ingham, N., and Ledger, S. (eds) *Exploring Experiences of Advocacy by People with Learning Disabilities*. London: Jessica Kingsley Publishers.

Earle, S., Tilley, E. and Walmsley, J. (2012) 'Who makes crucial decisions on reproduction and contraception?' *Learning Disability Practice 15*, 8, 34–35.

Graham, H. (2008) *Days Gone By: The History of Day Centres for People with Learning Disabilities in Croydon*. Open University Project. Available at www.open.ac.uk/hsc/__assets/ qbw0zopgkfu74nu62n.pdf, accessed on 13 June 2014.

Ledger, S. (2012) 'Staying local: support for people with learning difficulties from inner London 1971–2007.' Unpublished PhD Thesis, Milton Keynes, Open University.

Ledger, S. and Tilley, E. (2010) 'Reminiscence, identity and developing a living archive of learning disability history.' Paper given at LGTB Seminar, LM Archives, December.

Ledger, S. and Shufflebotham, L. (2006) 'Songs of Resistance.' In Mitchell, D., Traustadóttir, R., Chapman, R., Townson, L., Ingham, N., and Ledger, S. (eds) *Exploring Experiences of Advocacy by People with Learning Disabilities: Testimonies of Resistance*. London and Philadelphia: Jessica Kingsley Publishers.

Nind, M. and Vinha, H. (2012) *Doing Research Inclusively, Doing Research Well?* Report of the study: Quality and capacity in inclusive research with people with learning disabilities. University of Southampton.

Rolph, S. (1999) 'The history of community care for people with learning difficulties in Norfolk, 1930–1980: the role of two hostels.' Unpublished PhD thesis, Milton Keynes, Open University.

Rolph, S., Atkinson, D., Nind, M., Welshman, J. *et al.* (eds) (2005) *Witnesses to Change: Families, Learning Difficulties and History*. Kidderminster: BILD.

Tilley, E. (2006) 'Advocacy for people with learning difficulties: the role of two organisations.' Unpublished PhD thesis, Faculty of Health and Social Welfare, Open University.

Tilley, E., Walmsley, J., Earle, S. and Atkinson, D. (2012) '"The Silence is Roaring": Sterilisation, reproductive rights and women with intellectual disabilities.' *Disability and Society 27*, 3, 413–426.

Townson, L., Macauley, S., Harkness, E., Chapman, R. *et al.* (2004) 'We are all in the same boat.' *British Journal of Learning Disabilities 32*, 2, 72–76.

Townson, L., Macauley, S., Harkness, E., Docherty, A. *et al.* (2007) 'Research project on advocacy and autism.' *Disability and Society 22*, 5, 523–536.

Walmsley, J. (2012) 'Research unpacked: Thinking about a good life for people with learning disabilities.' *Learning Disability Today* Oct/Nov 2012, 12, 5, 21.

Walmsley, J. (1995) 'Life history interviews with people with learning disabilities.' *Oral History 23*, 1, 71–77.

Walmsley, J. with Central England People First (in press) 'Telling the history of self advocacy: a challenge for inclusive research.' *Journal of Applied Research in Intellectual Disability*.

Walmsley, J. with My Life My Choice (2011) Checking Up On DES: An Investigation into the Implementation of Annual Health Checks in Oxfordshire. Available at www. janwalmsleyassociates.com, accessed on 13 June 2014.

Walmsley, J. and Johnson, K. (2003) *Inclusive Research with People with Learning Disabilities.* London: Jessica Kingsley Publishers.

Walmsley, J. and Downer, J. (1997) 'Shouting the Loudest: Self-advocacy, Power and Diversity.' In Ramcharan, P., Roberts, G., Grant, G. and Borland, J. (eds) *Empowerment in Everyday Life.* London: Jessica Kingsley Publishers.

AN ACCESSIBLE HUMAN RIGHTS ACT

The Human Rights Act[1]

In this handout we have added pictures and photosymbols® to make the content of the Human Rights Act more accessible to people with intellectual disabilities. We did this by adapting the words from Schedule One – The Articles – and working with people with intellectual disabilities to add pictorial symbols. Thanks are due to Andrew Holman for images from 'Inspired Services', and also to 'PHOTOSYMBOLS®'

Human Rights

The Human Rights Act was set out in 1998 and came into force in the UK in 2000. Some points were added later.

For people with intellectual disabilities, knowing about the Human Rights Act is very important. It should help people and their allies protect their rights.

Human Rights Act Rights and Freedoms

The statements of the Human Rights Act uphold your rights to a number of freedoms.

---

1   United Kingdom *Human Rights Act:* Elizabeth 11. c.42 Schedule One. (1998) London, HMSO.

Article 2

The Right to Life – Your Life is Protected by Law

Article 3

Freedom from Torture, Inhuman or Degrading Treatment

Article 4

Freedom from Slavery or Forced Labour –you cannot be treated like a slave

Article 5

The Right to Personal Freedom and Liberty

Article 6

The Right to a Fair Trial in Public

Article 7

No Punishment without Law

Article 8

The Right to Respect for your Private and Family Life, Your Home and Correspondence

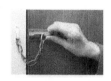

Article 9

Freedom of Belief, Thought and Religion

Article 10

Free Expression and the Right to Express Your Views

Article 11

Freedom of Peaceful Assembly (meeting others)

Article 12

The Right to Marry and Start a Family

Article 14

Freedom from Discrimination

Article 17

No one has the Right to Destroy or Abuse Rights

Article 1, Protocol 1

Protection of Property, No one Can Take Your Property Away, including the State

Article 2, Protocol 1

Everyone has the Right to an Education

Article 3,

The Right to Free Elections

Protocol 13 (agreed in June 2004)

No Death Penalty

THE LAW AND OTHER RULES
WE WORK WITH

Adapted with kind permission from Fanstone and Andrews, *Learning Disabilities, Sex and the Law* 2009, pp.3–5.

International and European laws and rules

There are declarations of rights that apply to everybody including some especially for people with learning disabilities. Some of these rights have been brought into our national law but others have no real power.

Religious traditions/rules

If you are a member of a faith group there may be rules about how you live, for example about sexual behaviour or contraception. These can apply to members of faith groups wherever they are in the world.

Local society's expectations

Break these rules and you could get stared at, shouted at or worse. For example, can people kiss in the street? What if they are the same sex? What if they are learning disabled or wheelchair users? Are the rules different? Can you approach people that you don't know? These rules are not written down but they affect people's lives significantly.

Family and cultural expectations

These rules are unwritten too, but can be even stronger. Anyone who is part of a family or cultural group has to behave in an acceptable way or risk being excluded. Disabled people may be excused some of these expectations but staff are expected to help people fit into their culture as much as possible. People who move house or develop friendships can find that there are differences between the culture of their new friendship group and that of their family or home area.

House rules for individual workplaces or living places

Every workplace or living place will have written or unwritten rules, for example rules about visitors, record keeping and acceptable behaviour.

Professional codes of conduct

Different professional groups have their own rules for their members, for example most professions have strict rules about confidentiality.

Regional or local guidelines

These could include child protection procedures or guidelines for the safeguarding of vulnerable adults. It is good practice to know about these and to work to them where they exist.

Employer's policies and guidelines

These are not the same as employment law which is legally binding. People with learning disabilities can lose their tenancy or placement and staff can lose their job if they fail to keep to the policies and guidelines of their organisation. Some employers have clear policies about sexual behaviour but others do not.

Custom and practice of staff

'How we've always done things here' is often the most powerful rule of all. Many legal myths start out this way and are then passed on by word of mouth or example. People are often astonished to find that other places and people do things differently.

The expectations of people with intellectual disabilities

People get used to how other people behave around them, and can be surprised and worried when things change. New rules, ideas and ways of doing things take some time to adjust to, however good they are. People's expectations may differ from the culture of the service. The culture of a service may be changing to become more or less tolerant of sexual expression.

THE SEXUAL RESPECT TOOL KIT

The Outsiders Trust has developed a Sexual Respect Tool Kit which can be found on its website (www.sexualrespect.com). It clearly sets out updated legal guidance for practitioners. These were adapted from the work of Claire de Than, senior lecturer in human rights and criminal law at City University. Claire is specialising in sex and disability.

1. It is illegal to have sex with a person where you are in a 'position of trust', even when both parties are over 16 and have consented. This will be relevant to teachers, carers and doctors, anyone who is in a supportive position and/or mentors of people with intellectual difficulties.

2. Not everyone has the capacity to consent but sex can still be legal in some cases even where people are not deemed to have capacity.

3. Discrimination against disabled people (including people with intellectual disabilities) is unlawful. Disabled people must have the same opportunities as others and reasonable adjustments may need to be made to facilitate this.

4. Female genital mutilation is illegal and counts as sexual abuse, so must be reported.

5. Forced marriages, for whatever reason, are illegal.

6. The legal age for sex is 16 for gay and heterosexual people.

7. Sexual discrimination is illegal and this includes orientation, for example lesbians, gay people, bisexual people and transgendered people.

8. In some situation it is possible for care staff and personal assistants to work with people with disabilities to support them to make arrangements to engage the services of an established professional sex worker.

9. Touching clients is a little complicated. Generally clients should not be touched without their consent. However, there are occasions when people need to be touched, to gain attention or support or reassure them. There are also emergency situations where it is not possible or practical to gain consent. Qualified medical or nursing professionals may touch their clients but not in a sexual way, or they may be convicted of a criminal offence.

Reproduced with kind permission from Dr Tuppy Owens.

SUBJECT INDEX

AUTHOR INDEX

Abbott, D. 170, 196, 197, 202, 230
Abela, A. 115
Anderson, J. 56
Andrews, S. 31, 145, 151, 204, 205, 207, 298
Anyon, Y. 257
Aspis, S. 264
Atkinson, D. 11, 16, 41, 48, 124
Azzopardi, A. 110, 123
Azzopardi Lane, C.L. 115

Bank-Mikkelsen, N.E. 53–4, 55, 57
Barber, F. 230
Barger, E. 125, 127
Barr, M.W. 49
Barrett, C. 123
Baxter, C. 142
Beckett, C. 207
Bersani, H. 32, 59, 290
Block, P. 60
Blunt, C. 269
Blyth, C. 211, 213, 214, 250, 254, 258
Boal, A. 85
Bonnie, S. 111, 115
Broberg, G. 49, 50, 57
Brock Committee 36
Brockley, J.A. 52, 54
Brown, HHHHH. 58, 59, 60, 123, 151, 168, 169
Bryde, R. 129
Bryman, A. 251
Buchanan, I. 58, 59
Buck, P.S. 51, 52
Buckinghamshire County Council 169
Burns, J. 196

Cambridge, P. 230, 250, 253, 254, 255, 256, 258
Campbell, B. 168
Campbell, J. 41

Care Services Commission for Social Care (CSCI) 193, 202
Carey, A.C. 56, 58
Carmody, M. 168
Carson, I. 212, 214, 254
Cassar, M. 115
Chambers, M. 129
CHANGE 127, 235, 236
Chapman, R. 153, 251, 264, 269, 271
Chivers, A. 251
Chuo-Houki 102
Churchill, J. 169
City of Westminster 151, 204, 206, 208
Community Care 145
Cooper, M. 124, 263
Council of Europe 115
Cox, P. 176
Craft, A. 39, 55, 57, 123, 166, 167–8, 169, 284
Craft, M. 39, 55, 167–8
Curry, M.A. 251
Curtice, M. 285
Cuskelly, M. 129

Dale, P. 51
Davey, M. 196
Davies, D. 127, 196
Dendy, M. 34, 48
Department for Constitutional Affairs 204
Department for Education and Employment 234
Department of Health 16, 147, 149, 151, 153, 156, 157, 169, 175, 176, 183, 196, 206, 284
Desjardins, G. 177
D'Espallier, A. 89
Diamond, M. 232
Diekema, D.S. 57
Digby, A. 51
Dillon, J. 123

Dingman, H.F. 53
Docherty, D. 17, 27, 197, 212, 214
Doe, T. 168
Downer, J. 226
Downs, C. 169
Drummond, E. 115
Durham County Council 146
Dybwad, G. 59
Dyson, S. 123

Earle, S. 175
Edgerton, R. 38, 53, 55
Elkins, T.E. 56
Emerson, E. 54, 257
Eriikson, E. 102
European Commission 89
Evans, D.S. 129, 170, 282

Fairbairn, G. 115
Family Planning Association (FPA) 21, 205
Family Planning Northern Ireland 127
Fanstone, C. 30, 145, 151, 204, 205, 207, 298
Farnan, S. 121, 123
Felce, D. 177
Feldman, D. 11
FGS Social Security 90
Fido, R. 49, 178, 179
Fitzgerald, C. 154, 196, 201, 254
Fitzsimons, N.M. 127
Forrest, M. 265
Foucault, M. 155, 259
FPA 297
Francis Report 146
Frawley, P. 42, 120, 122, 123, 124, 125, 126, 127, 129
Furedi, F. 169

Garbutt, R. 127, 231
Gerodetti, N. 49, 50